SUPERMARIONATION

CLASSICS

STINGRAY   THUNDERBIRDS   CAPTAIN SCARLET

AND THE MYSTERONS

 ITC

Dave Rogers

John Marriot

Chris Drake

Graeme Bassett

ITC
Entertainment Group

BOXTREE

This edition first published in Great Britain in 1993 by
Boxtree Limited

Stingray first published by Boxtree in 1992
Thunderbirds Are Go! first published by Boxtree in 1992
Captain Scarlet and the Mysterons first published by Boxtree in 1993

1 3 5 7 9 10 8 6 4 2

Designed by Millions Design
Printed and bound in Scotland by Cambus Litho Limited for

Boxtree Limited
Broadwall House
21 Broadwall
London SE1 9PL

A CIP catalogue entry for this book is available from the British Library.

ISBN 1 85283 900 7

CONTENTS

STINGRAY

CONTENTS

WELCOME TO LILLIPUT LAND

Gerry Anderson never intended to go into TV, let alone produce puppet films. Having entered the film industry in 1943 and worked his way up to the post of assistant editor at Gainsborough Pictures, he dreamed of directing feature films. 'I agreed to make the puppet films simply as a way of surviving,' he replied when posed the question: *why* puppets? 'At the time I had no interest in them. None at all. I'd never even seen one.'

His involvement in Lilliput Land began in 1956, when Gerry co-founded AP Films with Arthur Provis and 3 other directors — Sylvia Thamm (who later became his wife), special effects expert Reg Hill, and lighting cameraman John Read, who had handled the special effects

on several highly acclaimed British films, including *The Dam Busters*. Full of ambition and determined to make a name for themselves, the four of them set up office in an old mansion house called Islet Park down by the Thames at Maidenhead in Buckinghamshire.

As foolish as it may seem today, they expected people to ring up and order films like they ordered groceries from a shop.

Not surprisingly, the telephone (just the one, as having sunk their entire savings into the new company the partnership couldn't afford the luxury of an extension line) remained silent. The only letters they received were reminders for unpaid bills. The company was soon on the verge of bankruptcy. With the cold winds of failure threatening to blow away their dreams, the team swallowed their pride and decided to return to their previous occupations in order to earn money to keep their company alive; Gerry back to film editing, Sylvia by taking on film continuity work and Reg and John picking up where they had left off.

Fate took a hand when Roberta Leigh, a writer, called at their office with her idea of producing a series of puppet films entitled *The Adventures of Twizzle*. As Gerry recalls, she said, 'Look. I have these 52 fifteen-minute

Troy Tempest, at the controls of Stingray, the super-sub of the twenty-first century.

A publicity shot of Stingray. Note the numeral 3 painted on the pier wall.

Marina, the mute mermaid from Pacifica.

Hub of all activity at Marineville, the central Control Tower, the operations nerve centre of the World Aquanaut Security Patrol.

scripts. Would you be interested in making them?' He took less than a minute to confirm, that he would. 'It really wouldn't have mattered what the subject was. It just so happened that they were puppet films. We were on the breadline so the opportunity to do the series — to do *anything* — was simply too good to miss.'

The puppets used on *Twizzle* were made from papier mâché, with little black buttons for eyes and painted mouths; the storyline revolved around a little boy whose arms and legs would 'twizzle' and grow in length. 'Frankly, I was so ashamed,' Gerry remembered, confirming that whenever he met his friends in the feature film business and they asked him what he was doing, he would answer *sotto voce*, 'I'm making puppet films.'

It didn't take him long to forge a love-hate relationship with the puppets — he hated them enough to want to throw away the rule book, while focusing his mind on ways of improving the puppet-maker's lot. He decided the only solution was to make the *Twizzle* programmes as close to normal pictures as possible — 'really in order to maintain my self-respect.'

Until then, most puppet films had been animated by the use of strings and/or model animation — nicknamed 'pack shots' — which often resulted in jerky movements, and the entire laborious process was, by its nature, artistically limiting. Gerry and his team determined to change all that. Believing that a different technique could be evolved, the team tuned their minds to discovering a new way of surmounting the obstacles inherent in puppetry technique.

Gerry still remembers the hurdles they had to overcome.

'On series like *Bill and Ben* the puppeteers would stand behind a painted piece of hardboard scenery. They would be able to lean over this with the puppet and so be able to see the puppet's face, but because the puppets themselves could only work in front of a painted background, there was no depth and their shadows would fall across the backdrop. I wanted to change this. The first thing I did was to build an overhead bridge so that the puppeteers could stand over the puppets which meant that, in the case of Twizzle and friends, we were able to place cut-out models of hills into the set and space them out all the way down to the background and so get some depth into the scene. But this also meant that the puppeteers were looking down on their puppets and they couldn't see their faces, which meant it was extremely difficult for the operators to see which way the puppets were facing. Another problem was, because the mouths of the puppets in *Twizzle* didn't operate, the only way that the puppeteers could tell if a puppet was speaking was if it was nodding its head, which gave the puppets a terribly amateurish look.'

The problem was overcome when, early on into the production, a salesman visited the studio selling industrial television equipment. Gerry was quick to recognise the potential there. Despite the fact that the studio couldn't afford to do so, he purchased the lot and put it to immediate use. 'I hit upon the idea of mounting the television camera behind the cine-camera, with its lens looking directly through the cine-camera's eyepiece. So, instead of working blind, with the cine-camera operator being the only one who could see what was being filmed, we could now pipe his point of view through to the television monitors which enabled not just every-

In 'Plant of Doom', concerned that Marina is homesick, Troy suggests that she joins him aboard Stingray and guide him to her father's kingdom. Marina nods her agreement. Silly Troy. He never could resist a pretty face.

A publicity shot of Troy Tempest.

body working on the floor to see, but also the puppeteers working overhead. By looking down into the television monitors they now had a camera view of their puppets as they were being filmed, which allowed them to turn their characters in the right direction. We then reversed the scans of their monitors so that when they turned their puppets to the left, as viewed on the monitor, the puppets would also turn to the left.'

Delighted with the *Twizzle* series, Roberta Leigh asked the team to go on and make a new series of programmes, *Torchy, the Battery Boy*.

Armed with the experience they had gained during the previous series, and although saddled once again with a shoestring budget (each episode of *Twizzle* had cost £450, *Torchy* would cost just a few pounds more), Gerry and his associates pursued their dream of making puppet programmes on a spectacular scale — a search for perfection which led to a mass of innovations being brought in to improve the new show.

'We now had puppet heads which were made of plastic wood, heads that were hollow and had wooden eyeballs that could look to the left and right. They had mouths that could open and shut. The only problem was that the mouth was still being operated by a string. When the puppeteer pulled the string the mouth would open — but it wouldn't close. The solution was to invent a spring device to close it, but this meant the puppeteers had to give it a real hefty tug in order to overcome the spring mechanism, the consequence of which was that the head of the puppet nodded.' Eventually this was overcome to some degree by experiments made on two subsidiary puppets who had the beginnings of the Automatic Mouth Movement — the device that would revolutionize puppetry technique.

'On all the puppet programmes I've made, we would first of all record the dialogue,' Gerry recalls. This was then played back on the floor and the puppeteers would make the puppets mime the dialogue — in Torchy's case by operating the mouth with the string to sync the soundtrack. With the new system we were developing, we had installed solenoids (electro-magnets) into the puppet's head. We then brought in an electronics engineer who built a box containing a resistance-capacity network which, whenever the recorded dialogue was pushed through it, translated the words into pulses of DC current which would go up to the bridge where Torchy's puppeteer worked, down the wires holding the puppet and into the solenoid implanted in the puppet's head. When the current was flowing the solenoid became magnetic and pulled up a base plate that would open the mouth. When the current stopped the magnetism would stop and the return spring would close the mouth. The beauty of this system was, of course, the saving of time. The puppeteers no longer had to learn the dialogue in order to operate the mouths and the puppets were at last able to speak without their heads lolling about like a broken toy.'

Christine Glanville, the chief puppeteer on all the Anderson series since the *Torchy* series, describes how much more freedom of movement the AMM gave her when operating the puppets. 'It was a tremendous help, because it enabled us to concentrate on the action rather than the words. Prior to that we had to learn the lines, which wasn't really difficult, because the takes weren't very long, so one could memorise them easily. The difficulty was learning the space between the lines, so that one could start the mouth in sync with the dialogue.' She recalls that they didn't have cue-points in those days (a series of "pips", electrical starter points for the dialogue, piped to the puppet operators via headphones), so there was always a slight delay in operating the puppets' lips. 'As a consequence we would start late and catch up so that although we ended in sync, this made it very difficult for the editors because they couldn't sync up the words properly.'

Another departure from the restrictions imposed on the filmmakers by the two-dimensional backdrop sets was that, on *Torchy*, the sets had proper interiors; miniature rooms, complete with the trappings of everyday life.

'Exteriors had grass, bushes and trees dotted around the landscape. It was a great step forward,' Gerry remembers with obvious pride. 'For me, at any rate, the puppet series were beginning to look halfway respectable.' Respectable perhaps, but puppetry still wasn't paying the bills. Invited to make a further series of *Torchy*, Gerry considered his options.

A publicity shot of Sam Shore, the gravel-voiced commander of Marineville.

'I knew we were doing a great deal of development work at our studios — but we were doing it for somebody else. I thought it was time we should make our own films.' His associates agreed. Ideas were kicked around and they decided to make a pilot film for a series to be called *Four Feather Falls*, a Western written by Barry Gray, whom Gerry had met when he was working for Roberta Leigh. 'I asked him if he could compose as well. He said that he could, so he composed the music for *Four Feather Falls*, scripted the pilot and wrote the songs.' In total the pilot film cost the company £6,000 — £2,000 of which was paid to songsmith Michael Holliday, who was then a major star.

The pilot was shown on Granada TV, who put up the finance for 38 more episodes. Believing that success was waiting around the corner, the team realised that they required more space.

Throwing caution to the wind, they risked everything they had made and took an option on a disused factory premises on the Slough trading estate and set about converting this to their needs. Working from daybreak to midnight, they converted the unit into a film studio entirely on their own, cutting down the echo in the place by lining the walls with egg cartons and building and painting their own scenery.

The first real breakthrough in puppetry technique came on this series. Using an advanced version of the AMM for the very first time, Gerry and his team achieved a previously unheard-of high degree of synchronisation between dialogue and puppet movement. 'The series was really a huge step forward in production. We now had the whole of the main street to play with and the interiors of the saloon and the sheriff's office were beautifully made. We had managed to get

Marina and her father, pictured together in Aphony's throne room. From 'Plant of Doom'.

the puppets to do most things reasonably well now — but we still couldn't get them to walk! This was impossible. There were, of course, severe restrictions on what a puppet could do — or couldn't do. For example, if the wires were left slack by the puppeteer, they would coil and cast light and send off a hundred refractions. If the puppet operator didn't take the full weight of the puppet the character would slouch. If too much weight was taken, the puppet would become so light that its feet would sway from side to side like a pendulum.' This problem was eventually overcome by cutting to a waist shot and bobbing the puppet up and down to create the impression that they were walking.

Above all, *Four Feather Falls* was a great learning experience, one that would stand the team in good stead for the rigours to come. The Western series proved very successful and they expected Granada to ask for more. Granada didn't. It just took delivery and the team never heard from the company again. Once again AP Films had their backs to the wall.

Having learned by now that children needed lots of action and fast movement in their programmes, Gerry devoted his time to accomplishing ways of achieving the desired effect. 'It was a crazy situation. Here I was, stuck with puppets that couldn't even walk, let alone run, and I was faced with having to find a way of achieving even faster movements. There had to be a way.'

Gerry came up with the idea of creating a car, and so that there would be plenty of scope for stories, the car would be also a submarine that could fly. The idea was developed with Sylvia, and Reg Hill designed it, producing a superb brochure about its various workings. Such a vehicle would have to be *super* of course, so — *Supercar*, which enabled the puppets to seemingly whizz around at a break-neck pace. 'It was a bit of a cheat really, because the characters were being carried around in the vehicle,' said Gerry. 'It nevertheless achieved the desired effect.

'Then someone introduced us to Lew (now Lord) Grade, who funded the *Supercar* series and *Fireball XL5*, which was very successful and was sold to the American TV network, NBC.'

One day Lew Grade called Gerry to one of his usual 7.30 a.m. meetings and told him that he was going to buy his company. Gerry recalls: 'My company was very precious to me. Not financially, but the letterhead, the name, the van with the name painted on the side — I was really just a kid, it was *my* company and it was very important. So when he told me that he was going to buy my company, I was furious. I kept a poker face and remember thinking, "What a so-and-so cheek. Not, Gerry would you like to sell your company? Not, I'd very much like to buy your company, but *Gerry, I'm going to buy your company*!" And then he mentioned the price he was prepared to pay and I remember thinking, *what a splendid idea*! So he bought the company and ploughed a huge amount of money in and we opened these brand new studios in Slough — brand new factory units.'

It must be remembered that because the team were making puppet films, they didn't need the huge height that is required when making live action films. Because the sound was pre-recorded and only played back on the studio floor, they didn't require sound stages. Factory units were ideal. Gerry recalls that they spent an absolute fortune. 'We built stages. We had a property department, a scenery-building department, cutting rooms, the puppet building — it was a veritable fairyland and was the finest studio of its kind in the world. And our first production was *Stingray* . . . .'

Dressed in uniform or a tux, Troy is always prepared for a sudden emergency.

TROY, MARINA AND THE MEMBERS OF WASP

Unlike *Thunderbirds*, where the puppets' personalities were only sketchily outlined, in *Stingray* each puppet was given a highly detailed history, which added a degree of realism and depth when defining each character in the series. The hero was, of course, Troy Tempest.

Troy Tempest

Born in New York City in 2038, Troy was educated at the World Navy Academy at San Diego. Despite the fact that many of his schoolmates elected to train to become astronauts, Troy's interest in marine bionomics determined the next step in his career. Joining the submarine service at the age of 18, he forged a lasting friendship with fellow cadet George Lee Sheridan, a young man pursuing a degree in communication engineering. After showing outstanding bravery when under enemy fire, Troy was seconded to the Marineville WASP establishment, aged twenty-two and was promoted to the rank of captain and given command of the Stingray patrol vessel.

He has deep blue eyes, and his strikingly handsome face has a deceptively gentle look to it. Troy is conscientious and fearless as far as his career is concerned, but cautious and a bit of a dreamer in the romantic stakes. As far as women are concerned, he would rather be investigating an explosion at sea than finding ways to resist the romantic overtures of the women in his life: Atlanta Shore, daughter of the Marineville base commander, and Marina, the silent girl from the

sea. Both adore him with a passion, but Troy responds to their charms with indecision. Their relationship is that of friends, colleagues — at least as far as Troy is concerned! Atlanta makes no bones about it: she loves Troy to distraction, finds him intriguing and waits for the day he will reciprocate her love. Troy's feelings for Marina are somewhat confused. He finds it difficult to resist her exotic fluttering eyelashes, but shies away from her whenever Marina turns on the charm. His affection for her knows no bounds

Captain Troy Tempest, spearhead of the Marineville fleet and pride of the World Aquanaut Security Patrol.

'Why can't you whisper the words that my heart is longing to hear?' Marina and Troy, seen in the closing captions.

'Phones' Sheridan. His skill with the hydrophones have made him the envy of the fleet.

— as far as the job is concerned. But romance? He flits between the two of them enjoying the company of both while steadfastly refusing to say whom he prefers!

Spearhead of the WASP unit, Troy is already married — to his career!

Troy's voice was supplied by actor Don Mason.

Phones

Christened George Lee Sheridan, Phones was born in South Carolina. Fascinated by communication techniques when his father introduced him to radio as a child, Phones, a nickname supplied by his fellow cadets, due primarily to his skill on the Hydrophones, took a degree in communications engineering at the WNA in San Diego, before becoming a cadet in the WASP submarine arm. Rising rapidly to the rank of lieutenant, he was assigned to become Hydrophone Operator on Stingray at the suggestion of his friend Troy Tempest.

With Phones at his side, the Stingray captain can be certain that he selected the very best man for the job. Aged thirty-one, Phones may be a few years older than Troy, but he is a natural for the co-pilot's chair. There isn't a communications officer in the WASP unit to touch him. His skill with the hydrophones (short-range sonar equipment) is legendary, his piloting technique the envy of the fleet. Despite their status of commanding officer and subordinate, neither is senior to the other; the best double-act in the unit.

Down-to-earth, laid-back and cheerful, Phones is as brave as they come and can be relied upon in any emergency. He has to be, because the Stingray craft faces danger every time it sets sail!

American actor Robert Easton supplied Phones' voice.

Marina

Rescued by Troy and Phones after being captured and made slave by Titan, Marina escapes with the Stingray crew and becomes Troy's devoted aide.

Only 19 years old, she is the daughter of Aphony, ruler of the undersea city of Pacifica, a huge shell city on the bed of the ocean.

A tail-less mermaid from an underwater continent, Marina is unable to communicate vocally with her friends but nevertheless understands what is said to her and makes herself understood

Unable to communicate vocally with her friends, Marina puts her message across by the expressive use of her hands.

by the expressive use of her hands. The reason for her muteness is her love of her father and race: she was sworn to silence by Titan, who told her that if she were ever to speak again, her people and city would be destroyed.

A hybrid who can breathe just as well in water and air, legend has it that her race is the result of the union between a human and a mermaid — hence they have characteristics of both races; their flesh caucasian in colour, their eyes and hair green. She sometimes accompanies Troy and Phones on their missions in Stingray.

Marina can swim like a fish, her lithe, perfectly shaped human body being able to withstand great water pressures and she is equally well at home on the surface where she is able to remain for long periods without harm.

Passionately in love with Troy, she has formed a friendship with Atlanta, and engages in friendly rivalry with her for Troy's affections.

Troy and Phones, partners in mayhem. The best double-act in the WASP unit.

A character study of Atlanta,
daughter of the Marineville
commander Sam Shore.
She's intelligent and tough,
but her heart melts when
she's close to Troy.

Atlanta

Daughter of Marineville Commander Sam Shore, Atlanta is the assistant communications officer at the control tower, part of her job being to supervise Stingray's launch. All WASP craft must obtain her clearance before entering or leaving the base.

Born in California, since the death of her mother, the auburn-haired, brown-eyed girl has run the Shore household. A gifted cook, her kitchen is ultra-modern and functional and comes complete with a state-of-the-art hi-fi unit.

Like her father, the twenty-three-year-old lieutenant is disciplined and strong-willed. She has carved out her rise through the ranks on ability — not looks. The equal of any WASP operative, Atlanta conducts herself in a highly business-like manner — except, of course, where Troy is concerned.

She fell madly in love with the Stingray captain on their first meeting, and constantly tries to get him to propose — despite the fact that she suspects Troy is really attracted to Marina. Pushing this rivalry to the back of her mind, Atlanta treats the mermaid as a sister, although at times her behaviour towards her is distinctly cool — particularly when Troy appears to favour the girl from the sea.

Her voice is spoken by actress Lois Maxwell, the original Miss Moneypenny in the Bond films.

Commander Sam Shore

Christened Samuel Arthur, the WASP commander was born in Kansas in 2015. Leaving home at an early age, he ran away to sea and spent the early part of his life in the navy, rapidly achieving promotion through the ranks and taking command of a World Security Service submarine three years into his service. While out on routine patrol, his vessel was attacked by hostile aircraft. Crippled during the combat, he is chairbound and moves around in a hoverchair constructed by the WASP technicians. A highly-manoeuvrable conveyance, powered by a 186 cc hydro-combustion engine, this enables him to carry on his business in a somewhat aloof manner.

Handed the task of setting up the Marineville HQ, Shore eagerly accepted the challenge of forming and controlling the WASP base. To no one's surprise, he completed the task with the knowledge and ability of a man who knows where he is going — straight to the top.

A fine figure of a man with short, greying hair, Shore may be getting on a bit (he's 50), but everyone at the base acknowledges his ability to run Marineville in his gruff-voiced, authoritative manner. Indeed, the WASP personnel wouldn't

have it any other way, those close to him being aware that he's really a big softie at heart.

Sam's voice is provided by Australian actor, Ray Barrett, who also supplied the voice for Titan — Sam Shore's arch-rival!

Sub-Lieutenant Fisher

Twenty-two year old John Horatio Fisher was born in Oregon.

Atlanta's relief controller in the control tower, Fisher joined the Marineville team after a distinguished career as a World Navy Cadet.

Sometimes overly enthusiastic at his post, the sub-lieutenant has yet to qualify as a fully fledged WASP patrol boat captain.

Commander Shore and control room assistant Sub-lieutenant John Horatio Fisher, trainee aquanaut.

Oink

Having saved the Stingray crew on a mission to the Arctic Circle, Oink, Marina's pet seal cub, was adopted by Troy and Phones as the Stingray mascot when the baby seal stowed away aboard the vessel.

There is always villainy afoot, of course, particularly whenever the Stingray crew venture near to Titanica, the birthplace and domain of their foremost enemy:

Titan

230 marine years old, the olive-skinned Titan is the undoubted ruler of the kingdom of Titanica.

Cruel and vicious, he hates the land people with a vengeance and longs to dominate them all. A constant thorn in Titan's side is Troy Tempest, the man who dared to steal away his slave, Marina. Instilled with an intense hatred for the Stingray captain, Titan has sworn to invade the surface world and wipe WASP off the face of the earth.

Driven by his mad dreams of domination, he attempts to accomplish this with the help of his slaves, the Aquaphibians, who appointed Titan as their ruler after he had destroyed a giant squid that had threatened their existence.

Powerful though he may be, Titan is obsequious before Teufel, the mute fish god he keeps in a tank in his throne room, who he believes has supernatural powers and who is used to decide the fate of Titan's prisoners. If the fish god turns its back on the person in custody within one marine minute, the prisoner is sentenced to the undersea prison of Aquatraz!

Titan's voice was supplied by Ray Barrett.

X-2-Zero

In order to keep abreast of what is happening in Marineville, Titan employs surface agent X-2-Zero, a strange, creepy bug-like creature, to spy on the WASP set-up. Despite the fact that his employer treats him with total contempt, the dim-witted agent jumps to Titan's every command.

Shrewd and ruthless (or so he thinks), the 107 marine years old mealy-mouthed toady of Titan lives in a secret base on the Isle of Lemoy, a barren stretch of rock in the Pacific Ocean near to Marineville. Viewed from the air, the base appears to be an ordinary, dilapidated old mansion, but at the press of a button its rooms are transformed into a fantastic spy centre, complete with communication devices on which X-2-Zero makes direct contact with Titan via a huge marine screen.

Whenever he wishes to travel to Titanica, the surface agent hops aboard his one-man submarine, a sleek, fish-like craft driven by powerful engines. This is normally housed in a secret pen cut into the rock of the island.

A master of disguise, the silvery-blue, bug-eyed amphibian always manages to put his foot in it when devising another devious scheme to wreak havoc on Troy and his colleagues.

Actor Robert Easton portrayed X-2-Zero's voice.

The Aquaphibians

A race of physically monstrous Terrainians who serve as Titan's soldiers, these green-skinned, scaly-backed creatures are used by their ruler to put the frighteners on Troy and Phones.

Big, ugly and unbelievably stupid, these less-than-friendly aliens have bulging eyes and razor-sharp fangs, and are able to operate in or out of the water. They obey Titan without question. Though they can converse in primitive English, they normally communicate in a strange gurgling language.

Ordered into attack, their main weapons are their mechanical fish, known as Terror Fish. Manufactured in Titanica's undersea laboratories, these are capable of fantastic speeds. The fish-shaped craft carry a two-man crew who launch their high-powered missiles from their gaping mouths. Titanica can also launch the Terror Fish missiles from special launch ramps situated on the outskirts of the kingdom.

The voices of the Aquaphibians were supplied by a constant looped tape of bubbling water!

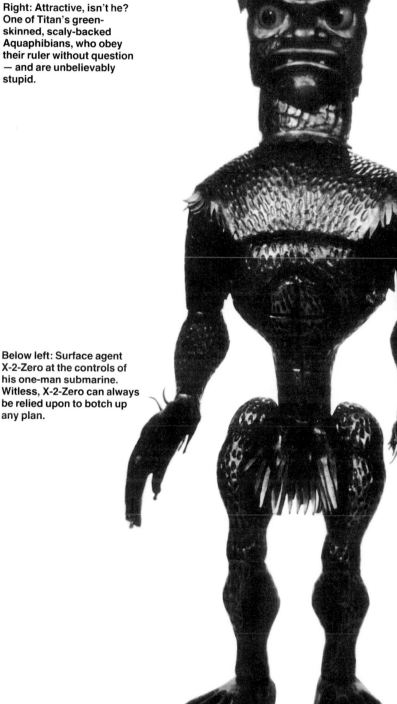

Left: Titan, ruler of the kingdom of Titanica, whose dreams of dominating the land people are thwarted at every turn by his spy, Agent X-2-Zero, who kneels before him.

Right: Attractive, isn't he? One of Titan's green-skinned, scaly-backed Aquaphibians, who obey their ruler without question — and are unbelievably stupid.

Below left: Surface agent X-2-Zero at the controls of his one-man submarine. Witless, X-2-Zero can always be relied upon to botch up any plan.

STINGRAY AND THE WORLD OF MARINEVILLE

It's the year 2065. United under a world government, the surface world is at peace. Having conquered the galaxy, man has turned his attention to the exploration of inner space, the oceans that cover three fifths of the world and provide a new source of mineral resources. But the sanctum is peopled by many alien races, some of them hostile to the surface people whom they see as invaders of their domain — creatures like the green-skinned Aquaphibians, a race of undersea warriors ruled by Titan, an evil despot who has sworn to invade the surface world and destroy the forces of the World Security Patrol, an international organisation set up to preserve world peace.

The hub of this organisation is the World Aquanaut Security Patrol (WASP), an ocean police force which patrols the seas of the world and protects the world from enemy threats. As its title implies, WASP is a security force, its role being defensive, not aggressive, its aim to maintain world peace.

WASP's most powerful asset is the sleek and deadly underwater craft Stingray.

Highly advanced, even by 21st-century standards, this atomic-powered craft — Mark III of a series of experimental WASP patrol/combat vessels — has been in service for 3 years, its success rate against attack from hostile forces making it the pride of the World Security Patrol fleet.

Its incredible speed — Mark 4 beneath the surface (equal to 600 knots) and a surface cruising speed of 400 knots — is achieved by using sea water which, sucked in and rapidly heated by its atomic generator, drives its twin Drumman hydrojets, giving the vessel tremendous thrust which enables Stingray to cruise and dive to depths never before achieved by a manned underwater craft. Its pressurised, honeycomb-laminated monocoque hull is able to withstand tremendous underwater pressures, thereby allowing the vessel to submerge almost vertically to previously unexplored depths of the ocean, where it can land on the sea-bed, no matter how uneven the surface, by lowering its retractable skids. On routine cruising manoeuvres, these skids are withdrawn into the vessel's undercarriage.

Completely self-contained, Stingray can remain at sea for six months at a time, its ultra-comfort furnishings providing the crew with a home-from-home facility. Used by the aquanauts whenever the vessel is being steered by its onboard Automatic Bosun, Stingray's relaxation bay houses the crew's wardroom, sleeping quarters, well-provisioned galley and equipment bays, each of which is accessed by descending the control cabin companion ladder. The wardroom itself contains a comprehensive reference/navigation library, complete with chart table,

A publicity shot of WASP's most powerful asset, the sleek and deadly, atomic-powered super-sub Stingray.

Right: When Marina, Phones and Professor Darren find themselves trapped in the bathyscape, Troy exits from Stingray on a sea-bug to give Titan and his henchmen a taste of their own medicine. From 'The Golden Sea.'

Above right: Atlanta can plot Stingray's progress on the Automatic Sea Map, which enables her to pinpoint any approaching vessel.

and, despite the shortage of space for off-duty leisure activities, offers the crew the opportunity to play a game of chess on the touch-button rotating chessboard. The companion ladder also gives access to Stingray's engine room and equipment storage bays.

When piloting the vessel, Captain Troy Tempest, WASP's heroic Stingray commander, sits to port and Phones to starboard. Always at their fingertips are the half-moon bridge steering columns, which retract into the main control console whenever the crew leave their chairs. Positioned between these and directly in front of the crew is the bank of operating controls, incorporating the vessel's Sting Missile — or Aquasting — launch levers and push buttons — both being used when firing Stingray's defence weapons — a depth gauge and the engine speed monitor clock. To the left and immediately behind the captain's chair, sit the vessel's auxiliary controls. Although the craft is designed in such a way that its crew have a wide field of vision and can see what is going on around them when the craft is submerged, an additional look-out facility is suspended from the ceiling of the control cabin adjacent to Stingray's hatch number 1. Known as the Surface Video Screen (SVS), this underwater television apparatus — somewhat akin to a periscope — enables the aquanauts to see and detect objects at a greater distance than the range of the human eye. (Hinged to allow the team to exit and enter, the SVS camera arm can be swung back whenever hatch number 1 is in use.) The SVS is also equipped with several other 'look and learn' devices.

Positioned on the wall adjacent to the captain's chair is the sound and echo equipment used by Phones to send out long-range signals which, returned to Stingray as echoes, allow the hydrophone operator to detect objects from as far as 4 miles away.

Several hatch compartments afford the crew the opportunity to leave the vessel when Stingray is submerged.

The main hatch, situated immediately in front of the control cabin, allows the team to exit Stingray in their deep-water aquasuits. Manufactured from a special pliant fabric, the suits protect the crew from the extreme underwater temperatures whilst allowing them freedom of movement. The face-masks of these are fitted with two-way receiver microphones and each of the team wears a wrist radio which allows them to communicate with each other over short distances.

Whenever the aquanauts depart on short reconnaissance dives, they hop aboard their Aquasprites: two-man underwater jeeps, capable of high — but limited — bursts of speed. Stingray carries two such craft, each being housed in the vessel's hull to the rear. More

anoeuvrable — and therefore put to more
equent use — are the team's one-man operated
abugs. Operating on compressed-air principles,
ese small, sleek vehicles — akin to one-man
bs — make it possible for the aquanauts to
opel themselves along at high speed and
plore places where it would be impossible for
ingray or the Aquasprites to penetrate. A third
ode of transport is provided by the Mono-
pters. Steered from the rear by jet packs, these
ord the crew the facility to hover in the air and
ove up or down, forwards or backwards at the
uch of a button. These prove particularly
eful in allowing the team to exit from Stingray
d propel themselves across to the shore.

Stingray's principal armament are its Sting Missiles. Armed with an explosive power equivalent to 1,000 tons of TNT, these deadly, atomic-powered darts can be guided by remote control. The craft carries a complement of 16.

At all times, the patrol vessel is in radio contact with its Marineville control base, thanks to the 21st-century discovery of achieving a means of transmitting radio waves through water.

Stingray cannot fly, but it can leap out of the water, salmon fashion.

It's a question Gerry Anderson has been asked many times: Why should people sit in seats and then slide down a pole, straight into the submarine? Why not just have them race down the stairs and board like anybody else? His reply: 'At that time, British, American and Russian pilots were sitting in Atom Bombers day and night, so that if the call came, bang, they were away. It was that that prompted me to launch Stingray in this fashion. I thought, if you want to get away in a hurry . . . .'

The Stingray crew is alerted to their latest mission via the Videophone link between WASP headquarters in Washington and the Central Control Room in Marineville. Spurred into action, Troy and Phones drop whatever they are doing, cross to the Injector Bay — a recessed area set into the wall of the Standby Lounge — position themselves into one of 3 injector seats (chair number 3 being used by Atlanta whenever she joins the crew) and await further orders — usually while contemplating aloud what they are letting themselves in for this time!

Told by her father, Commander Shore, to sound launch stations, Atlanta depresses the appropriate button on her computer console and sets in motion the Stingray launch sequence.

Alerted to action by the high-pitched, staccato drum beat emanating from the speaker directly above their position, Troy and Phones push forward the injection chair-release levers. The floor beneath them slides open and the aquanauts are transported swiftly down long injector

tubes to the flooded subterranean compartments that lie several fathoms beneath the Marineville complex, each of which is big enough to house several sea-going craft, to their destination, Pen Number 3, in which Stingray is docked.

Deposited into the vessel via hatch number 1 — situated in the submarine's conning tower — the crew find themselves directly in command of Stingray's operational instrument banks. Should Marina join them on a mission, her entry to the sub is achieved via the hatch immediately adjacent to the SVS periscope. Their chairs locked into position by hydraulic clamps, Troy orders Phones

Stingray can leap out of the water, salmon fashion, in order to evade a hostile craft; in this case, Titan's Terror Fish.

Phones and Troy are transported down the injector tubes – their destination, Pen Number 3 . . .

. . . and Stingray, which sits supported on its hydraulic-powered, elevated pen support.

PEN 3
STINGRAY

STINGRAY

3

to release the injection tubes. The tubes retract, the hatch is sealed and the hydrophone operator signals to Atlanta to release the elevators. The computer-controlled, hydraulic-powered elevated pen support platform does the rest. Lowering the vessel and its crew to the pen floor, it pulls aside its giant clamps and Stingray is free to power-up its engine. Given the order to accelerate (more often than not, 'Acceleration Rate 1'), the vessel builds up speed. The docking pen door slides open and, *whoosh*, Stingray is propelled forward through the aperture and out into the inky-blue ocean tunnel beyond. Above them in the control room, Atlanta tracks the vessel's progress on her tunnel scanner. Confirming that

Stage 1 (a successful launch) has been completed, she releases the control that opens the ocean door — a huge extrance/exit door, constructed of 12-inch thick steelite, a tough, rust-proof metal compound — giving Stingray access to the ocean. In receipt of Troy's verbal confirmation 'Sea borne', Commander Shore briefs the crew on their mission.

The injection tubes withdraw, the locking-clamps fall away and the vessel descends to the ocean floor, ready to power-up its engine. Ordered to accelerate, Stingray propels itself forward . . .

. . . and zips out through the Ocean Door into the inky-blue ocean, ready to face another dangerous mission.

Located in the Pacific Ocean, somewhere on the west coast of North America (its true location is known only to a handful of hand-picked, highly placed, senior members of government), Marineville is situated 10 miles inland (or 20, depending on the source material one reads.) Revolutionary in design, the WASP base is a completely self-sufficient community capable of surviving alone for a period of 3 years.

Having harnessed the ocean's tide movement to drive its atomic pile generator, the township produces its own lighting, heating and air-conditioning. In times of power-failure, the generating plant can be backed up by the nearby reserve power plant, which, able to draw and convert the sun's solar energy into electricity, drives the Marineville dynamo. Built on the edge of the ocean, the plant has a water purification filter to convert salt water into fresh drinking water to fill the requirements of, among other Marineville establishments, the community hospital.

Equipped with ultra-modern health-care devices, like the wall-mounted diagnostic machines, the four-storey complex employs a team of 300 medical men and nurses, each of whom are experts in their chosen field. On duty 24 hours a day, the doctors and nurses are serviced by a fleet of jet-propelled ambulances. Capable of speeds up to 150 mph, these miniature hospitals-on-wheels come complete with their own operating theatre and airlight suspension to ensure that no time is lost — or medical expertise spared — when conveying their patients to the medical base. Garaged in bays beneath the hospital, each vehicle is linked to a medical team by a videophone. High on the hospital's agenda is the research carried out in the marine laboratories, including ways of discovering how man can best adapt himself to a marine existence.

Befitting the ultra-modern design of the community, the Marineville living quarters are luxurious in the extreme. WASP and civilian personnel live side by side in the apartment and housing

Prisoners of the Varls, the Stingray crew plot the course of the alien missile on the video map. When the light reaches the end of its course, Marineville will cease to exist! A pulse-pounding moment from the episode 'Emergency Marineville.'

mplex situated near to the control tower.
eisure facilities include every type of sports and
creational activities, shops and a theatre. Get-
1g about in Marineville is simplicity itself, by
opping aboard one of the hovercars which
ovide a link with all works areas. Operating
1 a cushion of air, induced by the downward
rust of their engines, the hovercars are a
ompact and highly efficient method of transport.
apable of achieving a top speed of 200 mph, it
kes the hovercar no time at all to deposit its
ssengers at their destination point. Senior
ASP officials drive around in high-powered
aff cars, which, as with all Marineville vehicles,
e radio-linked to their control base — a

security move, taken to ensure that no one,
neither civilian or WASP personnel, can stray
further than the base perimeter control points.
Should they do so — accidentally or otherwise
— they are certain to run into the WASP guard
units who man the checkpoints day and night;
admittance and exit being allowed only on the
production of a top-security pass.

The centre of all activity at Marineville is the
Control Tower. Mounted centrally above the
ops building, it is not unlike an airfield control
tower, but that's where the similarity ends. Its
exterior dimensions belie the interior. Housed
here is a complex of offices, planning rooms,
research departments, conference rooms and

The Central Control Tower is from where Commander Shore controls the WASP organisation, supported by his daughter, Atlanta, who operates the banks of computer-generated communications consoles.

When under hostile attack, the entire Marineville complex is lowered beneath the surface to the safety of an underground emplacement by enormous hydraulic support ramps.

relaxation lounges. At the heart of the tower stands the Master Control Room, the nerve centre of WASP HQ, a room of spartan appearance decked out with a myriad of intricate machinery, computer consoles, banks of highly sensitive communications monitors and row upon row of transmitting machines. It is from here that the WASP patrol vessels receive their operational orders from Commander Shore who controls the activities of the WASP organisation in an authoritarian manner, sometimes under direct orders from WASP headquarters in Washington, via the Videophone link, a television link-up device which allows the caller to see as well as hear the person to whom he is talking. However, if required, vision can be eliminated at the touch of a button.

During an hostile attack, 'Battle Stations' is sounded and a well-organised operation sends the entire Marineville complex beneath the surface to the safety of the underground emplacement, making it quite invisible from above. 'Battle Stations' procedure is tested daily to ensure maximum efficiency.

The control tower descends first, followed by the living quarters, the military installations, power plant and parking bays, each being lowered to the depths by huge hydraulic support platforms. Enormous steel and concrete shutters seal the base from the outside world, protecting it from any attack.

Safe in its subterranean lair, Marineville can retaliate with a variety of defence devices. Vital to its defence are the underwater interceptor missiles, deadly rockets which, concealed beneath the sea-bed very close to Marineville's ocean approaches, can destroy hostile craft within a range of 12 miles. Powered by magno-dynatomic engines and capable of underwater launch speeds of more than 150 knots, the base has an arsenal of these. The second arm of its defence are Hydromic missiles — huge rockets capable of speeds up to 25,000 mph. Stored underground, these remote-controlled darts are fired from launch pads. Kept on constant alert are the Marineville hypersonic aircraft, vertical take-off search and strike fighters capable of flying at fantastic speeds.

The WASP jet squadron takes off. Their mission, to bombard the 'Pink Ice', in which Stingray is trapped, with their Hydromic missiles.

Fired from launch pads, the WASP Hydromic missiles are Marineville's second arm of defence.

STINGRAY'S OPPONENTS: A CLOSER LOOK AT THE ALIEN CRAFT

Despite what Gerry Anderson says, not all models were highly detailed in structure. As Jim Millett and Dave Tremont, co-founders of *The Model Smiths*, a TV Special Effects studio based in Queensland, point out, various alien craft encountered by Stingray on its undersea missions were often made on the spot, from whatever materials were at hand.

Jim and Dave were responsible for the creation of the highly detailed miniature scale models used in television's *Mission Impossible* (1989 version), commercials for the Toyota 'Chillies'

motor car (1990), Air New Zealand (1990) and the children's television series *Tip Top Muffins* (1991).

According to Jim and Dave — and they should know — the *Stingray* team had just the one in-house model maker, Eric Backman, who created the models depicted here on a workbench set up in the studio, the main models being made by Mastermodels — later known as Space Models. The models came from a variety of sources: plastic model kits, cardboard, metal tubing, styrene sheeting, balsa wood, and bits of material scavenged from all over the place.

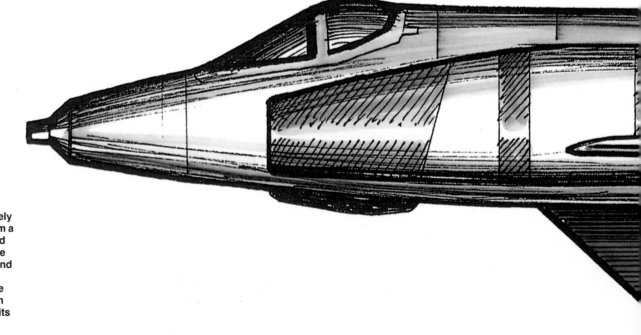

Alien craft from 'Sea of Oil'

The model is approximately 12 inches long, made from a Delta Dart kit. A shortened tail fin is mounted with the base of an Atlas rocket, and a fin from a 'Jupiter C' kit serves for the engine. The main wing is upside down and has other assorted bits added.

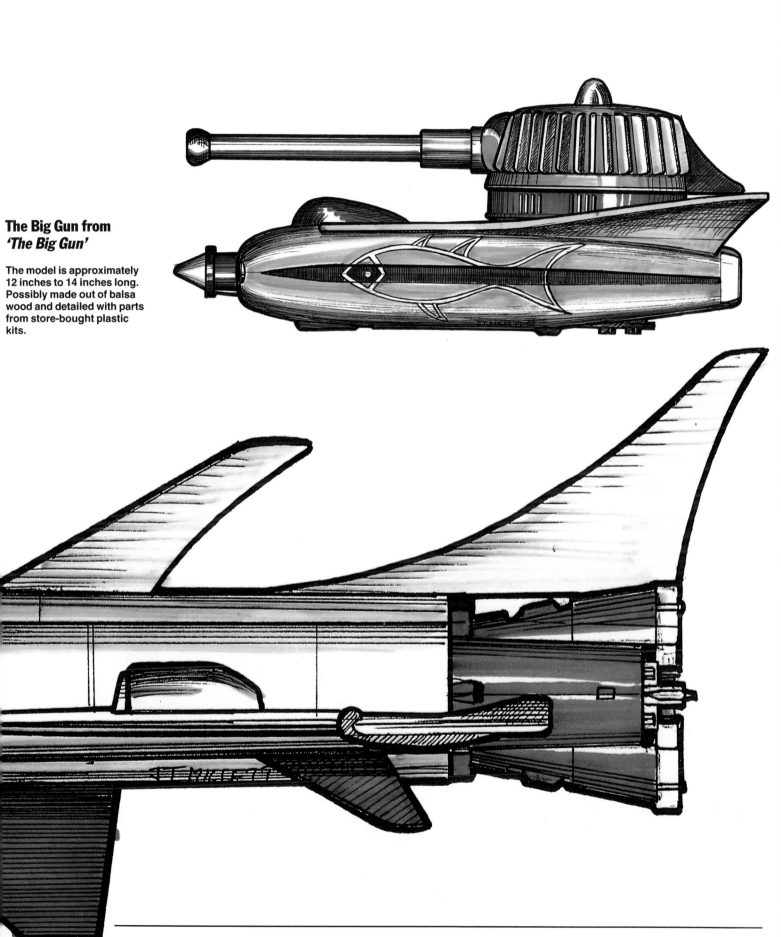

The Big Gun from 'The Big Gun'

The model is approximately 12 inches to 14 inches long. Possibly made out of balsa wood and detailed with parts from store-bought plastic kits.

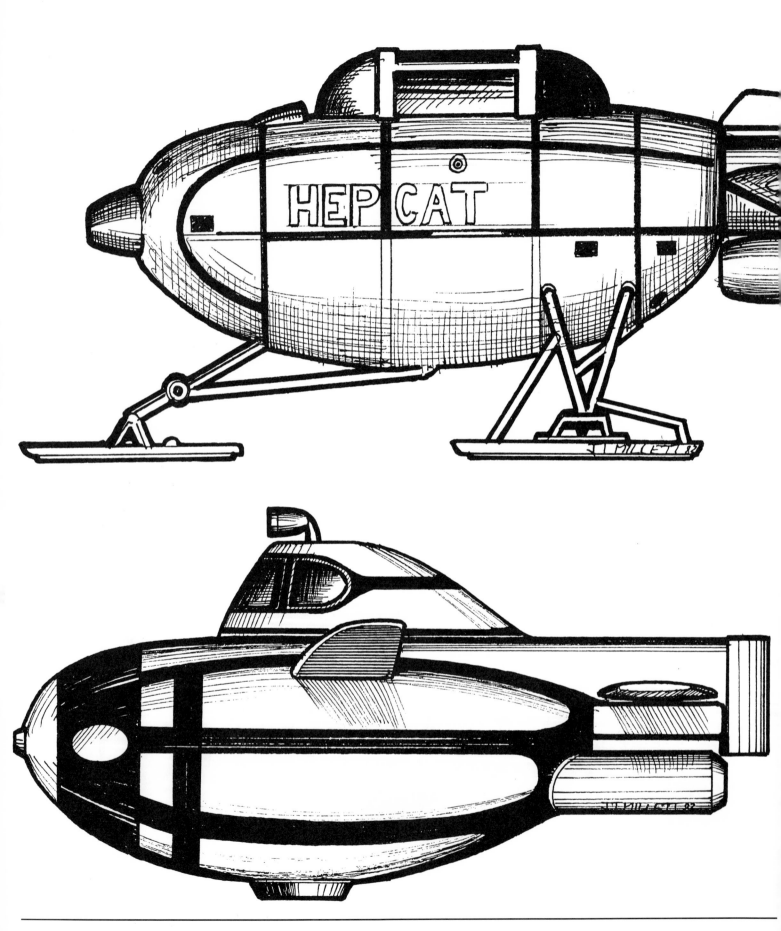

(LEFT)
Hep-Cat from *'Rapture of the Deep'*

This is the same model as the one used in 'Ghost of the Sea' with added detail to nose and tail, plus aircraft wings and decals. The canopy is similar to the one on 'Supercar.'

(BELOW LEFT)
Unidentified Hostile Craft from *'Ghost of the Sea'*

The model is approximately 10 to 14 inches long. It is most probably made out of balsa wood, detailed with kit bits and aircraft wings. This one is a re-dressed Hep-Cat.

(BELOW)
Bathyscape from *'The Golden Sea'*

The model is approximately 12 inches long, made out of balsa wood, with kit bits for dressing, as well as plastic and metal tubing.

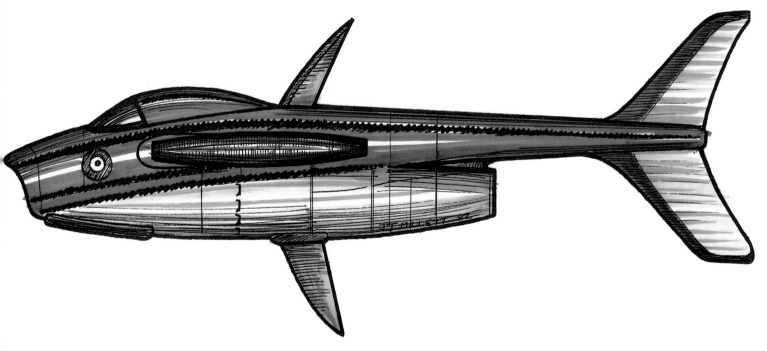

Agent X-2-Zero's Craft

This was made from an X5 Aircraft kit. The basic fuselage has added fins as well as pods on its side to cover up the holes where the main wings had been removed.

Alien Craft from *'Pink Ice'*

The model is approximately 10 to 12 inches long. It is most probably balsa wood with plastic kit pieces added for effect.

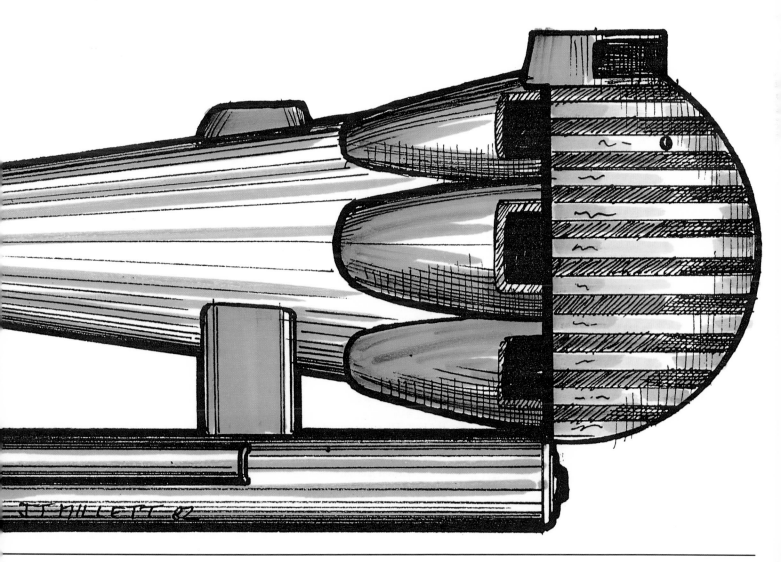

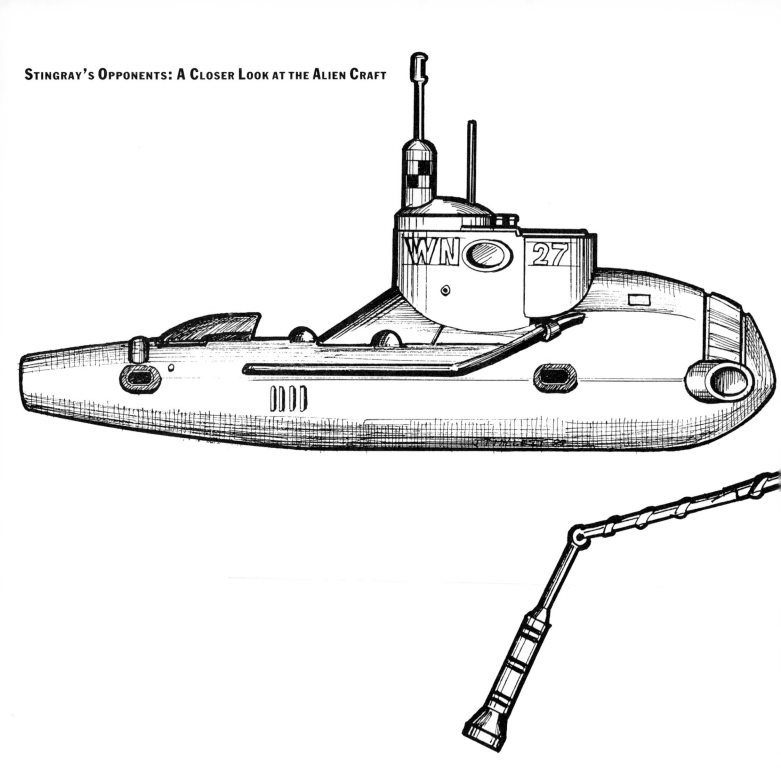

Navy Sub 27 from *'Man From the Navy'*

The model is approximately 12 inches long, and is from a toy or kit racing car with added conning tower and bits of plastic for detail. Redressed and repainted, this model was used several times for publicity shots, as well as used in an episode of *Thunderbirds*.

Alien Towing Craft from *'Trapped In the Depths'*

The model is approximately 10 inches long. It is basically wood on a ribbed tube with a removable top for access to the towing line. It is detailed with plastic kit parts.

Downbeat from *'Tune of Danger'*

The model is approximately 16 to 18 inches long. It has a balsa wood body, with plastic side pipes. The conning tower has pins for rivets and decals from aircraft kits. Decals on nose are from a Hot Rod kit.

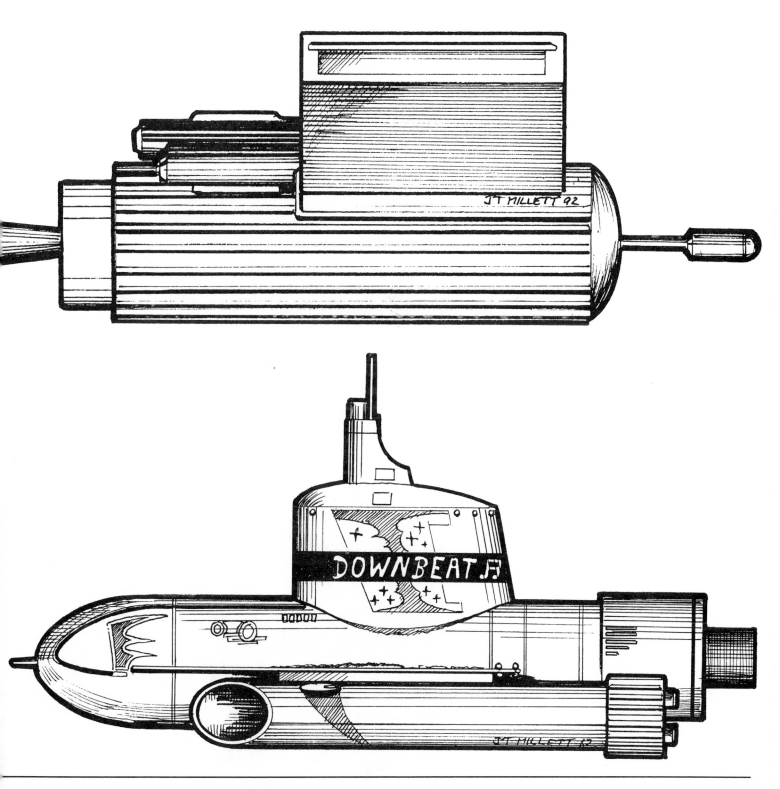

'Anything Can Happen in the Next Half hour!'

Stingray (The Pilot)

Ordered to investigate strange explosions at sea, Captain Troy Tempest and Phones set sail in Stingray and encounter a mysterious underwater race ruled by Titan, the tyrannical ruler of Titanica. Several hours into their mission, Stingray is attacked by a giant mechanical fish and the super vessel is sent crashing to the bottom of the ocean. Its pilots are taken to Titan's underwater palace, and a trial is held before the mighty fish god, Teufel, whom Titan believes to have supernatural powers. Found guilty, Troy and Phones are sentenced to death. Back in Marineville, Commander Shore mounts an aerial search and decides to bomb Titanica with hydromic missiles — leaving his WASP team with only thirty minutes in which to engineer their escape. Help comes from Marina, daughter of Aphony, ruler of the peaceful undersea kingdom of Pacifica and Titan's slave. She helps them to escape and accompanies them back to Marineville to become a permanent member of the team.

Script: **Director:**
Gerry & Sylvia Anderson Alan Pattillo

This episode has no on-screen title, but is commonly referred to as The Pilot.

'Standby for action. Anything can happen in the next half hour!'

'Who are you? Where am I?' asks Troy in the pilot episode. Titan supplies the answer. Troy is the first Terranean to set eyes upon the underwater kingdom of Titanica. Bad news for Troy — until Marina lends a hand

 WASP 2 **Plant of Doom**

Conscious that Marina is feeling homesick, Troy agrees to take her to see her father in Pacifica. Made aware of this, the vicious Titan sends agent X-2-Zero to the domed city with a seemingly beautiful flower in a glass bowl, the cover of which, when removed, gives off an exotic but deadly perfume. Returning to Marineville, Marina presents the flower to Atlanta who removes the glass cover and collapses. Suspected of an assassination attempt, Marina is arrested. Believing her innocent, Troy determines to discover the truth by leaving the uncovered flower in Marina's possession. If she ignores it, this will be proof of her guilt. Marina sniffs the deadly perfume and everyone realises that she is the victim of duplicity. Now recovered, Atlanta invites Marina to be the guest at a dinner in her honour.

Script:
Alan Fennell

Director:
David Elliott

 WASP 3 **Sea of Oil**

Accompanying Troy and Phones on a special mission to investigate the destruction of an oil-drilling rig which breaks into pieces to the accompaniment of weird, high-pitched humming noises, Atlanta is captured and taken to an underwater city. Discovering that its inhabitants are responsible for the oil-rig disasters but are really a peace-loving race who believe that Troy is trying to destroy their city, Atlanta becomes alarmed when told that a bomb has been planted on Stingray. This will explode as soon as the craft submerges. Enter Oink, Stingray's pet seal, who saves the day by pushing the bomb overboard. Aware that the WASP team will attempt to rescue her, Atlanta hits upon the idea of spelling out her name in the International Distress Code. Stingray picks up the signal and, reunited with Atlanta, Troy sorts out the misunderstanding with the city dwellers.

Script:
Dennis Spooner

Director:
John Kelly

'Aphony, the peaceful one. Cultural lord of the oceans. Great leader of the famed city of Pacifica . . .' Surface agent X-2-Zero turns on the charm when presenting Marina's father with the 'Plant of Doom', which gives off an exotic but deadly perfume.

When all seems lost, Troy and Phones turn the tables on Gadus and his henchman, perpetrators of 'The Hostages of the Deep' . . .

4

Hostages of the Deep

A distress signal from Admiral Carson, a former member of WASP, requests Stingray's aid — but it also contains a code warning of a trap. Carson, who lives in retirement with his wife on the island of Lull, is being held prisoner by Gadus, an underwater despot whose aim is to destroy Stingray and its crew. The trap fails. When Stingray proves to be too large to follow Gadus's underwater craft to its base in a submerged cavern, Marina leaves the craft and heads for the tunnel, Troy and Phones following minutes later in their Aquasuits. Captured by Gadus and his henchman, Marina is placed upon a stone slab. Above her hangs an evil-looking swordfish, from whose nose comes a long, razor-sharp, jagged-edged sword. When all seems lost, Troy and Phones enter the cavern, and rescue Marina, the Admiral and his wife.

but not before the underwater despot, Gadus, has taken Marina hostage at gunpoint!

Script:
Alan Fennell

Director:
Desmond Saunders

WASP
5

Treasure Down Below

Having purchased an old treasure map, Phones is disappoined when Troy is disinclined to suspend judgement and refuses to have anything to do with a treasure hunt. However, when Marina alters Stingray's course and takes the craft close to where the map denotes the treasure is buried, Troy finally agrees to investigate. He gives the order to dive and the craft is caught in a whirlpool which swirls them into an underwater cave. They find the treasure inside it, but are taken prisoner by two fish-people. Offer of rescue comes from a Captain Black, but Troy refuses to meet his terms. The WASP crew fight the fish-people and Troy escapes, leaving Phones and Marina behind to face their punishment. When Troy steals back to the cave, he finds his friends strapped to torture racks. He saves the day, of course, and puts an end to the underwater pirates' careers.

Script: **Director:**
Dennis Spooner   Alan Pattillo

WASP
6

The Big Gun

Sent to investigate the mysterious destruction of three Pacific islands which have been wiped out in the course of one week, the Stingray crew encounter enemies the like of which man has never seen before. They succeed in destroying an unidentified craft which attacks them, and Marineville scientists learn that the materials used to build the craft come from one of the deepest parts of the sea. On patrol again, Stingray comes under attack. Evading destruction, they track the mysterious vessel deep into a subterranean sea where they discover an underwater city. When the pressure on Stingray's hull increases, Troy and Phones lose consciousness. Marina, however, being an underwater creature herself, stays alert and manages to fire a Sting missile which saves their lives and destroys the underwater city. As a result of the crew almost losing their lives, and conscious that Stingray must be prepared to go to greater depths of the ocean, Commander Shore puts in hand further experiments to enable the craft to do so.

Script: **Director:**
Alan Fennell   David Elliott

He may look friendly — but this alien being is responsible for the destruction of three Pacific islands, courtesy of his tank-like craft 'The Big Gun.'

The Golden Sea

When a team of underwater scientists discover a way of mining gold from the seabed, Titan, the ruler of Titanica, uses the opportunity to strike at Stingray, which has been assigned to keep in contact with the scientists, take them supplies and return to Marineville with the gold they have mined. Making use of a giant swordfish which is capable of giving off an electrical charge that will destroy both Stingray and the scientists, Titan seizes his chance and attacks. Aware of their impending doom, Troy elects to stay behind in Stingray while Phones and the mining team escape in a bathyscape. Unknown to them, Titan has placed a sounder device on the escape vehicle. The swordfish attacks, sending an electrical charge through the bathyscape, throwing everyone inside to the floor. But Troy turns the tables by removing the sounder device that he had placed on the escape vehicle and placing it on Titan's craft. It is Titan himself who receives a shock.

Script:
Dennis Spooner

Director:
John Kelly

Boarding 'The Ghost Ship', Commander Shore and Phones fall into a trap engineered by an underwater creature who, on sentence of death, forces them to contact Troy in Stingray.

The Ghost Ship

A mystery galleon, enshrouded in heavy fog in a part of the ocean where fog is unknown? Commander Shore joins the Stingray crew to investigate this strange occurrence first hand. Reaching the spot described by the WASP jet liner which disappeared after calling in the report, the Stingray crew spot the ghostly galleon in dense fog. Leaving Troy at his station, Shore and Phones decide to explore the ship, keeping in contact with Troy by radio. The two men fall into a trap, engineered by an underwater creature named Idotee, who, on threat of death, orders Shore to instruct Troy to join them on board the galleon. Troy does so, and springs a surprise. Having filled his air cylinders with laughing gas, which he releases the second he boards the ghost ship, Idotee exits laughing.

Script:
Alan Fennell

Director:
Desmond Saunders

Countdown

Titan's surface agent, X-2-Zero is at it again, this time hatching a master plan to wipe Marineville off the face of the earth. Disguised as an authority on teaching mute people to speak, he puts his plan into operation when Troy agrees to Marina spending some time at the 'Professor's' clinic. Having taken Marina prisoner in his underwater craft, X-2-Zero lies in wait for Stingray to return from a routine patrol, his intention being to enter Marineville some minutes before Stingray arrives. Using tape-recordings of Troy's voice, he gains access to the Launch Tunnel and docks his vessel there — leaving Marina tied to a bomb timed to explode when Stingray arrives. When Troy arrives, believing him to be an impostor, Commander Shore and Atlanta sound the alarm. Atlanta saves the day — and Marina's life — by hitting on a way of confirming Troy's identity with seconds to spare.

Script:
Dennis Spooner

Director:
Alan Pattillo

Tired, Troy and Phones trip off to bed. Determined to beat the 'Countdown' Atlanta carries on alone, expressing the wish to complete Operation Decorate — a top secret scheme to welcome Marina back to Marineville.

The master of disguise, Agent X-2-Zero applies make-up and a wig that will fool the WASPs into believing that he is a Terranean. This time he adopts the persona of Professor Saunders, an authority on teaching mute people to talk. A scene from the episode 'Countdown.'

The Ghost of the Sea

Commander Shore relives the past horrors of the injury which has left him a cripple. He remembers how his one-man craft was severely damaged in combat with an unknown enemy, and how his life was saved by a mysterious stranger he has never seen since — a man he calls 'The Ghost of the Sea'. The mysterious stranger is suspected of having destroyed an oil rig at the place where Shore was injured, so, to lay the legend of the Ghost once and for all, Troy suggests that his commanding officer should return to the scene. On their way there, Stingray comes under attack from an hostile aircraft, but escapes unharmed. During the skirmish, Shore recognises the man who saved his life and Troy is instrumental in repaying the commander's debt by saving the stranger's life. In return the grateful man signals that he wishes to make peace. No further oil rigs will be destroyed.

Script:
Alan Fennell

Director:
David Elliott

'Who are you? What do you want with us?' Troy asks the hostile duo responsible for 'Emergency Marineville'. Troy trembles at the reply. The underwater beings mean to wipe Marineville off the face of the earth.

In order to gain the secret of Marineville's defence system, Agent X-2-Zero dupes Troy into saying a few simple phrases that Marina will recognise: like the password Troy uses to request entry into Ocean Door . . . . . . Phones is taken in too, and blurts out the other codewords that will open the Ocean Door.

Emergency Marineville

...ent to investigate when mysterious missiles are ...red at Marineville, Troy and his crew discover ...n island from where the missiles are being ...unched underwater. Spotted by the enemy, the ...rew are taken prisoner, locked in a cell and told ...e devastating news that a major missile attack ... to be launched at Marineville. When Marina's ...fe is threatened, Troy is forced to plot the best ...ourse for the missile attack. However, while the ...nemy sleeps, Troy and Phones escape from ...heir cell and put in motion a plan to make

known their plight. When the Marineville battle-stations are put on alert in the face of the missile attack, nothing, it seems, can avert disaster when the first missile strikes. It does so with a thud instead of an explosion. The message Troy has hidden in its explosive head is read by Commander Shore, who mounts an immediate rescue operation which ends in defeat for the enemy.

Script:
Alan Fennell

Director:
John Kelly

Marina joins Troy and Phones aboard Stingray to investigate the mysterious missiles which have been fired at the WASP base in the episode 'Emergency Marineville'.

There was never a shortage of underwater aliens for the Stingray crew to combat or aid, creatures of all shapes and sizes. It's hard to tell whether this one's friend or foe!

WASP 12

Subterranean Sea

Looking forward to a vacation, the Stingray crew have their leave cancelled and are ordered to investigate the depths of the Subterrain. Rather than take a holiday alone, Atlanta returns to duty. Venturing into uncharted seas, Troy and Phones dive into a deep shaft and find themselves on a beautiful desert-like plateau. Leaving Stingray to investigate further, they find themselves trapped by a cascade of water. Swimming for their lives, they are able to get back to their craft. Attempting to locate the shaft, they discover a second underwater chimney and, in danger of running out of oxygen, are forced to enter it. To their amazement, the shaft leads them to a beautiful tropical island deep below the Subterranean Sea. Imagine Atlanta's surprise when she receives a postcard from her friends saying what a lovely vacation they are having!

Script:
Alan Fennell

Director:
Desmond Saunders

WASP 13

The Loch Ness Monster

Admiral Denver is a believer. Commander Shore is sceptical. Does – or doesn't – the legendary Loch Ness Monster exist? In order to find out, the Admiral orders Stingray to travel to Scotland and run the legend to ground. Arriving there, Troy and Phones are met by two Scotsmen, Jamie and Andy, brothers who invite them to spend the night at a 'haunted' castle. The search for the monster begins early next morning and the men are astounded when a ferocious-looking dragon attacks them. In self-defence, the Stingray crew destroy it with their Sting missiles – only to find, much to their amazement, that the monster is a fake, an ingenious mechanism which, it is revealed, has been rigged up by the brothers to attract the tourist trade. The two brothers beg Troy not to reveal the truth and so the Stingray captain puts in a negative report which leaves the argument between the Admiral and Commander Shore unresolved.

Script:
Dennis Spooner

Director:
Alan Pattillo

The Invaders

Captured by a race of underwater creatures when they rush to answer a distress call from a weather station, Troy, Phones and Marina are interrogated about Marineville and the WASP defence system. They reveal nothing and are allowed to leave. However, unknown to them, their thoughts have been translated into pictures on a hidden monitor screen and they have revealed vital secrets. Returning to Marineville, Troy, suspicious of their quick release, discusses the matter with Commander Shore, who agrees to tighten up security. But the enemy outfox them. Instead of attacking from above, they burrow their way into the base from below, make their way to the Control Room and place Shore and his daughter Atlanta in custody. Fortunately, Troy – who is piloting Stingray into the base – overhears a radio conversation between the invaders and their prisoners. Realising what has happened, he sounds the general alarm. The invasion attempt is thwarted and a message to Marina, who is still in Stingray, leads to the invaders receiving a nasty surprise.

Script:
Dennis Spooner

Director:
David Elliott

 ## Secret of the Giant Oyster

About to depart in Stingray, Troy receives a surprise when two divers surface in front of him. When questioned, the men reveal that they are amateur divers and have discovered an enormous, priceless, pearl. Unfortunately, they were diving in WASP-controlled waters, where civilian exploration is forbidden. Pretending to be interested only in the reward for finding the pearl, they relate that the oyster bed is protected by thousands of satellite oysters, with the giant oyster opening for only a few seconds at certain intervals. Believing that the pearl could be put to technical use, Commander Shore details Troy and one of the divers to explore the oyster bed. This worries Marina, who is aware of the legend that whoever removes the pearl from its bed will be overtaken by bad luck. She need not have worried. Though Troy soon finds himself in trouble, the satellite oysters protect their own and by doing so, save not only the giant oyster, but the lives of Troy and the would-be thief.

Script:
Alan Fennell

Director:
John Kelly

If Troy Tempest's role model is James Garner, Marina's is obviously Brigitte Bardot!

WASP 16 Raptures of the Deep

On routine patrol, Troy rescues two seamen whom he finds in difficulty after they had been searching for what they believe to be a forest of jewels on the bed of the ocean. Having satisfied himself that no such forest exists, Troy turns Stingray for home. The craft suddenly becomes short of air and, overcome by lack of oxygen, Troy sinks into delirium. He dreams that he has found the jewel forest and is living in a beautiful palace, with Marina and Atlanta as his servants and Phones obeying his every call. But then the palace comes under attack, its walls crumbling in ruins around him. He looks around for a weapon. He sees none. He cries for help, his words echoing back from the walls. He awakens with a jolt – to find Phones bending over him and realises with a mixed feelings of regret and relief that it was all a dream.

Script: Alan Fennell

Director: Desmond Saunders

'Oh Great One. Do you require anything?' Troy does. Atlanta can peel him another grape and Marina should play her music soft and mellow. Well, anything is possible when Troy is dreaming the 'Raptures of the Deep'.

WASP 17 Stand By for Action

Troy is very disappointed. A film unit has moved into Marineville to film the WASPs at work – but Troy cannot play himself. The part is to be filled by a famous movie star. Unknown to anyone, the producer of the film is none other than agent X-2-Zero, his movie just another scheme to dispose of Troy. When every attempt to give our hero the kiss of death ends in disaster, X-2-Zero scampers away and returns to his island at Lemoy. The filming continues, however, and when the mock battle scene organised by the long-gone X-2-Zero turns into a real one, it is Troy, and not the movie star impersonator, who saves the situation. Troy becomes a hero in more ways than one for, having previously swooned over the handsome film actor, Atlanta and Marina once more focus their affections on their real-life hero.

Script: Dennis Spooner

Director: Alan Pattillo

Recognize Johnny Swoonara? Yes it's Steve Fireball XL5 Zodiac sporting a black wig. Zodiac's jet car also turns up in Stingray, driven by Troy Tempest.

WASP 18 The Disappearing Ships

Marineville receives a signal about the disappearance of three disused freighters which have been sunk in Shipwreck City before being blown up by remote control. Troy and Phones are off on their travels again: their orders, to clear up the mystery. Their search takes them to the ocean floor, where they find the three vessels lying silent and deserted, not too far away from four other old shipwrecks, which have lights shining out of their cabins and portholes. Swimming over to investigate, the Stingray crew find themselves confronted by the leader of a nomad tribe whose people are using the wrecks as homes. Warned by Troy that one of the ships is about to explode, the nomad refuses to believe him. The explosion takes place and jams the door of the ship they are in, blocking off their only avenue of escape. A second freighter explodes and Troy realises that they have less than ten minutes left before it is their turn. Engineering their escape in the nick of time, Troy promises the nomads that, in future, all the old freighters will be given to them as homes.

Script:
Alan Fennell

Director:
David Elliott

Troy need not have worried. Having previously had eyes for no one but Johnny Swoonara, Marina and Atlanta once more focus their attention on their real-life hero.

The Man From the Navy

It's a three-handed feud. Having developed a distaste for a boastful naval captain who arrives at Marineville to demonstrate a new missile, Troy determines to prove Stingray's superiority. Learning of the mock attack, X-2-Zero throws in his oar by planning to take advantage of this to fire real explosives instead of dummies at Stingray. The naval captain's ship is taken over by Aquaphibians who force the navy man to launch the live missiles. But Troy outmanoeuvres them and returns to Marineville. Astounded by what has taken place, Commander Shore orders the naval vessel back to base. The Aquaphibians desert ship, leaving the captain to face Commander Shore's wrath and a court-martial. Troy, however, believes and confirms the captain's story: he encountered the mechanical fish which serve as the Aquaphibians' craft. Released from custody, the captain nevertheless continues his boastful attitude and everyone rejoices when he leaves.

Script:
Alan Fennell

Director:
John Kelly

Titan makes contact with X-2-Zero on the surface agent's marine screen: this time in order to make things hot for the boastful 'Man From the Navy.'

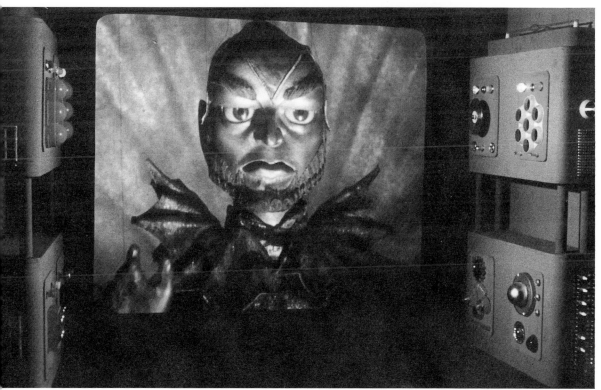

WASP 20 · Marineville Traitor

Troy cannot believe what he hears: Commander Shore, accused of being a traitor. A vital piece of equipment has been stolen and the evidence points to the commander. Despite pouring scorn on the charge, Troy must nevertheless do his duty. Shore is taken into custody and locked in the Marineville jail. However, what Troy does not know is that it is all a trap to catch the real traitor, who now reveals himself when he approaches Commander Shore and invites him to join forces with him. Shore pulls a gun, but the spy – a member of the station tracking team – beats him to it. Shore manages to turn on his wrist radio and the whole conversation is heard by Troy and Phones in the control room. Realising that the Commander is in great danger, they race to his rescue and place the real traitor under arrest.

Script:
Alan Fennell

Director:
Desmond Saunders

WASP 21 · Tom Thumb Tempest

The alert has been sounded, so Troy and Phones wait in the standby lounge ready to set off on another mission. Troy hates this part of the job, the waiting around until they receive further orders from Commander Shore. Impatiently, he calls to his senior officer to find out how much

Overheard by the WASP team, Commander Shore faces the dangerous task of unmasking the 'Marineville Traitor' who, when Shore turns down his offer of a partnership, pulls a gun on the Marineville head.

longer they have to wait. Shore snaps back: don't ask too many questions. The warmth of the lounge makes Troy drowsy and he nods off to sleep and dreams a fantastic adventure. Prior to dozing off he had been watching the fish in the aquarium and thinking how confined their life was. In his dream, Stingray shrinks to miniature size and sails through the fish tank with its Tom Thumb-size crew. The imagined adventure begins. Beset by Titan and his agents, they attempt to escape. To their horror, they are unable to get Stingray out of the fish tank. All looks lost until, at that point, Troy wakes up. Looking around him he sighs with relief when he recognises the comfortable furnishings of the standby lounge.

Script:
Alan Fennell

Director:
Alan Pattillo

WASP 22 · Pink Ice

Bombarded by reports from all parts of the globe that oceans are being frozen over by a mysterious pink liquid, WASP Commander Sam Shore sends Troy and his team to investigate. Arriving at an area covered in pink ice, and finding a crack in it, Troy submerges the craft. An examination of the surface establishes that the ice is a man-made substance and not a freak of nature. Someone is deliberately causing chaos to the world's shipping lanes. But why? Why would anyone want to cripple all industry and communications on earth? As they discover when they sail some miles further out to sea, the answer lies with an unseen enemy, who bombs them with more of the pink ice. In seconds Stingray is well and truly lodged in an ice pack – unable to submerge or move. Desperate situations call for desperate measures, so Troy radios a distress signal to Marineville and requests they bombard the area with hydromic missiles. Within minutes the WASP craft is free – free to react to a second attack from the enemy, whom they send to the depths of the ocean with their Sting missiles.

Script:
Alan Fennell

Director:
David Elliott

The Master Plan

Cruising near to Titanica, Stingray is attacked by an Aquaphibian terror fish, whose missiles strike the WASP sub in the stern. Fighting back, the Stingray crew sink the mechanical fish with a sting missile. Going outside to inspect the damage, Troy is attacked by one of the enemy who shoots a cloud of purple liquid at him and then disappears. Troy appears to be unaffected, but on the way back to base he collapses. Taken to the Marineville hospital, the medical team give their verdict: Troy has been poisoned. No antidote is available and Troy has only a few hours to live. Hope appears when Titan contacts them by radio: he has the antidote and will exchange it for Marina, his one-time slave. Despite being given orders to the contrary, Marina swims back to Titanica alone, gives herself up and the antidote is sent. Back on his feet again, Troy determines to go after Marina. Joined by Phones, he succeeds in entering Titanica where, after a grim battle with the Aquaphibians, he rescues Marina.

Script: Alan Fennell

Director: John Kelly

'Now watch closely, X-2-Zero,' says Titan. His plan is simplicity itself. The Terror Fish will disable Stingray, thereby forcing Troy Tempest to leave the stricken craft and make himself a target for Titan's scaly-backed Aquaphibian soldier, who attempts to switch out Troy's light forever. He doesn't succeed, of course, despite being a pawn in 'The Master Plan.'

24 Star of the East

El Hudat, the leader of an eastern country, wishes to become a member of WASP. Midway though his negotiations with Commander Shore, however, news reaches Marineville that El Hudat has been deposed and his brother has seized power. As El Hudat is no longer eligible to represent his people, Shore calls off the negotiations. Frustrated by this turn of events, the enraged visitor accuses the Commander of being behind the revolt, which in turn sees him thrown out of Marineville. Next morning, however, the Commander discovers that El Hudat didn't leave alone? Marina is missing too. Tracking El Hudat in Stingray, Troy radios the villain, demanding he return her unharmed. El Hudat replies by opening fire on Stingray, and Troy narrowly escapes death. Piloting the sub into a crash dive to trick El Hudat into believing that he has scored a direct hit, Troy manages to sneak aboard the enemy gunboat, overpower its captain, rescue Marina and return to Marineville. Hearing that the revolt against him has been quelled, El Hudat attempts to pick up the negotiations where he left off. There's just one snag; WASP law calls for criminals to pay for their crimes, so a delighted Commander Shore sees to it that El Hudat cools his heels in the Marineville jail.

Script: Alan Fennell

Director: Desmond Saunders

The sequel to Star of the East *is outlined on page 66.*

25 An Echo of Danger

On routine escort duty, Phones picks up unusual sounds on his hydrophones, which leads the Stingray crew to investigate. While doing so, the oil tanker they were escorting catches fire and its valuable cargo goes up in flames: Phones is accused of dereliction of duty. When, at the hearing, he is unable to produce any evidence to support his claim, Phones is relieved from duty pending a medical report. It's a trap of course, yet another scheme by agent X-2-Zero – who now appears on the scene as the psychiatrist from whom Phones accepts help. It was X-2-Zero who planted the transmitter which gave off the signals Phones had heard, but which was switched off when Stingray approached. Having convinced Phones that he is unfit for duty and should retire from the service, X-2-Zero turns his attention to Troy, but this time he is thwarted, thanks to Sub-Lieutenant Fisher, who has accompanied Troy on patrol. Thanks to the lieutenant's warning that Stingray is about to be attacked, X-2-Zero's plan ends in failure and Phones heaves a sigh of relief when he is reinstated by Commander Shore.

Script: Dennis Spooner

Director: Alan Pattillo

26 Invisible Enemy

Upon receipt of a distress signal, Stingray sets sail and discovers a small lifeboat. In it lies a mysterious stranger who is apparently in some kind of coma. Taken back to Marineville, the man is examined by doctors but fails to respond to treatment. Unaware that they have installed a deadly enemy into their HQ, Troy and his crew return to patrolling the seas. The unfortunate stranger is in an hypnotic trance, induced by an alien underwater race who control his every move. Despite being an innocent bystander, the man has been ordered to render Marineville helpless by putting everyone there in a similar trance. It is fortunate then that Troy returns and discovers what has happened. With Marina's help he is able to reverse the hypnotic spell and bring Marineville back to life before the aliens launch their attack. Their fiendish plot in ruins, the aliens retreat. Their innocent victim is cured and receives no punishment for his part in the unpleasant affair.

Script: Alan Fennell

Director: David Elliott

A publicity shot of Stingray from the TV 21 comic.

Deep Heat

It's a routine mission – until Stingray is sucked down to the ocean floor! The crew try everything to get back on course, but nothing works. Left with no option but to investigate this strange occurrence, they find themselves travelling beneath the Earth's crust. Here they discover two weird underwater beings who admit to having lured the WASP vehicle to their domain. They are victims of a terrible fate and require help. Their base is sitting on top of a volcano, which is soon to erupt and will completely destroy their last stronghold. The crew agree to help. But, when the strangers discover that there are only two sets of Aqua-gear, they pounce on Troy and Phones robbing them of theirs, and leave them to die. But Marina refuses them entrance to Stingray and they are forced to return to Troy and Phones and attempt to persuade them to get Marina to open the hatch. Once bitten twice shy, the WASP team are ready for them and it is they who become masters, with the underwater beings held as prisoners.

Script:
Alan Fennell

Director:
John Kelly

Summoned by Titan, Teufel the mute fish god is there to decide Troy's fate. If the fish god turns away from the prisoner with the space of one marine minute, Troy's goose is cooked – the penalty is death! A scene from the pilot.

In Search of the Tajmanon

The crew are used to mysteries, but the one which they now face stands as one of the most baffling they have encountered. Contacted by archaeologist Professor Graham, the crew listen in silence when he tells them that the Palace of Tajmanon – submerged 40 years earlier when a dam was built – has disappeared! Joined by Atlanta, they set out to solve the mystery and one clue after another leads them to the wilds of Africa, and a man named Hassan El Hamra. Hostile at first, when El Hamra recognises Professor Graham as an old colleague, he welcomes them and takes them to his stunningly beautiful palace – the Palace of Tajmanon, which, rescued from its watery grave by El Hamra's people, was removed from the sea-bed stone by stone to be rebuilt in darkest Africa.

Script: Dennis Spooner

Director: Desmond Saunders

Titan Goes Pop

Agent X-2-Zero seldom gets things right. This time he's made the mistake of his life. Informed that the red carpet treatment is being afforded to a visitor to Marineville — a man titled 'The Duke' — and assuming that the visit is being made by a VIP he lays plans to kidnap the visitor. Having succeeded in renting his island home to the Duke, he drugs him and takes him to Titan's underwater palace where, interrogated by Titan, the Titanican ruler forms the opinion that the Duke is an ally – well, why else would the Duke use his strange powers to throw Titan's people into a frenzy. And so begins Titan's introduction to pop music. X-2-Zero has goofed again. Their prisoner is in fact, Duke Dexter, a pop singer who was visiting Marineville to entertain the station personnel. Congratulated on the fine job he is doing, Dexter is allowed to return safely to Marineville. Some time later, when Titan and agent X-2-Zero tune their television monitor into the Marineville wavelength and see Dexter whipping the WASP audience into a frenzy, they can't help but congratulate themselves on this excellent piece of sabotage they have pulled off under Troy Tempest's nose!

Script: Alan Fennell

Director: Alan Pattillo

WASP 30 — Set Sail for Adventure

With the arrival at Marineville of Admiral Denver, the scene is set for the navy man and Commander Shore to become involved in another of their habitual arguments, this time with Shore refusing to acknowledge that the WASPs of today would be unable to stand up to the rigours of crewing an old-fashioned sailing ship. So it is that Phones and Sub-Lieutenant Fisher join Admiral Denver's crew on an ancient sailing vessel. Unknown to Denver, Troy decided to follow them in Stingray. Trouble soon raises its head. A strong wind blows up and the admiral is knocked unconscious, which causes him to lose his memory and do very strange things — like casting Phones and Sub-Lieutenant Fisher adrift in a small dinghy! Sighting Stingray, Admiral Denver fires at it, but Troy gains the upper hand. Knocked unconscious again, the admiral recovers in the Marineville hospital, with his memory restored, but believing he has successfully crossed the Pacific and back in a galleon. Neither Commander Shore nor Troy has the heart to tell him the truth!

Script:
Dennis Spooner

Director:
David Elliott

Original prints carried the title given. Later transmissions had no on-screen title in some TV regions.

WASP 31 — Tune of Danger

Unaware that the next time they give a concert it could well be their last, the WASP jazz group travels to its next venue – a gig for Marina's father, Aphony, in his underwater city. Agent X-2-Zero is responsible. The jazz group's agent — an ally of X-2-Zero — has planted a bomb inside the bass-player's fiddle, which will explode when it is played. In this way it is hoped that vital WASP members will be done away with. Fortunately, Troy stumbles across the secret when he picks up a secret message from X-2-Zero on his car radio. However, despite Troy's efforts to warn Marina and her father, Troy himself is captured and very nearly burnt alive when the shack in which he is imprisoned is set on fire. When the fire alarm sounds, Troy escapes in the panic and propels Stingray at full speed to head off X-2-Zero's latest assassination attempt.

Script:
Alan Fennell

Director:
John Kelly

Unaware that the next concert they give could well be their last, the WASP Jazz trio, strum out their 'Tune of Danger' — a 12-bar piece that could end with a bang!

Captained by Lt Fisher, Stingray has fallen foul of X-2-Zero's latest plot. There is but one way to save him, so Commander Shore puts into action a 'Rescue From The Skies priority' and Troy is flown to the stricken craft's location in an Arrowhead jet plane.

WASP
32

Rescue From the Skies

Aboard Stingray with Sub-Lieutenant Fisher, Phones leads the trainee through shooting practice, using a variety of mechanical fish as targets. But X-2-Zero has learned that the exercise is taking place and has smuggled a device into the firing range. Fisher hits it. It explodes, causing severe damage to Stingray and almost costs the trainee his life. Worse still, to ensure complete success X-2-Zero has placed a stick bomb on Stingray's hull. Timed to explode by remote-control, this will completely destroy the WASP vehicle. Finding this out, Commander Shore and Troy decide that the only way to save Stingray's crew is from the air. Troy is flown to the craft's location in an Arrowhead jet plane. Ejecting into the sea, he swims underwater to Stingray, locates the bomb and begins his attempt to remove it from the hull. It's a dangerous task. He accomplishes it, of course, thereby sabotaging X-2-Zero's nasty surprise yet again.

Script:
Dennis Spooner

Director:
Desmond Saunders

Unaware that Marina is being held prisoner, Troy and Phones set out for the underwater fish farm run by Professor Cordo. They will soon become 'Trapped In The Depths'.

WASP 33 — The Cool Cavemen

It's dream-time again. On standby duty, Troy isn't sure as to whether he will be able to attend Marina's fancy dress party. Advised by Commander Shore to catch up on his sleep in case he is called for duty, Troy falls to sleep. He dreams of underwater cavemen who plunder the cargo of a vessel carrying radio-active material. Joined by Phones he attempts to stop them – but the pair dance with death before the adventure fades and Troy wakes up. Relieved to find that it was only a dream and that his tour of duty is over, Troy knows now what he will wear as his fancy dress — a costume that will delight and amaze Marina and her guests. To his horror, however, when he attends the party dressed in what he believed to be a highly original costume, he discovers that everyone else has had the same idea: all the guests have arrived dressed as cavemen! Despite this, Marina's party is still a great success.

Script:
Alan Fennell

Director:
Alan Pattillo

WASP 34 — A Nut For Marineville

Returning to Marineville after a routine patrol, Troy and Phones have an amazing story to tell. They were attacked by a powerful alien craft. Stingray scored two direct hits but the enemy ship was undamaged. Concerned by this, Commander Shore calls in outside help to design a new, more powerful missile: having established its superiority, the alien craft is bound to return. The man Shore turns to is Professor Burgoyne, very much the 'egg-head' type of scientist, whom the commander is loath to visit. The two get off to a bad start when Burgoyne overhears some of Shore's comments about him, so the professor rubs salt into the wound by demanding that he be given a workshop completely isolated from the rest of the Marineville personnel. Shortly afterwards, when a gigantic explosion blows up the Professor's lab, everyone assumes that Burgoyne has killed himself. He appears within minutes to announce that his experiment was a triumphant success. His work requires refinement, which will be done on board Stingray when the craft goes to meet the enemy ship. Launched at sea, the Professor's missile destroys the alien craft and Marineville is saved. Even Commander Shore is well-disposed towards the Prof.

Script:
Gerry & Sylvia Anderson

Director:
David Elliott

Trapped In the Depths

Professor Cordo has lived under the sea for so long that he has become unbalanced and holds a race of underwater people completely under his power. Atlanta, who is taking a course on an underwater fish farm run by Cordo, finds this disturbing but is able to do nothing. However, when she accidentally discovers that the Professor is hatching a plot to take over Stingray and use it to attack the land masses, her attempts to contact Troy — who is also visiting the fish farm — are thwarted when Cordo informs her that he has hidden a gun nearby which he threatens to fire if Atlanta makes one false move. Meanwhile, returning to Stingray, Troy and Phones are astounded to find that the vessel is only a mock-up: the real Stingray has disappeared. It is, in fact, on its way to Marineville, manned by Cordo's underwater slaves. With only a limited amount of air in their breathing tanks, Troy and Phones succeed in distracting Cordo's attention long enough to save Atlanta. Overpowered by the aquanauts, Cordo is forced to recall Stingray, thus thwarting his evil scheme.

Script:
Alan Fennell

Director:
John Kelly

His first mission complete, Troy relates the events surrounding his capture by Titan, and Commander Shore now realises what they are up against: whole races of people living under the sea. Some bad, some good. Some to help, some to fight!

WASP 36 Eastern Eclipse

Still held prisoner in the Marineville jail for offences against the WASPs, Eastern Dictator El Hudat is offered the chance to escape by agent X-2-Zero. Aware that Ali Khali, El Hudat's brother, is on his way to Marineville, having escaped after the revolt in which he lost his power, X-2-Zero offers to exchange the brothers, who are identical twins, and thus return the imprisoned El Hudat to power. All X-2-Zero seeks in return is that El Hudat will assist him in conquering Marineville. Posing as a lawyer. the surface agent renders the visiting brother unconscious, instals him in his brother's cell, and smuggles El Hudat out of Marineville and back to his own country. Discovering the swap-over, Troy welcomes Ali Khali aboard Stingray and they set off in pursuit of his treacherous brother. They engage X-2-Zero's vessel before it reaches its destination and during the scuffle, both the brothers fall into the sea. Fished out, they present a problem. No one knows which brother is which. As both men lay claim to being the real Ali Khali, Commander Shore determines that the only sure way of keeping them both out of trouble is by locking both men away. The Marineville jail now holds two identical prisoners, and once again X-2-Zero's plotting disappears in a puff of smoke.

Script:
Alan Fennell

Director:
Desmond Saunders

See page 58 for Star of the East.

WASP 37 A Christmas To Remember

It is Christmas, and everyone at Marineville is determined to make it a Christmas to remember for the small orphaned son of an ex-WASP aquanaut, who is spending the Yuletide holiday at the base. Troy in particular treats the boy to some unexpected excitement when the orphan is allowed to join the Stingray crew in an effort to solve the mystery of an enemy aircraft which has apparently been abandoned by its crew. To help

them solve the mystery, Troy suggests that they re-enact the battle in which the aircraft was engaged. While Phones pilots the enemy craft, Troy and the boy track the vessel in Stingray. Suddenly the radio link between the two craft goes dead. Unknown to Troy, one of the enemy crew who had concealed himself in a secret compartment of the apparently abandoned craft is now holding Phones at gunpoint. His intention is to lure Troy over to the enemy craft to investigate. Troy is not so easily fooled of course. He not only saves Phones, but also solves the mystery of the missing crew. Their mission complete, the WASP team and their guest return to Marineville for a very memorable Christmas.

Script:
Dennis Spooner

Director:
Alan Pattillo

Original prints carried the title given. Later transmissions had no on-screen title in some TV regions.

WASP 38 The Lighthouse Dwellers

When the decision is taken to close down a lighthouse because its winking light confuses planes making for a new airfield, the lighthouse keeper, Frank Lincoln, is retired. But after the

Mistaking the lighthouse beam for the runway beacon of the Arango Air Base, the pilot of Flight 127 lowers his undercarriage — and crashes into the ocean. The Lighthouse Dwellers have claimed another victim.

ight has flashed for what should have been the last time, it blinks on again, its intense light pelling instant disaster when an incoming plane mistakes the lighthouse for the landing strip and crashes into the ocean. Unable to understand what has happened, Commander Shore sends the Stingray team to investigate. They soon learn the truth, which is that the lighthouse is being used by an underwater race of people as a source of energy to provide light and heat for their city. Believing that the land people have shut down the lighthouse deliberately, the undersea people have taken Frank Lincoln prisoner when he returned to the beacon to discover why the light had come on again. Troy acts as go-between and Commander Shore is delighted to arrange for the sea people to have a constant source of power.

Script:
Alan Fennell

Director:
David Elliott

WASP 39

Aquanaut of the Year

After a hectic party to celebrate his 'Aquanaut of the Year' award, Troy slips back to his room to snatch some well-earned rest. No chance! Much to his dismay he soon finds himself the subject of a *'This is Your Life'* programme. Having recounted several exciting moments from the aquanaut's career, the TV host puts the vital question to Troy: 'Are you and Atlanta more than good friends?' Troy hesitates. Then, before he can reply, the alert is sounded and the Stingray crew have to race to the stand-by lounge to ready themselves for another mission. As Atlanta remarks, 'There just isn't time for romance in the World Aquanaut Security Patrol.'

Script:
Gerry & Sylvia Anderson

Director:
Alan Pattillo

Trained to stay cool under any circumstance, Troy nevertheless feels the heat when Stingray is sucked down to the ocean floor and receives the 'Deep Heat' treatment.

'STANDBY FOR ACTION!' STINGRAY IS LAUNCHED

The Creators and Puppeteers Speak Out

Stingray arrived on British TV screens in 1964, and creator Gerry Anderson remembers why he was so enthusiastic about the futuristic underwater setting. 'After *Supercar* people started to say to me, "I see that you are into science fiction now." I remember thinking, what do they mean? *Fireball XL5* equals science fiction! I never thought of it in that way. But what a good idea. That's a new direction in which to go. We'd done the sort of Toytown, Noddy kind of pictures. We had covered the Western. We had been to outer space. So, in an endeavour to do something different, we decided that the time was right to deal with the sea and a craft that sailed underwater.

'One must bear in mind that we had a brand new studio, fully equipped with state-of-the-art gear, so we were able to tackle what was then a fairly difficult subject to do with puppets. What's more, we were filming in colour for the very first time.' Indeed, it must be remembered that *Stingray* made television history by being the very first British television series to be filmed entirely in colour — a move designed to ensure an American TV network slot.

This brought a whole new set of problems.

Although the Americans had been transmitting TV programmes in colour for 9 years, British television audiences were still viewing programmes in black-and-white; the official launch of colour TV in England being July 1967, when BBC2 covered the Lawn Tennis Championships from Wimbledon, so AP Films had no reference

as to how colour looked on television. In order to familiarise themselves with the conditions that existed when doing so, the company decided to make a short test film of *Stingray* (filmed on Sam Shore's Marineville control tower set) which Reg Hill took to NBC in America. The news wasn't good. The colours they had used were too bright, resulting in crude colour separation; reds bled around the edges and blues tended to reflect on other objects on the set. As a consequence — and in the knowledge that the programme would be transmitted in black-and-white in the UK — the team had to repaint most of their sets. Gerry

Piloted by Tom Thumb Tempest, the miniaturised Stingray approaches the ocean door that leads the crew to a frightening adventure in the confines of a fish tank.

WORLD AQUANAUT SECURITY PATROL

Always a hive of activity, the
Marineville Control Room is
linked to WASP HQ in
Washington by the
Videophone (see inset.)

explained: 'As far as the rest of the world was concerned, the difficulty was that if a person wearing a red-coloured shirt stood in front of a dark background, in colour you could differentiate between the two, because the red was a different colour. However, in black-and-white, a dark red shirt comes out looking black, and so they merge. So, although we were filming in colour, we didn't really have the benefits of filming in colour because we knew that as soon as the programme was finished we were going to make black-and-white prints.' To overcome this, the directors would have the sets decorated as normal, and then the lighting cameraman would look through a tone glass which would give him an idea of how the scene looked in monochrome.

The problems with colour didn't end there. *Stingray's* art director, Bob Bell, remembers how he spent a great deal of time consulting with the wardrobe department in order to meet the requirement of finding colours for the puppets' costumes that would enhance both the characters and the set on which they appeared. It was no good at all having a puppet in a red costume walking on to exactly the same coloured set, as both would merge and the puppet would totally isappear. One also had to take into account the olour of the character's hair. So if a dark-haired uppet was used on the set a dark background olour had to be avoided otherwise the hair ould get lost. Colour separation was a job for ne lighting cameraman, so many meetings would ave to be held between him, wardrobe and the rt director well in advance of filming.

The desire to pick up sales in America was the eason for having the characters speak with merican accents. On the cowboy-based *Four eather Falls* the producers were obliged to have neir characters delivering dialogue in a mid-estern drawl (a cowboy asking a villain to kindly raise your hands above your head, would ou? There's a good chap' would have been udicrous). By the time *Stingray* came around, Gerry and his associates had learned their lesson ell. Conscious of the fact that 60 per cent of the ntire world revenue of sales of their programmes ame from the United States, and unless a rogramme recouped its production cost the dds of doing a further series were zero, they

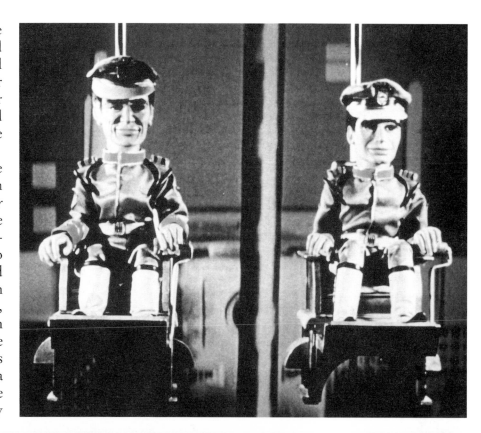

wonder what we're letting urselves in for this time?'

's the negative side of tlanta's job, the nerve-acking vigil of waiting for roy to renew contact when tingray is under attack. The rain on the WASP peratives' faces says it all.

determined above all that their films would sell well in the USA. 'By this time, I had learned that as children's programmes the puppet shows were very, very expensive, because working with puppets you achieve very little footage each day,' said Gerry, relating that there were really only two choices open to him. 'One was to make *Stingray* a British show and have an American representative character appear in the stories, which had been done before and I felt was offensive to British audiences and probably phoney to the American audience, or to make it an American story and virtually an American production. At the time there were lots of American pictures being made in this country, pictures that were obviously acceptable in the States and were equally acceptable here, so I thought that this was the route that was least hurtful to British people and the most acceptable to the Americans. That was my reasoning, to make sure that in America they were watching a genuine — what *appeared* to be a genuine — American production, but over here people were watching, hopefully, a good quality American show — which they were used to watching anyway.'

Despite what many people think, Gerry never prepared a production brief (a bible, to advise writers and directors as to what they could, or could not, do with the format of each series). How then did he approach each new programme? Never short of ideas, he simply took the bull by the horns when the time came to do so. 'The term "bible" and the whole business of producing a bible came from America and was something I learned about in the fullness of time. We didn't produce a bible for a number of reasons. First of all, it was in the early days and we didn't even know this method of working. Secondly, I had a philosophy that I follow to this very day, which is to produce the first script — which would be very lengthy in terms of pages, because every time we went on to a new set it would describe the entire set, or, in the case of a new character, describe the new character — so in some respects the first script incorporated a lot of the material which today would be in the so-called production bible. I would always restrict the scripting so that we were no further ahead than we needed to be, because we would go through a process of evolution. You see, if you are working on a live-action show, you can talk about all the various

An aerial view of the WASP Marineville Base.

Will Marina be saved from a fate worse than death? Can Troy rescue her? Or will the beautiful fish girl be fried? Marina, close to blowing her top in the episode 'Emergency Marineville.'

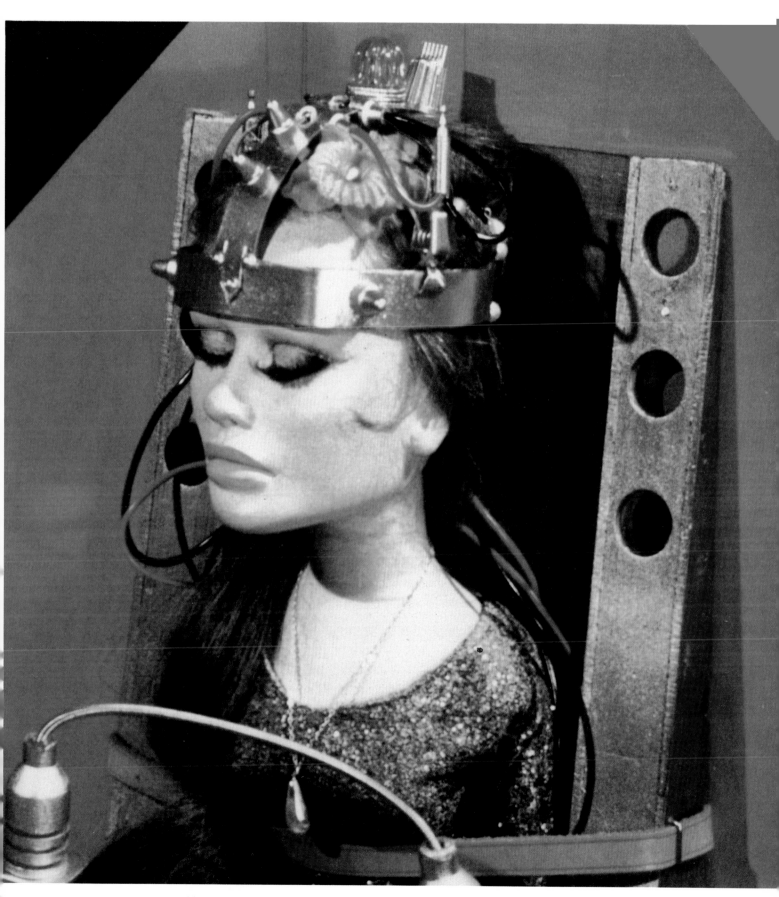

The film crew at work. *Left to right*: On the puppet gantry are: head puppeteer Christine Glanville and her assistant, Yvonne Hunter. Note the crew member taking a light reading before filming begins.

actors that you think might play the part and everybody immediately has a mental image of that character. With a puppet, you have no mental image at all. So we would describe Troy Tempest as a square-jawed hero with a sense of humour and twinkle in his eye, and from that description the puppet-maker would sculpt the head. Then, in discussion, we would say, "Make him good-looking, a hero with a sense of fun; something like James Garner." And from that brief the puppet-makers would make the face. When the face was finally accepted, we would then cast a voice and say to the voice artiste,

"Here is the script and here is the face," and they would come up with the voice. We would then put the two together on the screen. We would now have a character which might be as envisaged, or somewhat different, the advantage being that we were now able to say to the writer, come and see *Troy Tempest*. So he sees the character and begins to write with that character in mind. So Troy Tempest is beginning to evolve. The same technique is applied to the sets. At first we write about Marineville: Interior: Control Room — for which every writer has a different mental image. But once it has been built and filmed, now they know what they are talking about. So I always kept the script restricted to one episode ahead of the episode in production, so that this process of evolution could carry on. It would evolve.'

Christine Glanville, who, prior to joining Gerry's team on *Torchy* as head puppeteer, had been employed on *Twizzle* as a puppet operator by Joy Laury, was one of the team of sculptors responsible for making the puppet heads. 'There was myself, Mary Turner and John Brown, who were the sculptors, and I was lucky enough to have an assistant, a girl called Yvonne Hunter. Mary Turner also had one, Judith Shutt, but poor John did everything himself. In the early days, say on *Fireball XL5*, we had an artist who drew the characters' faces for us, although sometimes these didn't work out and we had to deviate from his impression of how the faces should look. On *Stingray* we had no reference at

all, apart from film stars' faces, like James Garner's. I did Atlanta, Titan and X-2-Zero, who was based on Claude Rains. John Brown did Sam Shore and Phones, and Mary Turner did Marina and Troy. The characters were presented to us as types. So one would mould a type of face — say, based on James Garner — and we would say, "Well, yes, but James Garner has got a sort of dimple here" or "his eyebrows are crooked", so the characters turned out to be more portraits than types. Christine (who herself may well have served as the inspiration for the Tin-Tin character from *Thunderbirds*) recalls being given no brief at all for Titan. So, taken at the time with Laurence Olivier, it was his face she had in mind when creating the character.

As *Stingray* was the first series on which the puppets had facial expressions, changes were required in moulding techniques. The sculptors would first make a Plasticine head, which was

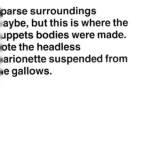

parse surroundings maybe, but this is where the puppets bodies were made. Note the headless marionette suspended from the gallows.

Marina looking winsome and lovely in her undersea kingdom.

then painted (because a lot of people couldn't picture what the stone-coloured face would finally look like), wigged and photographed. The Plasticine head was then cast in rubber, which in turn was cast into several fibreglass heads which, as far as was possible, had neutral expressions. The automatic mouth movement was installed next, together with a piece of flexible kid leather, which went between the puppet's lower lip and chin, and operated the character's lower jaw, together with two strings in the back of the head that would operate the character's lip and eye movements — the strings being specially made and blackened so that they wouldn't shine on camera. Hand and leg strings were only attached to the puppets when it was necessary for them to walk or reach out for something, as otherwise they would hang in front of the puppet's face. The next stage was to apply the character's facial expressions; a frown, a smile, a slight curl of the mouth, a raised eyebrow. Then the 'smilers' would be introduced — that is to say, a smiling head, not another puppet — and a blinking head, on which the eyes moved from side to side, the plastic eyes being assembled with a track-rod at the back of the eye-socket so that the eyes could move in unison. An entirely different head would be used whenever the puppet's eyes needed to be closed. Then the sculptors would start smoothing them down with sandpaper. Christine Glanville remembers that they spend a tremendous amount of time sandpapering the faces. 'Week after week was spent smoothing them down with several grades of emery cloth and filling in each blemish with a material known as Bondapaste, until the surface was as smooth as silk. Then the heads were put together with the bodies made by John Blundell and Eddie Hunter, and the puppets were handed to the wardrobe mistress, Elizabeth Coleman, to be wigged and dressed. Most of the female characters had real hair because their hairstyles had to be changed regularly. The wigs were combed and sprayed with hair fixative, which meant that the hair became clogged up and frequently had to be washed to keep the hair nice and sleek.'

As amazing as it may sound, the next step echoed the routine employed by a live-action production. The puppets were given a screen test to ensure that they photographed properly!

A splendid selection of puppet heads, including several 'Revamps' — the fibreglass heads used over and over again as guest artists. And is that *Fireball XL5's* Robert the Robot tucked away on the top shelf.

There were other puppets as well: ones that didn't require the refinements of their fellow artistes. Known as 'revamps', these were fibreglass heads shaped rather like a chicken's egg. These had two eyes and a slot for the mouth and although they would have the AMM machinery inside the head, they would have no face. Accumulated as the series progressed, these would be used in the role of guest artistes. Using Plasticine, the sculptors would fashion the revamp head into a totally new character. Given a beard, a wig, a pair of spectacles and a lick of paint, the revamp could be used over and over again, taking on the personae of as many different characters as were needed. When the episode was over, the Plasticine face was removed and the revamp was ready to adopt a new face.

The problems continued to be manifold: one of the overwhelming ones being changes in facial expression. Unfortunately puppets cannot smile on cue, yet it had to look as if they could. This was achieved by changing the puppet heads for

Puppets always look good in close-up, says Christine Glanville. How true — as witness the publicity shot of Marina.

different shots and cutting the film together in the editing room. For instance, if there was a serious-looking puppet who was about to smile, the director would cut away to another character for long enough so that when the camera came back and the sombre character which had appeared earlier was smiling, it was believable that the smile had formed during the cut-away. Nor could they talk properly — despite the AMM mechanism. Although this was accurate for about 90 per cent of the time there were certain words that the AMM would miss. So the filmmakers employed a 'lip-sync operator' who, whenever the pre-recorded dialogue was played back on the floor, was required to override the missed dialogue and key those words in manually.

There were many other drawbacks, but none greater than the restrictions placed on the puppet operators themselves.

Gerry Anderson's main regret was that the team never cracked the problem of finding ways to make the puppets walk convincingly. Christine Glanville agrees. 'We could never do a good walk,' she explained, pointing out the drawbacks from a puppet-operator's point of view. 'You can do a good puppet walk, which is perfectly adequate for the stage, but when you do this on film, it's hopeless. The camera picks up everything; every swing of the foot, every discrepancy in the puppet's movement is amplified. When you've got a puppet like Twizzle or Torchy — who were caricatures anyway — you could get away with it to a certain extent. But on the later programmes, starting really with *Stingray*, there's an awful lot you can't get away with, because there the puppets began to look like real people and weren't as caricatured, so consequently they just looked liked monsters.'

It's a fact of course, that because all the puppets prior to *Stingray* had to have heads large enough to get the AMM machinery inside, the puppet-makers had inadvertently created caricatures, in as much as the puppet's heads were disproportionate to their bodies. Christine explained the technical difficulties of having the characters walk through doorways. 'If you wanted the puppet to walk through, you had to have a slot above the door, because the wires would catch the top of the door jamb. So when we used to zoom in to a close-up of the puppet,

someone would whip out the top of the door frame and the puppet would bob his way through.' Such problems didn't apply when a puppet had to look out through a window. 'The puppet could be on the inside, with the strings on the outside. With the window pushed open, you could pull the character through,' she said, confirming that puppets always look good in close-up. 'It's when their feet are dangling that they don't look very convincing.

'The thing about puppets is, they can't move any faster than the speed of gravity. If you let them go, they will only drop as fast as the speed of gravity will allow. So if you have a puppet that is obliged to dodge down quickly behind something, all you can do is drop it. The way you get over that is to have the floor puppeteer holding it whilst it is being filmed from the waist up. At the required moment the floor puppeteer pulls the puppet down quickly and you get a convincing shot.' The floor-puppeteer on *Stingray* was a girl named Zena Ralph.

Marineville Commander Sam Shore relies on a motorised hoverchair for mobility. The story of how he came to be crippled was told in the episode 'Ghost of the Sea'.

THE MAGICAL WORLD OF SPECIAL EFFECTS

The sheer amount of effort and ingenuity that went into the making of *Stingray* is amply demonstrated by the expertise and wizardry of *Stingray*'s art director, Bob Bell. Bob, who joined the team on the *Torchy* series as Reg Hill's assistant (a post he retained until being promoted to art director when Reg Hill was appointed Associate Producer on *Fireball XL5*), had more than enough problems to contend with, because of the attention which had to be given to the smallest detail — absolutely everything, not least of all being the acquisition of props. 'The main problem, of course, was that we had to make *everything:* from knives, forks, spoons, through

to chairs, tables, pianos — whereas on a live-action production I would have hired all the furniture, on the puppet shows we had to manufacture all things from scratch. Even the pictures on the wall had to be specially made. If a picture was a background picture, one seen for only a moment, we might possibly find something suitable in a magazine. We'd cut this out, paste it on a board, frame it and place it into the set. If it was a featured picture, one on which the camera would linger, this had to be painted by the studio artist. So just about everything had to be made.' There was one exception to this. Bob struck lucky when he noticed whilst on a tour of a toy

An outsider's view of the Marineville WASP complex, admittance and exit being allowed only on the production of a top-security pass.

Note the plastic knife and plate held by the waitress. Art Director Bob Bell purchased these from toy shops. The wine glass had to be made specially.

The studio prop room complete with its treasure trove of miniature props, including a miniature painting used throughout the series.

department, that cups, plates and saucers from a doll's tea service were exactly in proportion to the size of the puppet's hands.

Bob was also responsible for the water tanks used so dramatically in the series. Several different size tanks were used, the largest being 8 ft long, 4 ft high — inclusive of its metal base stands — and 6 inches in width. Designed to allow the filmmakers to do tracking shots, there were two of these, one in regular use by the main unit, the second being reserved for special effects. As the team were using two stages for the first time, the tracking tanks were supplemented by several different sized aquarium tanks; a small one employed for still work, and others which allowed the unit to continue filming until the main tank was ready to be used. Made of double-walled, armoured plate glass by the people who made the aquarium tanks for the London Zoo, these mobile tanks had a capacity of 2,000

gallons. These were specially manufactured as a result of the disasters in the early days. Bob remembers that on the day the very first tank — made originally of tempered plate glass — was test-filled, the tank exploded under presure and hundreds of gallons of water flooded the studio floor.

Once set up, the tanks were filled with many different sizes of the same species of tropical fish. This was done in order to give the illusion that when filming through the side of the tank, the effect was not one of big fish and small fish, but *close* fish and *distant* fish — the small fish looking as if they were some distance further back. Behind this would be a cyclorama — a curved wall or backcloth — which was painted to represent the sky or the sea-bed. Wave movement was created by a bank of electric fans and a light would be shrone though an Ulser lamp — a rotating piece of board with different size holes

cut into it — to create a pattern on the sea-bed, the sea floor itself being represented by layers of sand and pieces of seaweed. The device worked perfectly — when shooting underwater sequences. Shooting Stingray and other craft moving across the surface of the tank was an entirely different ball game.

The difficulty in this instance was concealing the metal edge of the tank furthest away from the camera — in other words, the horizon as viewed through the camera lens. Despite the fact that the tank was filled up to its brim, the slightest movement of water meant the metal rim would be picked up by the camera. Working in conjunction with Reg Hill, Gerry Anderson came up with a system to overcome this.

'The system we used was to build troughs all the way around the tank and to over-fill the tank with water. Now, the front and the sides of the tank were probably 2 inches higher than the back, so that when it was over-filled, the water had nowhere to go but over the back edge of the tank and into the trough. The water collected in the troughs was then piped back into the tank by automatic pumps, so we now had a constant waterfall effect over the rim of the tank, which gave us a totally clean horizon.'

Gerry credits Reg Hill with playing a highly significant role in helping to develop some of the basic techniques of combining special effects with water, and in particular for creating the triangular water tank — in fact it was more

Capable of a surface cruising speed of 400 knots, Stingray can surge through the ocean like a dolphin, leaving barely a ripple in its wake.

Attacked by an alien underwater craft, Stingray gives chase to the vessel, a war machine piloted by the man known to Commander Shore as 'The Ghost of the Sea'.

tapered', something like an Italian ice cream cone laid on its side with the camera lens looking from the base of the cone towards its mouthpiece. As could be expected when dealing with tanks containing thousands of gallons of water, moving the tanks around proved quite a problem for water is very heavy. Conscious of this, and of the fact that whenever the filmmakers panned their camera along the surface of the tank there would always be a vast area of water on either side of the camera that was never in shot, Reg Hill designed the new tank along the lines of a camera lens — in other words, triangular. This also reduced the weight of the tank by a third and allowed the crew to move the tank around with comparative ease.

Reg was also responsible for the design of the huge tower block which was erected at the back of the special effects studio, enabling FX director Derek Meddings to attach a painted backing

cloth into the tower and winch down another in minutes. Prior to this Derek had had the problem of replacing a backing cloth depicting a day scene with one painted with a night sky. Although he used to group all the day shots and night shots together, this was still terribly time-consuming. Now he had a whole range of backing cloths to select from.

Having joined Gerry's team on the *Supercar* series, Derek stumbled into special effects by accident. During the filming of the *Supercar* episode 'Amazonian Adventure', a sequence in the script called for Doctor Beaker to pound the keyboard of an organ so heavily that the instrument finally collapsed. Destroying the organ was easy, one simply attached wires to the instrument and yanked it apart to order — an effect which the team had used time and again. Enter Derek, then an assistant director, who attempted to convince the filmmakers that he could achieve the desired effect in truly explosive fashion. After a long discussion over the merits

of which method to use, Gerry Anderson nodded his agreement. Off went Derek, to return with several boxes of fireworks, from which he removed the combustible powder. Making up a charge, he crammed the device into the innards of the organ, then detonated it by remote control. The organ was demolished in a sheet of orange flame. Doctor Beaker's operator Christine Glanville jumped back in fright — which caused the puppet to react — and the production team recognised instantly that they could do this more often. They created their first FX department on the very next series.

Most people believe that special effects are all about creating explosions and fantastic volcanic eruptions. Nothing could be further from the truth. While it is fair to say that the FX team spend the majority of their working lives creating miniature — *convincing* miniature — catastrophes of one kind or another, what many people aren't aware of is that they use their wizardry in a hundred different ways. Fondly referred to as

An explosive shot of the deadly darts is fired by remote control when the Marineville complex is underground.

'the toy makers' by their movie-making colleagues, their greatest challenge is to convince the public that what they are seeing is real. An example of this might be that whenever a new model was tried on the set — say a plane taking off — it seldom looked natural. Because the models were very small and very light, an aircraft's wheels would skid across the tarmac without traction. This is where the FX team came in. By mounting the model's wheels on a block of foam rubber, Derek Meddings and his crew would give the model its own independent suspension and as if by magic, the wheels of the aircraft would now move across the tarmac independently of each other. Initially even this didn't look right, until, by a process of trial and error, the filmmakers learned to turn the camera at 120 frames a second — instead of the usual 25 frames a second — and pull the model through the miniature set at great speed. Played back in slow-motion, the model now appeared to be travelling at normal speed, its wheel movement being slow and lumbering, thereby creating a truly realistic effect. Because they were filming this kind of shot day after day, the crew became expert at knowing when the effect would look right.

Stingray returns from another successful mission.

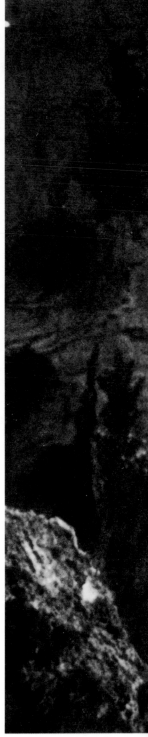

Supermarionation is go!

The high-speed camera trick was used when creating the effect that Stingray was cleaving its way through the water like a dolphin. Using several different models, some of which were waterproofed and weighted, the controllers would 'fly' Stingray between the water tank and the backing cloth on wires. When played back at normal speed, the bough waves churning out from the vehicle's tail created the highly realistic effect that Stingray was operating not in a water tank, but a huge ocean. Later on, when this technique had been mastered, Derek Meddings added more realism to the scenes by running a very fine plastic air-line into the tank. Pumping air through this, he could then create a burst of bubbles which were seemingly coming out of the top of a diver's helmet. This fooled everybody, the transparent air-line being disguised with foreground pieces of rock and seaweed.

There were, of course, other hazards to deal with.

Camera trickery came in useful when creating the impression that the puppet characters were swimming, which of course they weren't. Their aqua-suits never even got wet. This again was achieved by shooting at high speed. Christine Glanville remembers how this was accomplished. 'Unlike Troy and Phones, who wore aqua-suits, Marina simply swam, with her long hair billowing out behind her — an effect we achieved by having fans placed along the bridge, facing upwards, to blow her hair about. We mastered the swimming effect by thundering along the bridge at break-neck pace, dragging the puppets along behind the water-filled tank.' She remembers thinking to herself that this was going to look horrible, but then she saw the results in play-back. 'The puppets looked very good. Marina looked as though she was really swimming, with her feet floating out behind her.' Achieving the effect was very noisy indeed, so the scenes had to be re-dubbed later.

The grace and speed of a
dolphin: able to breathe just
as well in water as air,
Marina is equally at home on
terra firma or in the ocean.

WASP 7

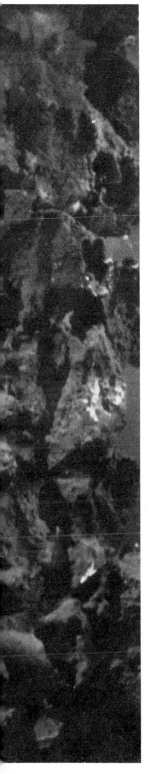

In an attempt to evade Stingray, the Big Gun dives into the deepest depths of the ocean.

'My pictures are synonymous with explosions and destruction,' Gerry Anderson conceded in a matter-of-fact way. 'People think that we used to take models and blow them sky high. We didn't, of course; we couldn't afford to. If we wanted to blow a car up, we would lock off the camera so that it couldn't move, photograph the car, stop the film, take the car out of the shot and replace it with a polyurethane bag containing explosive and put recognisable bits of the car over it. We'd then shape the polyurethane bag very roughly into the shape of the car, turn the camera over at high-speed and detonate the explosive charge. As seen on the studio floor, it would literally go bang, like a firework. But because we were filming at high-speed — and therefore retaining slow-motion — when we played back the film it would be like a mushroom explosion, with all the little pieces of debris spinning in the air amid the smoke. We would then take the shot of the car and the explosion and cut the two together. Things happened so swiftly that the eye could believe the vehicle had exploded. It hadn't, of course. The car was put to one side to be used again.'

Gerry holds his team in high esteem. Indeed, he doubts whether he would be where he is today without them. 'Because we were working in colour for the first time, we were going for models with a high degree of detailed finish — which, when filmed for the first time, turned out to be an awful disappointment. They looked like toys. So we then created what we called "the dirtying down shop." As soon as the pristine models were completed, we sent them to the shop for painting. Say there was an enemy fighter plane. All the cowlings around the engine would be painted as if they were burned by the heat of the engines. The paintwork around the cockpit door would be rubbed away where the pilot would board and disembark. The fuselage panelling would be marked on. The under-

91

In the episode 'The Master Plan' Titan's unarmed missile ploughs its way into the Marineville complex. Its cargo? The antidote that can save Troy's life. What on earth can the despot be thinking of?

carriage would be dirtied and the whole model would be aged, so that it didn't look as though it had just come off the assembly line. This gave a great deal of realism to the models.'

These were just a few of the difficulties that had to be overcome before the filmmakers could convince the public that the puppets had personalities of their own, their own distinctive mannerisms and even, one would swear, their own thoughts.

In retrospect, Gerry Anderson remembers Lilliput Land as being a beehive of frenzied activity. Working on the programmes was very hard work — and he loved every minute of it, despite the fact that his input often meant that he worked an 18-hour day. With two full-blown units filming separate episodes simultaneously, at any given hour during the production, there would be a writer coming in for discussion

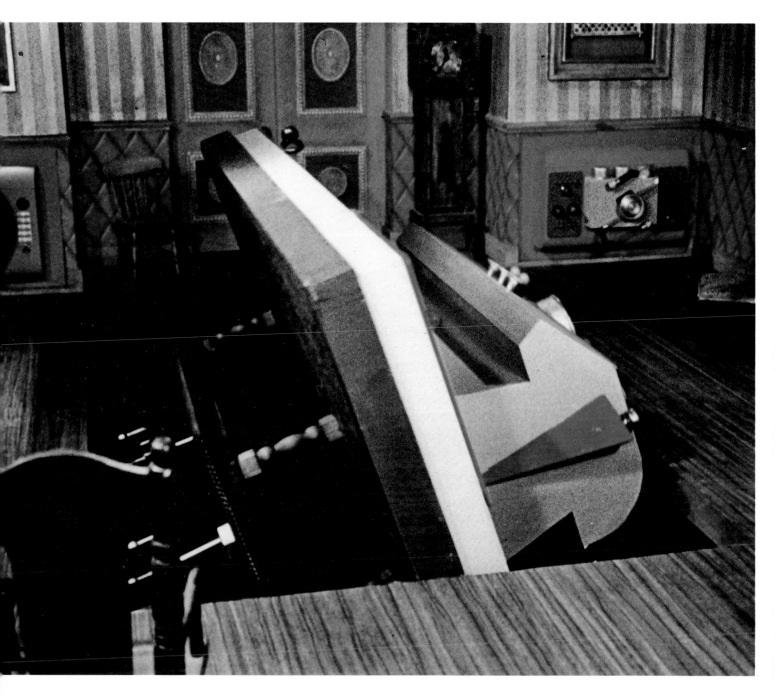

regarding a new storyline, another writer delivering his first draft and another script being finalised by the directors. There would be an episode in production and another one in preparation. A film would be in the cutting room, one would be in the dubbing theatre and another would be at the laboratory being printed. Sets, props and revamps were being made and the voice artistes would be recording their dialogue in the dubbing room. Life in puppet land was busy, busy, busy.

Christine Glanville and Bob Bell are in harmony in their assessment of Gerry Anderson. 'The thing about Gerry was that he was always wanting to prove that each film was an improvement on the last!'

And Gerry Anderson's view of his own work? 'I suppose it's fair to say that because I never wanted to make puppet films in the first place, I was trying — foolishly — to take the puppet and turn it and its settings into total reality, because I believed that broadcasters would eventually say,

X-2-Zero's dusty old house becomes transformed at the touch of a button. The chandelier flashes on and off and the dining room table and chairs revolve to be replaced by the surface agent's control console.

"This man is wasting his time. We really ought to give him big, major movies to make." And so with that philosophy, I became hypercritical. I mean, I couldn't see anything without it being wrong in my eyes. I was trying to bring a sense of reality and believability to the programmes, trying to make them work. There have been times, here and there, when, if I was sitting in a theatre with a receptive audience and they laughed or I sensed that they were very quiet at a funny or tense moment, then, just very occasionally, I would think, "Hey, that was good." Since then I certainly haven't been a sort of fading Hollywood star who watches my pictures every day and night and bathes in the glory. I'm very much a person of tomorrow. One who is more than happy to talk about the past when people ask me to. But left to my own devices I would never think back.'

Gerry's then-latest saga of puppetdom was introduced on 4 October 1964. *Stingray* had been launched and Supermarionation was GO! Hugely successful, *Stingray* sold to well over 100 markets in the USA and was dubbed into nearly every language in the world.

A precursor of things to come, two years later the Anderson team would produce their greatest triumph, *Thunderbirds*.

Thunderbirds would become a milestone in TV history and the programme that would transfix the public and achieve blast-off in a way that previous Anderson vehicles had not.

Confessing to his limitations as both writer and speller, Gerry and his wife Sylvia went to Portugal to write the pilot script, 'Trapped in the Sky'. Gerry would dictate his ideas, carrying the convolutions of the script in his head.

The weird rescue vehicles, invented by the week for the show, as well as Thunderbirds 1-5 themselves, were a fantasy expression of Gerry's fundamental interest in aircraft and spaceships. Intrigued, too, by early space missions, Gerry remembers that when President Kennedy claimed in 1961 that America would send a man to the moon in 10 years, Gerry himself prayed that he would live long enough to bear witness to the event.

AN
APF
TELEVISION PRODUCTION

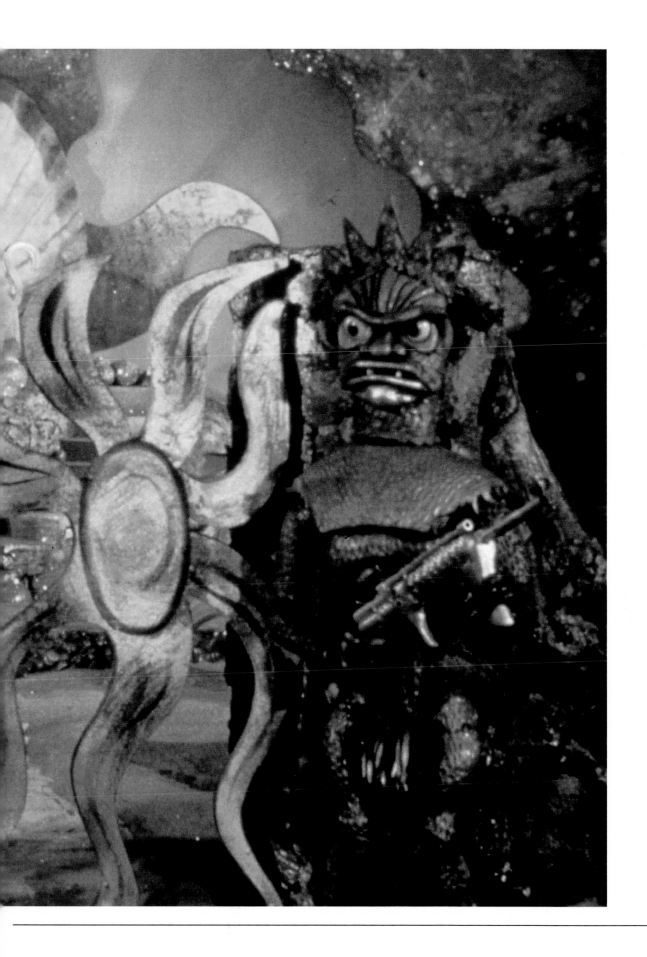

THUNDERBIRDS

ARE GO!

Contents

THUNDERBIRDS LIFT OFF

Thunderbirds is a great enigma. Once again the series has astounded with its ability to attract and hold, excite and thrill, as well as intrigue and captivate television audiences of all ages. Small children, teenagers and more mature viewers who affectionately remember the programmes first time around switched on in their millions to watch the series on BBC2. They have been hooked again by the fantastic Thunderbirds space craft, International Rescue, and the perilous missions in which they are engaged.

Since the early days enthusiasm for Thunderbirds has continued to build until it has become one of the most recognised and most talked-about series ever shown on television. The interest is truly international: from the series' earliest days to the present time the ITC Entertainment Group has been successfully licensing the series to television networks throughout the world. Thunderbirds has impressively demonstrated its ageless appeal.

A new generation has now proved its enthusiasm with the high viewing figures and by its clamour for Thunderbirds merchandise.

Exactly what it is that attracts – the exciting storylines, the magic of the puppets, the incredible craft or the extension of unbelievable fantasy into a series of compelling possibility – Thunderbirds continues on its successful path.

It could never have been envisaged that all these years later the series would still be functioning in top gear, enjoying a continuing craze of commitment which right up to the present time truly remains an enigma.

Despite his penchant for innovation and exploiting the latest techniques, Gerry Anderson had not the slightest inkling that 'Thunderbirds' would transfix the public and achieve blast-off in a way that his previous vehicles had not.

Confessing to his limitations as both writer and speller, he and his wife Sylvia went to Portugal to write the pilot script, 'Trapped in the Sky'. Gerry would dictate his ideas, carrying the convolutions of the script in his head. Derek Meddings took his lead for the craft from Gerry's descriptions in this first script, which he dictated to Sylvia over four sessions.

Alan, Brains, Gordon, Scott
and Virgil on Tracy Island
(left). Scott, seated at Jeff's
desk, has taken command in
the episode 'Atlantic
Inferno', ready to co-
ordinate the craft of International Rescue.

Jeff Tracy, co-ordinator of International Rescue, seated at his desk.

An aerial view of Tracy Island (below).

The weird rescue vehicles, invented by the week for that particular show, as well as Thunderbirds 1–5 themselves, were a fantasy expression of Gerry's fundamental interest in aircraft and spaceships. Whereas it would take the airline industries years to improve on speed, range and the number of passengers carried, Anderson, Meddings and the team could instantly create craft of stunning ability. Intrigued, too, by early space missions, Gerry remembers that when President Kennedy claimed that America would send a man to the moon in ten years, Gerry himself prayed that he would live long enough to bear witness to the event.

The secret organisation International Rescue was created by the bottomless pockets of millionaire entrepreneur and ex-astronaut Jeff Tracy; it comprised all manner of state-of-the-art craft and hi-tech gadgetry which would prise individuals from the sort of sticky jams that would have overwhelmed conventional equipment. Working under a thick veil of secrecy on Tracy Island, itself situated non-specifically in the Pacific Ocean, Jeff was spurred on by the sudden death of his wife, which left him with five sons – Scott, Virgil, Alan, Gordon and John – who formed the backbone of his ever-eager rescue squad.

Intelligent and imaginative back-up is provided by the likes of friends-turned-agents (Lady Penelope Creighton-Ward and Jeremiah Turtle *et al.*) who assist the Tracy clan with an effective blend of cunning, caring and charm, while scientific guru and major boffin Hiram K. Hackenbacker (alias Brains) seems only to have to blink through his thick-lensed glasses in order to produce the most advanced scientific wizardry, not to mention the supercharged craft themselves, from thin air. His much-coveted Thunderbirds speed from Tracy Island to the requisite disaster zone, vanish back into the ether and, despite the efforts of an assortment of nasties and ne'er-do-wells, can never be traced right back to base.

The Hood, the key villain throughout the series, is desperate to glean even the slightest detail of the International Rescue operation. The

A portrait of Hiram K. Hackenbacker, more commonly known as 'Brains'.

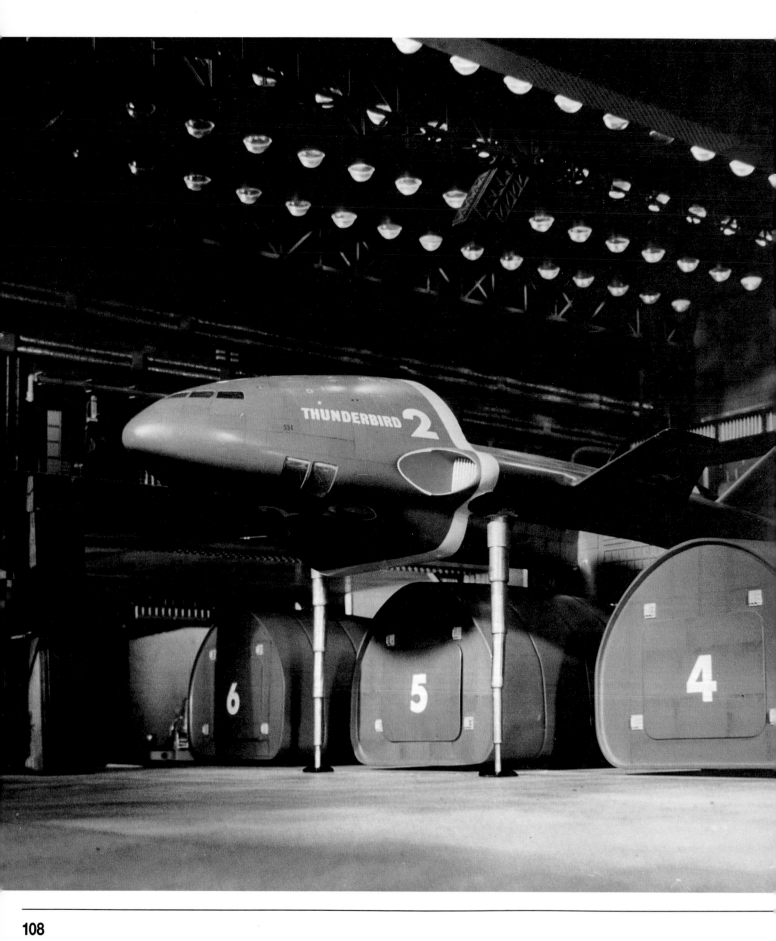

heartless half-brother of Kyrano, Jeff Tracy's faithful manservant, he is able to influence Kyrano through his disconcerting voodoo-styled hypnotic powers.

However, even the perpetual conniving of the Hood can never penetrate the fortress of Tracy Island. Appearing to the casual eye as merely the paradise home of the Tracy family, its rocks conceal the four Thunderbirds supercraft, while Thunderbird 5 is in a state of constant orbit, picking up Mayday calls from every corner of the globe.

The series took its title, of course, from the five rescue vehicles themselves.

Thunderbird 1 is the supercharged rocket-plane which catapults mission-leader Scott Tracy

towards any danger zone at a speed of 15,000 miles per hour, so that he can make on-site decisions as soon as possible.

Thunderbird 2 is the giant bug-shaped cargo-transporter which carries the appropriate rescue gear in any one of its six huge pods. Virgil Tracy is in command here.

Thunderbird 2 (left) sitting over Pod 5; this large craft can select from a number of pods to help with its rescue missions.

Thunderbird 1 returns to the ship Ocean Pioneer II in the episode 'Danger Ocean Deep' (below).

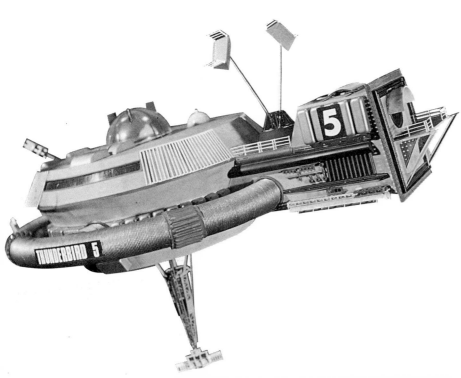

Thunderbird 3 is a vast spaceship which can effect in-space rescue missions and act as a shuttle to Thunderbird 5. This is in the safe hands of Jeff's youngest son, astronaut Alan Tracy.

Thunderbird 4 is compact enough to be carried in one of the massive pods by Thunderbird 2. A mini-submarine, it hogs centre-stage during underwater emergencies and deep-sea disasters. Gordon Tracy is its aquanaut pilot.

In geo-stationary orbit above the earth, Thunderbird 5 is both space station and communications satellite which is primed to home in on every radio and video signal in the world. Oldest son Scott Tracy is the pilot who can feed instant emergency signals back to his brother Jeff, ready to deal with any crisis.

Thunderbird 5 (above), space station and satellite communications centre, acts as the gathering unit for the world's distress signals.

A real image of the earth is used as the backdrop to this scene of Thunderbird 3 orbiting the planet (left).

Thunderbird 4 tows an underwater well-capping device to stem the flow of oil from the seabed in 'Atlantic Inferno' (right).

EVERY CHARACTER A STACCATO SUPERBRAIN

Though the Thunderbirds themselves upstaged their pilots when either in full flight or mounting a tricky rescue operation, it was the puppets themselves who softened proceedings with their human traits and benevolent tones. Although little background information on each character was squeezed into the series, enough is available to build up a composite picture of each individual.

Jeff Tracy

The lantern jaw and determined frown of Jeff Tracy embody the rugged spirit of the man who founded International Rescue. A thrusting pioneer who would be no stranger to John Wayne, his basic decency caused him to found his squad so as to weed out the assorted rogues and counter the catastrophes regularly bringing the world to the brink of disaster.

As befits his spirit of soaring adventure, Jeff was born and raised on a Kansas wheat farm by a father who combined his sharp mathematical insights with driving a combine harvester for a living. This may well explain Jeff's abiding fascination with complicated machinery as well as his own mathematical prowess.

He carried out his military service with the American air force and progressed smoothly to the rank of colonel before joining the much-fêted Space Agency Project. Here he excelled as an astronaut and his skill and enthusiasm soon enabled him to become one of the first men on the moon.

Jeff's easy ride to fame, glory and space conquest was abruptly ended by the tragic early death of his wife while she was giving birth to their youngest son, Alan. 'Thunderbirds' must have instinctively predicted an era of domesticated New Age men and househusbands when Jeff abandoned his neon-lit space career to return home and bring up his five healthy sons.

A publicity shot of Jeff Tracy, wearing, unusually, Brains' International Rescue uniform.

A Christmas family portrait.

With his mechanical bent well to the fore, Jeff embraced the worlds of civil and construction engineering and, as befits his awesome track record, soon became one of the richest men in the world. Performing an enviable juggling act between work and rearing his children at the same time, his new work also gave him plentiful contacts which would prove useful in the founding of International Rescue. Conveniently funded by Jeff's millions, the team operate under a thick veil of secrecy from Tracy Island, itself situated non-specifically in the Pacific Ocean.

His workaholic nature, entrepreneurial spirit and grand ambition have never diminished his genuine feeling for his fellow-man. Born on 2 January 1970, he's now fifty-six, head of a crack space-age team and showing no signs of slowing down. He has almost to be forced to go to Australia by his offspring when he is offered a much needed break on Lady Penelope's ranch.

Though warmhearted and occasionally humorous, Jeff has no trouble at all in being decisive or fixing an errant son with a gimlet eye. In *Thunderbirds Are Go* he rages at Alan for leaving the base unmanned; yet he is applauding the same son by the end of the adventure.

His abiding zeal to improve International Rescue by even the smallest detail gives evidence of an obsessive personality, and Jeff is indeed sometimes irked by his all-out drive. In *Thunderbird 6*, for example, he is frustrated by the conflict between his desire for a further machine and his inability to fathom what its function ought to be. He can, however, be readily boosted by visiting admirers like Tony and Bob Williams in 'Cry Wolf' or Chip in 'Security Hazard'. Whenever a mission is under way, Jeff is firmly in charge on Tracy Island, offering mature middle-aged wisdom to his orbiting sons. Decent to the last, he knows when his hard-working boys are in need of a break and so lets them cut loose for a while. See *Thunderbirds Are Go* for further details. The voice of Jeff Tracy was given full expression by Peter Dyneley.

Scott Tracy

An unsurprising fusion of Dad's intellectual dazzle and gritty masculinity (he reads books and eats steaks), Scott Tracy, born on 14 April 1996, at thirty is the eldest of Jeff's boys. He is admiringly named after the astronaut Scott Malcolm Carpenter. This dark-haired *Wunderkind* was educated at both Yale and Oxford and, like his father before him, joined the United States Air Force where he was decorated on numerous occasions for valour and bravery.

The pilot of Thunderbird 1, the rocket-powered reconnaissance plane whose speed of

Jeff Tracy enjoying a game of billiards.

5,000 miles per hour matches Scott's lightning brain, he is always first to land at the disaster zone, where he ably assesses the situation and decides what kind of rescue equipment is needed. When it finally arrives, Scott's lack of arrogance enables him to assist in even the most menial tasks. He is also happy to co-pilot Thunderbird 3, where he is of much help to his brother Alan, while his seniority places him firmly in command of the island headquarters whenever his father is absent.

A fast-talking, quick-thinking bright spark who, like his father, enjoys a good joke, he is characterised by a curt decisive speech-pattern, while his final words often trail off into the ether.

As physically powerful as he is knowledgeable, and with the confidence to make instant decisions, he radiates his father's tireless energy and survives on very little sleep. His untroubled nature never dents his determination to win through, while his turquoise uniform and pale sash and band (his on-duty attire) make him instantly recognisable.

His voice was played by actor Shane Rimmer.

Scott Tracy in command on Tracy Island while Jeff is on holiday in Australia, relaxing on Lady Penelope's ranch.

Virgil Tracy

Possessed of an intensity which has by-passed his brothers, Virgil certainly has the most serious nature of all. Born on 15 August 1999, his gravity of demeanour lends him a maturity which obscures his mere twenty-seven years.

An accomplished graduate from the Denver School of Advanced Technology, his mechanical dexterity makes him the ideal pilot of Thunderbird 2, International Rescue's heavy rescue craft and vast transporter. In this capacity, he ends up driving any number of complex vehicles which Thunderbird 2 has brought along for the complicated rescue mission. Just like his brothers, he is never blinded by technology to real human need, and is quite happy to endanger his own life if it means saving others. Virgil takes part in almost every daring encounter in which International Rescue is involved.

Named in tribute to astronaut Virgil Grissom, his looks and colour call his mother to mind, and he thus enjoys an especially close relationship to his father Jeff. Yet Jeff is careful never to let his affection for the young man slide over into favouritism, for that would disrupt the balance and well-being of the entire team.

With medium-brown hair, and sporting a yellow sash and a belt while on duty, he tends towards the monosyllabic. Direct to the point of bluntness, he offers an array of immediate and fixed opinions which are unfailingly correct. Generally fearless and blessed with iron resolve, Virgil does, however, assess the importance of fear without which, he feels, there would be foolhardiness. He believes he owes it to those he is rescuing not to jeopardise their lives in any cavalier act of disregard.

An intriguingly complex creation, Virgil is both music buff gifted pianist and talented artist, and these traditionally non-macho leanings (a debt, perhaps, to his mother) make him a regular butt of his brothers' predictable jokes. Well disposed to the last, Virgil does not, however,

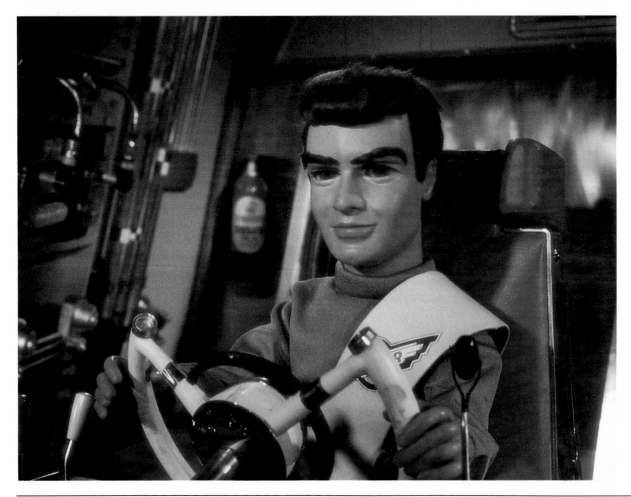

Virgil at the controls of Thunderbird 2, the heavy-duty carrier craft.

old his brothers in lesser regard. Displaying a particular penchant for jazz, he has also cleverly composed the 'Thunderbirds' rousing theme tune. Barry Gray might thus be a touch confused.

First David Holliday, then, for the second series, Jeremy Wilkin lent their vocal talents to Virgil.

John Tracy

Taking his name from John Glenn, the first American to orbit the earth, John, aged twenty-five, was born on 28 October 2001. With the fair hair and dashing looks of a popular matinée idol, John is certainly the dreamer of the group. This is just as well, since he leads a solitary life aboard Thunderbird 5, International Rescue's space station which is in a state of permanent orbit, high above Earth. It has to be properly manned so that distress signals, picked up by Thunderbird from frequencies across the globe, can be beamed back to base and so kick-start the team into their rescue missions.

His time at Harvard University gave him a superb knowledge of electronics and specialist skills in laser communications, while he also trained as an astronaut. The quietest and most intellectual of all the boys, he also shares his father's active interest in astronomy. His sealed-off existence in Thunderbird 5 allows him ample opportunity to pursue his hobby, while his natural patience is a prerequisite of the job.

The discovery of the quasar system is accredited to John, as are four substantial textbooks on astronomy and outer space. A slightly dour character, his intellectual abilities outshine his action-man experience, and he rarely participates in an actual rescue mission, a worthy exception being 'Danger at Ocean Deep'. John is, however, athletically able and, despite his slightly less muscular build, received many athletics awards at school which he naturally attributes to sheer mental agility. His brother Alan replaces John on Thunderbird 5 for a month at a time, when he assumes command of Alan's Thunderbird 3.

Wearing a lilac sash and belt, John's voice is given life by long-term Anderson associate Ray Barrett.

Gordon Tracy in the cockpit of Thunderbird 4, the small versatile submarine craft of the International Rescue fleet.

Gordon Tracy

Born on 14 February 2004, Gordon is distinguished by both frivolous banter and a sense of perky fun which place him attractively at odds with the harsh intensity of Virgil and the intellectual dreaming of John. Whether teasing his younger brother Alan about being in love, as in 'End of the Road', or embarking on some other joky escapade, he is often rebuked by his stern father.

Yet he is a keen contributor to the rescue team who can switch from light-hearted antics to committed responsibility in a flash. He is, in fact, the skilled aquanaut in charge of Thunderbird 4, a highly versatile submarine which is suitably equipped with top-strength underwater lighting, powerful cutting gear and a flexible grappling-hook. Thunderbird 4 is usually transported to the rescue site by Thunderbird 2.

This auburn-haired blue-eyed twenty-two-year-old undersea specialist has a particular affinity with water and has an unsurprising liking for all kinds of water-sports from water-skiing to skin-diving.

Named after astronaut Leroy Gordon Cooper he became an expert on oceanography in the Submarine Service and World Aquanaut Security Patrol where he invented a breakthrough underwater breathing apparatus, an improved version of which is employed in the exclusive service of International Rescue. With a strength and tenacity which underlie his good-natured high spirits Gordon is one of the world's fastest freestyle swimmers and, in fact, won an Olympic medal for the butterfly stroke. At WASP, Gordon was put in command of a bathyscaphe in which he spent a year underwater so as to study seabed life and marine farming methods. A short time before International Rescue began to function he survived a dreadful crash in his hydrofoil speedboat which capsized at 400 knots and was completely destroyed on impact. After spending four months in a hospital bed, Gordon returned to action with high spirits reined in a bit and a healthy new respect for the sea, though he will always remain the team's greatest prankster. He can be picked out by an orange sash and belt and the voice of David Graham.

Alan Tracy

A blond-haired baby-face who is as reckless as he is romantic, twenty-one-year-old Alan is the youngest of the brothers. Born on 12 March 2005, he was named after Alan B. Shephard, the first man to play golf on the moon, which Alan himself has visited many times. Aside from carrying out his stints aboard Thunderbird 5, he is the astronaut mainly responsible for Thunderbird 3 and is assisted in this task by Scott. He studied at Harvard University where he developed a rocket and, much to the annoyance of his tutors, actually launched it. It veered right off course, shattering every window at the University of Colorado. Jeff then decided that, in order to teach his impulsive son a sense of responsibility, Alan should also train as an astronaut, and his subsequent success in that field has borne out Jeff's faith in him.

Though a terrific sportsman, partygoer and racing-car driver (this latter enthusiasm lands him in trouble in 'Move and You're Dead'), he enjoys the quiet contemplations of archaeology and regularly wanders off to the less visible corners of Tracy Island to pore over rocks and potholes. This never interferes, however, with his utter dedication to International Rescue and to his father, who nevertheless sometimes treats him like a wayward schoolboy.

Such friction is highly visible in 'The Perils of Penelope' and *Thunderbirds Are Go*.

Though it is never fully written into any one script, Alan, the misty dewy-eyed romantic of the family, does seem to be involved with Tin-Tin, the daughter of the Tracys' loyal man-servant Kyrano. He is, in fact, the only brother in love with another of the characters. We only see evidence of this supposed relationship through Tin-Tin's attention to other men. In 'End of the Road', an old family friend, Eddie Houseman, visits the base and causes Tin-Tin to gasp in admiration. Alan's short-fuse jealousy is calmed by Grandma, whose mix of tact and gentle conniving brings the twosome back together again. Though also having to woo Tin-Tin back in 'The Cham Cham', where she gushes over Cass Carnaby, or in 'Ricochet', where she is transfixed by a mere mortal, Alan has learned neither to take her for granted nor to confuse her

Alan Tracy, youngest of the brothers, is pilot of Thunderbird 3 and rotates monitor duty aboard Thunderbird 5 with John.

A rare portrait of Lady Penelope Creighton-Ward.

FAB 1, Lady Penelope's pink Rolls-Royce, leaving Glen Fields airbase.

with the furniture. Despite his sex appeal as an impulsive blond bombshell, he remains single, the clue to which may be his giveaway remark in *Thunderbird 6*: 'The life I lead at International Rescue is too dangerous to ask anyone to share it with me.'

Voiced by Matt Zimmerman, he sports a fetching off-white sash and belt which are a perfect match for his stunning blond hairdo.

Lady Penelope

Born on 24 December 1999, and voiced by Sylvia Anderson, Lady Penelope Creighton-Ward is a twenty-seven-year-old aristocrat who is the key member of International Rescue's all-important network of undercover agents. Working from her large stately home in rural Kent, she is the globe-trotting British agent for International Rescue whose top-drawer elegance stands in amusing contrast to her constant girlish craving for intrigue. Her travels for International Rescue include tracking down a pack of criminals in 'The Imposters', opening a road in 'Atlantic Inferno' and dazzling all at a party to celebrate the success of a solar generator.

A grand lady who even had her own comic strip in *TV21*, she appears to those ignorant of her secret life as someone who really lives for lunch, yet she is a tough, if always charming, adversary to those who would disrupt world peace.

Polite and well mannered to the last, she is both a chic dresser who follows world fashion and a big-hearted altruist who will always bring help of all kinds to beleaguered unfortunates. Like her willing crook-turned-sidekick Parker, she has a child's enthusiam for electronic gadgets and, even if they can only perform the simplest task, will at once install them in her house or pink Rolls-Royce, FAB 1, which transports the odd couple on relaxing excursions in the countryside.

The only other luxury transport in her life is FAB 2, a yacht she enjoys on global jaunts. It was one of those trips which enabled her to meet Jeff Tracy, who, seeking an agent in Europe, was enchanted by Lady Penelope, who was already active as a successful spy. Jeff insisted she tackle a very difficult test and, after she succeeded with great ease and aplomb, he invited her on board. Her cool poise and steel nerves help her in the behind-the-scenes handywork which has pushed many an International Rescue mission towards triumph.

Aside from a distaste for American coffee, this single-minded pursuer of all hardened criminals is frightened witless by mice (see 'The Mighty Atom' for evidence of this). This fear combines amusingly with her upper-crust preference for

understatement to create fun moments in the midst of adventure: in *Thunderbirds Are Go* she explains to Parker, 'I don't think there is much need in looking for survivors,' or 'Oh dear, just when I am expecting visitors – three coach-loads, too. How inconvenient.' Her persistence and top-drawer Englishness are effectively satirised in 'Day of Disaster', where she declares firmly 'In my house everything stops for tea.'

Zena Relph, couturier to Lady Penelope, recalls the puppet and the period with great affection.

'I first became involved with Gerry when I replaced the wardrobe mistress on "Fireball XL5" when she went down with measles. I was, in fact, a floor puppeteer on "Stingray", before being asked to dress Lady Penelope for "Thunderbirds". Along with Sylvia and Betty Coleman, I'd leaf through *Vogue* for suitably exotic outfits, which appeared on Lady Penelope at the rate of one a week. The costumes were always made of silk, wool or cotton so that they would move with the body.'

Lady Penelope in the drawing room of her stately mansion, which was based on Stourhead House in Mere, Wiltshire.

A full-time magician, who once worked on a Russian cruise ship, Zena recently designed an off-white wool dress and re-created the mink coat from *Thunderbirds Are Go* for Lady Penelope's starring role in a Swinton Insurance commercial.

Parker

Born on 30 May, and possibly fifty-two years of age, Parker is Lady Penelope's sidekick who has been transformed from seedy crook into loyal butler, chauffeur and all-in-one aid. The joint appearance of Parker and Penelope in the pages of *TV21* gives us background knowledge of their relationship. It seems they met when Parker was trying to steal Penelope's car but was foiled by an anti-theft alarm. Instead of being handed over at once to the police, Parker, much to his surprise, was recruited by Lady Penelope, who could readily spot a resourceful ex-con, even if initially she had to press Parker into service with the help of a gun. The television series does, however, suggest that they may have joined forces after Penelope's assiduous trawling of the underworld for a useful assistant. For Penelope to be of value to the Tracy boys, and be able to squash criminals underfoot, she sometimes has to slide gracefully to just the wrong side of the law where Parker can help her pick locks and blow safes.

Blessed with the slightly surreal first name of Aloysius, but better known to his former associates as Nosey on account of his most obvious facial trait, Parker is reputed to be the best safe-blower in the world and has a reputation for unswerving loyalty and sound mechanical ability, which proves useful in tinkering with FAB 1.

Penelope's seductive charm and gentle persuasion eventually sent Parker down the road of total devotion to ' 'er Ladyship', and he was never once offended by her insistence on educating him in matters of etiquette. In the manner of a broad cockney, he is apt to preface all vowels with 'h', as in 'hinformation' and 'hadmiration'. Yet Parker's origins still betray themselves when it comes to food (in 'Vault of Death' he pronounces to Lilly the cook: 'Stew – me favourite'), and he can never quite shake off his grubby associates. They can either provide much

A rare picture (above) of Parker at Scott's mobile control – perhaps waiting for his cue during the production of a 'Thunderbirds' episode. . .

useful information or alternatively cause trouble, as does Light-Fingered Fred in 'Vault of Death', in which Parker is torn between loyalty to his new cause and to his former associates. In fact it is the conflict between his new social position and his rough past, as evidenced in his convoluted speech-patterns, which constitutes the best comedy in the series.

Although Parker was initially conceived as simple dramatic support to Lady Penelope, he would actively upstage her on many occasions because of his intrinsic amusement value. He would become more popular with many fans than even the dashing superheroes and was indeed the favourite character of Gerry Anderson himself.

While Gerry & Co. were still at the planning stage of 'Thunderbirds', they would regularly visit a traditional English pub near Cookham called the King's Arms. They were often served by a very decent waiter named Arthur, who had once been in the Queen's service at Windsor Castle and, in the appreciative manner of Parker enjoying his new liaison with upper-crust England, would give detailed accounts of life with Her Majesty. A wonderfully rich, lively character, Arthur was assiduously studied by David Graham who, once he had been selected as the voice of Parker, visited the pub on a number of occasions. With identical vocal and

A portrait of reformed ex-con Aloysius 'Nosey' Parker, now butler to Lady Penelope.

other mannerisms to Parker, Arthur never knew he had become an international hero; and Gerry, sensing that Arthur would not be best pleased at such vast recognition, never summoned up the courage to tell him. Gerry even believes that such knowledge would have destroyed Arthur who, unwitting to the end, sadly died a few years later.

Actor and voice artist David Graham, who is an accomplished veteran of the theatres of London's West End, the National Theatre and the BBC, first met Gerry when he was playing a villain in a television film, directed by Gerry, for the Martin Caine series. 'I was just a working character actor. I'd always been good at voices and, when Jerry said he hoped to do a puppet-based production, I said I'd like to give it a try. Before "Thunderbirds", in fact, I did "Four Feather Falls", "Supercar". "Fireball XL5" and "Stingray".'

Although he gave life to Gordon, Brains and Kyrano, David will always be linked with Parker in the public imagination. David admits that he 'never dreamed Parker would become a cult figure, though, along with Brains, he's certainly my favourite character. I created a fantasy life for him and indeed revived him last year when Gerry was making a charity speech at the Grosvenor House Hotel. Gerry had a model set with Parker on it, and my pre-recorded dialogue, which was in pure Parkerese, was pumped into the room.'

Lady Penelope and Parker relax at Bonga Bonga, Penelope's Australian ranch.

Brains

A loving parody of a teenage boy wonder is the dour bespectacled Hiram K. Hackenbacker (alias Brains), inventor of all the dazzling machines for International Rescue and, when he has a spare moment, currently translating Einstein's theory of relativity into Latin.

Though not one of the Tracy family, he nonetheless brings complementary brainpower to their collective skills, and, self-critical to the last, he is never at ease with his creations and is consequently often to be found modifying and tinkering with his machines. Never to be found scuba-diving or chasing Tin-Tin, his off-duty relaxation includes the study of trigonometry and thermodynamics, while he is forever cooking up new and radical ideas for improving Brainman, a robot who once beat him at chess.

Reduced to the status of orphan when a hurricane destroyed his Michigan home, Brains was twelve years old when he was adopted by a professor at Cambridge University who immediately found evidence of Brains's analytical prowess and dazzling intellect. Nothing proved too overwhelming for Brains to absorb or learn.

Jeff Tracy, after he had conceived International Rescue, realised that a switched-on superbrain would be necessary to help him accomplish his plans, and went on an extended world tour in search of a genius. Jeff eventually descended on Paris, where Brains was nervously delivering a deep-delving high-octane lecture in a palace of culture and knew at once that this was the man for him. Brains, acknowledging that Jeff was a decent entrepreneur who could save mankind, accepted Jeff's mighty challenge without pause for thought.

Neither Brains's intense bespectacled stare nor his nervous stutter prevent him from reacting to the pressure of circumstance, so that he is able both to advise the others ('Pit of Peril', 'Day of Disaster', 'Sun Probe', *Thunderbirds Are Go*) and find the courage to join in ('Lord Parker's 'Oliday', *Thunderbird 6*). In the midst of gung-ho astronauts and whizzing supercraft, Brains is a comforting island of comic solemnity.

The voice of Brains was provided by David Graham.

Brains, genius behind Jeff's dream of International Rescue.

Kyrano

Like Brains and Parker before him, Kyrano is voiced by David Graham and displays the same touching loyalty to Jeff and the boys, to whom he has been manservant for such a long time that he has also become Jeff's friend. Of Malaysian extraction, he feels that there is nothing he would not do for his masters and exudes a relaxing warmth to all around him. Like most others in the cast, Kyrano is one of the world's finest in his chosen skill, which in his case happens to be botany. Kyrano did, in fact, spend several years at Kew Gardens, where, as a consultant botanist, he advised on Asian orchids.

Kyrano was once active at the Kennedy Space Center where Jeff first met him. Already predisposed towards the adventurous world of astronauts, he was engaged in the discovery of ways of producing synthetic food from plants which could then be concentrated into tablet or paste forms to feed astronauts. This experience was a launch-pad for Kyrano, who quickly became a culinary wizard, and such was his excellence that he was soon installed as head chef at the Paris Hilton. Needless to say, Jeff and the boys eat well at all times.

Kyrano's father made sizeable fortunes from his vast estates and rubber plantations, but Kyrano himself, instead of inheriting his right and proper share of his father's will, was tricked out of his wealth by his malevolent half-brother, the Hood. It is the Hood who exposes Kyrano's minor flaw by exerting a sometimes mesmeric hold over him, and he is quite happy to exploit Kyrano's good nature by using him as an unwitting pawn in his prolonged attempts to crush International Rescue. Kyrano, however, has long since reacted against his half-brother's greed by replacing any interest in the material world with an enthusiasm for inner harmony, and this he has certainly found on Tracy Island.

The Hood

The Hood, so named after his inventive array of disguises, was thus able to offer endless dramatic possibilities to the script-writing team. Abusing his hypnotic inexplicable power over his kindly half-brother, Kyrano, he can often temporarily outwit the Tracy brothers, whom he will try to thwart as often as possible so as to glean the priceless plans of Thunderbirds 1–5.

Never referred to as 'the Hood' as such in the series, he creates harrowing disasters which are designed to trap the Tracys; yet, even with the element of surprise on his side, he can only ever come close to securing the prized plans. In 'Martian Invasion', for example, after filming Thunderbirds 1 and 2, he speeds off to a potential buyer but is forcibly stopped in his tracks by the Tracys.

He is feared as the world's foremost villain and, in complete contrast to the gentle features of Kyrano, he has a hard evil stare which is accentuated by outsize eyebrows and a mean, chiselled face. A huge man who can reduce the innocent to jelly by simply standing still, he is chiefly interested in dispensing with truth, justice and all things civilised in his mad pursuit of vast wealth. If only he had his huge hands on those Thunderbirds blueprints, he would auction them to the highest bidder.

The Hood, though generally working alone from his hard-to-locate temple in the bowels of the Malaysian jungle, is quite prepared to use unsavoury riff-raff and maladjusted lawbreakers to achieve his aim, and he can be seen causing much trouble in, for example, 'Trapped in the

Tin-Tin (right), Kyrano's daughter, and the Hood (left), Kyrano's half-brother, work on opposite sides; Tin-Tin is loyal to International Rescue while the Hood plots to obtain its secrets.

Sky', 'Martian Invasion', 'The Edge of Impact' and 'Desperate Intruder'. As ruthless and un-feeling as he is expert in voodoo and black magic, he will willingly trample on all those around him should the need arise, and he is often engaged in blackmail to keep his whereabouts secret. Though he is blown up for good in *Thunderbirds Are Go*, his enduring strength and naked ambition enable him to descend magically from the ether in time for his appearance as the Black Phantom in *Thunderbird 6*.

Tin-Tin

Tin-Tin, whose name is Malaysian for 'sweet', is the enigmatic daughter of Kyrano and therefore unlikely half-niece of the Hood. Embodying, like all the others, the pervasive heavy emphasis on solid family values and a decent education, she was educated in America and Europe at the insistence of Jeff, who incurred the expense because of her father's loyal devotion.

After graduation, she joined International Rescue and became unwittingly involved in the very first rescue mission, 'Trapped in the Sky',

where a nuclear bomb is discovered on board the Fireflash aircraft on which she is travelling. She is also involved in 'Sun Probe; and 'The Cham Cham' in which she helps Lady Penelope.

Her high-level knowledge of mathematics, engineering and complex technical theories makes her an ideal choice as assistant to Brains, and the genius twosome can often be seen grappling with an advance laboratory experiment. Strictly supervising the maintenance of all the organisa-tion's machines, she has thus repaid Jeff's kind-ness in funding her education. As fashion-conscious as Lady Penelope (Tin-Tin designs her own clothes) and as robustly athletic as Gordon (she particularly enjoys water-skiing and swimming), Tin-Tin combines the passive femininity of the East with the free-thinking determination of the West. Susceptible, too, to romance, she is dazzled by Alan, who is glued to her side, yet she tweaks his nerve-ends by jolting him out of his complacency and on to his toes. Alan is consequently both intoxicated by and disturbed in love.

Grandma

Perhaps old age has got to Grandma since, although she is taken to Tracy Island by Alan Tracy in 'Move and You're Dead', where she is introduced to viewers, she had actually graced 'Sun Probe', a much earlier episode, with her presence.

Forgetful or not, she weaves her way in and out of the series and is primarily a dramatic cipher who feeds lines to the principals in order to move proceedings on. Never actually con-firmed on screen as Jeff Tracy's mother, she is, however, presumed to be such, is drawn in sketchily and is sometimes taken for granted by her fellow-puppets. Yet she does mastermind a clever solution to secure the release of a helpless bank clerk who is trapped in a Bank of England vault. With the knowledge that an abandoned underground railway line passes conveniently beneath the vault, Grandma suggests to the boys that they blast their way in from the railway line to the bank. She is not really given credit for her well-hatched plan and so is the only character in the series not to be continually applauded for her resourcefulness and intelligence.

HOW TO SAVE THE WORLD

Jeff Tracy had originally planned his operations so that Thunderbirds 1-5 would undertake all the heavy work. Thunderbirds 1 and 2 could cope with both the air and the ground, Thunderbird 3 specialised in space, Thunderbird 4 in water, while Thunderbird 5 was an orbiting satellite which picked up distress signals from across the globe and fed them back to base. There must, however, also have been a mystery satellite to home in on that side of the planet which Thunderbird 5 was incapable of covering.

Jeff soon learned that, because of the complex variations in rescue operations, more equipment would be necessary, and one brand-new rescue vehicle a week became a thrilling highlight of each show, transported to the danger zone by Thunderbird 2 in its hangar-shaped pods.

Thunderbird 1 is perhaps the most striking and invigorating of all the craft. With blue base, dynamic rocket body and purposeful red nose, it is always first to launch from Tracy Island, and its superior speed enables it to reach the rescue zone first. Then decisions can be made by Scott as to how the rescue can be best effected. In case of unsavoury threats, Thunderbird 1 is also fully armed.

In order to simplify Scott's tasks at high speed, all of Thunderbird 1's controls are automatic where possible. The check-lights which grace the top of the panel are set above a multi-purpose television screen on which normal communication, route maps and touchdown conditions can be readily projected. Thrust and flight controls

are mounted conveniently on both arms of Scott's swing-seat, which will change position automatically to keep him upright during the dramatic switch from vertical to horizontal flight.

Also armed is Thunderbird 2, which, decked out in suitably utilitarian green, is not only the principal heavy-duty craft but also the transporter of a complex array of rescue gear in any one of its six huge pods. Jeff's second son Virgil Tracy is in command here.

Scott Tracy shifts Thunderbird 1 into horizontal flight on its way to another rescue site.

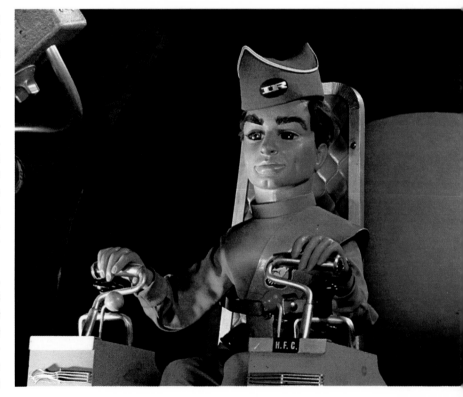

Thunderbird 1 roars into the
sky from its secret hangar
beneath the swimming pool.

Designed for space rescue and as a shuttle to the far-flung Thunderbird 5, Thunderbird 3 is a thrusting orange rocket whose three distinctive fins support the three rocket engines at the base. This is in the safe hands of Jeff's youngest son, astronaut Alan Tracy.

Thunderbird 4's gleaming yellow fuselage allows it to stand out under water, where it undertakes all of International Rescue's water rescue work. Compact enough to be carried in one of Thunderbird 2's pods, it also has a mobile lighting trough at the front which can probe the murkiest corners of the seabed, as well as a batch of high-tech extendable equipment and weapons which can be used when the trough is lowered. Gordon Tracy is its aquanaut pilot.

Piloted by John Tracy, Thunderbird 5 is International Rescue's circular space station which, aside from banks of necessary receiving equipment, also has a docking hatch and docking ramp for Thunderbird 3.

Since solitary periods in space can place John under great strain, luxury rest facilities have been thoughtfully provided in Thunderbird 5. Attractive features include a huge television screen and a well-stocked film library, a central table, comfy sofa and easy chair. Any number of drinks can silently emerge from beneath the table at the mere touch of a button.

John's concealed record-player, shelves of books and single pot-plant, which is growing in nutrient solution (horticulture being a favourite hobby of John's) all add to the super-soothing ambience. All-round air-conditioning ensures that John does not break into a sweat during his policing of the world's distress calls.

A high-grade computer assists him in this task. Programmed to select all messages which contain words like 'help', 'emergency' and 'rescue' in every conceivable language, it then transmits them to every corner of the satellite so that John cannot possibly miss any of them. John, needless to say, spends much of his time in orbit in the study of languages.

Although John's days are usually spent alone, at times he rotates his monitoring duties with his youngest brother, Alan. During these periods, John takes command of Thunderbird 3, adopting for a month at a time a quite different role in the missions of International Rescue.

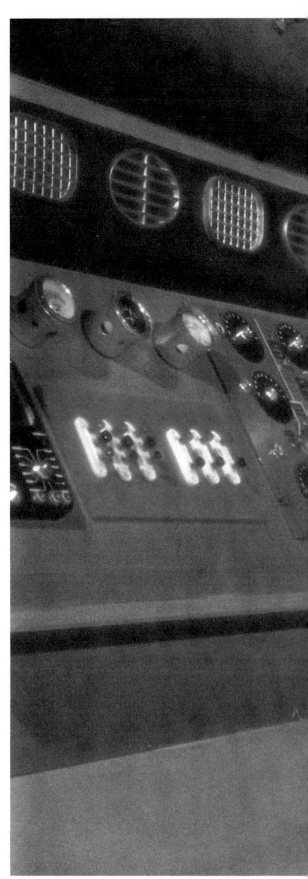

John monitors the world's communications aboard the Thunderbird 5 satellite.

A major part of the weekly international thrill was due to the intoxicating launch procedures, even though they employed stock footage which was dropped in time and again. Grasping that only tiny models were going through a complex sequence of tricky motions, emulating the speed and vapour of real craft only added to the enthralment of a global audience.

Passed through a sequence like a chocolate bar in a space-age wrapping factory, Scott stands on the revolving floor and wall in the Tracy lounge. His hands clutch the two wall-lamps, which in turn activate the wall and spin him right round into the bay of Thunderbird 1. The wall assumes its normal position, Scott stands on a gantry platform which instantly feeds him out towards the rocket. The gantry touches the nose, the door panel slides open and the pilot steps on to the chair footplate. He sits in the chair, which revolves to face the other way. With well-oiled slickness, the door closes, the gantry retracts and

Thunderbird 1 moves effortlessly down a chute on a bogie, inching its way beneath the house itself. Now ensconced in its blast-proof launch-bay, Thunderbird 1 gets ready to blast its way through the swimming-pool which adorns the front of the Tracy villa.

The pool works hydraulically and conveniently moves silently to one side to get out of Scott's way so that he can promptly vanish towards the danger zone. Once airborne, he announces his successful lift-off to his father via his own portrait, which along with those of his brothers, is mounted on a wall opposite his father's desk. When at work, the boys appear in these photos in uniform and sash; when not, the cover-up photos turn the boys into a semblance of relaxed professional golfers. With Scott having switched to horizontal flight, he can readily manipulate the movable wings (a feature guaranteed to generate alarm on most conventional aircraft) which can both increase stability and enable

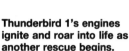

Thunderbird 1's engines ignite and roar into life as another rescue begins.

vertical landings and lift-offs. In 'Trapped in the Sky', for example, Scott announces to the British commander at London Airport that he has no need of a runway but can land vertically instead.

For Virgil, the build-up to the launch of Thunderbird 2 is much more dramatic. As he stands to attention in front of a picture of a rocket in the Tracy lounge, the picture tilts him back so that his feet are higher than his head and slides him on a custom-built padded trolley right into the cockpit of Thunderbird 2. With the picture now back in place, Virgil reaches a point

in the journey where the chute levels out and he is spun round on a mini-turntable so that he is now feet-first. The turntable tilts up, and Virgil is propelled down the chute into his pilot seat which, when his feet strike a footplate, springs up and frees the chute. The seat clicks on to a seat column, and the chute vanishes out of the door.

Virgil now sets in motion the conveyor belt which carries the six huge green pods underneath the craft. Each pod contains various rescue apparatus. Once he has selected the required

This publicity shot shows Thunderbird 1 with its wings open; this normally only takes place when the craft is in horizontal flight and nearing its destination.

pod, Virgil lets his craft squat down on it and he clamps it into place. While this has been going on, the cliff-face which hides Thunderbird 2 slides down, while two rows of palm trees obediently bend over to give Thunderbird 2 the required wing-clearance. Had the trees never been planted, the wide airstrip would have given an obvious clue to the whereabouts of International Rescue. The trees, which are planted in a nutrient solution, are located alongside fire-fighting sprays which rise from the ground when Thunderbird 2 needs to be doused down after an emergency landing as in 'Terror in New York City' when a World Navy ship, realising that Thunderbird 2 is too slow to be a missile but too quick for an aeroplane, yet knowing nothing of International Rescue, launches an attack.

Its heavy bulk moves slowly along the airstrip-road, comes to a halt and is then elevated forty-five degrees in the air by hydraulic pumps which push that particular section of road skywards. A smaller road section to the rear of Thunderbird 2 also opens up to take the full blast

from the craft and thus conceal any signs of lift-off. Like Scott in Thunderbird 1, Virgil can quickly switch to vertical manoeuvres.

Should International Rescue be required when visitors are present on Tracy Island, Jeff has absolutely no problem in steering them towards soundproofed windowless rooms, where they remain until launch procedures are over, completely unaware and content in the lap of luxury.

The most amusing launch of all occurs when a travelling sofa propels (normally) Scott and Alan towards Thunderbird 3. With the boys ensconced in the sofa in the middle of the living-room, Jeff

The heavy transporter, Thunderbird 2, prepares to follow Thunderbird 1 to the scene of action, carrying one of the various pod-contained vehicles which are piloted by Virgil (below).

couches a button which sends them down to an underground chamber. The settee now adorns a trolley on rails, a duplicate model shoots upwards into Jeff's living-room, where a missing sofa might raise eyebrows. The first trolley stops, the sofa glides on to another ramp which pushes Scott, Alan and sofa inside the rocket. The ramp returns to the base of the rocket, while the boys are taken up into the cockpit by lift. They have never left the sofa at any stage, except to pilot Thunderbird 3 from within its comforts.

Thunderbird 3 takes off through the oddly shaped Round House that sports a concealed hollow centre which, even when revealed, is still only visible from the air.

Thunderbird 4 is normally carried to any danger zone in Pod 4 by Thunderbird 2. Hovering above the water, Thunderbird 2 simply drops Pod 4 into the water, where it floats; a door opens and Thunderbird 4 is launched on rails into the water. On completion of its mission, the yellow one-man submarine climbs back up the rails into the pod where it finally swivels round on a turntable in readiness for its next escapade.

However, if need be, Thunderbird 4 can be launched from Tracy Island on a slipway which is actually Thunderbird 2's launch-ramp. It can also be launched into the sea from a jetty at the end of the road. 'Terror in New York City' bears witness to this latter procedure where, after the World Navy has impeded the operations of International Rescue, Jeff insists on sending

Thunderbird 4 to New York. The only moments of drama in which Thunderbird 5 is involved occur when Thunderbird 3 docks at the static spaceship.

The craft themselves are matched by the pink dazzle of FAB 1, Lady Penelope's gadget-heavy Rolls-Royce which is driven at all times by Parker. It must sniff out criminals more effectively than a tracker dog, for in 'Trapped in the Sky', where Jeff informs Penelope that The

Thunderbird 3, largest of the craft, soars into space (left).

Thunderbird 4 launches into the sea from Pod 4. In 'Operation Crash Dive' (left) Thunderbird 4 cuts the engines from the stricken Fire Flash allowing it to float to the surface and the crew to be rescued.

A rare production shot of FAB 1 outside a table-top set of Creighton Manor; clearly visible is the camber which allows the camera to film on ground level while increasing the perspective.

opening night of *Thunderbirds FAB* at London's Mermaid Theatre.

The car which acts as a fitting symbol for Parker's cockney comedy and Lady Penelope's undiluted class was a complex creation. Three sizes of the shocking-pink Rolls were constructed for the series. The large vehicle was complemented by both a tiny six-inch model and a six-foot puppet-size version, the latter being used most of the time. At least as much a star as the glamorous Thunderbird 1 or the comical Thunderbird 2, FAB 1 was constructed by professional model-maker Wag Evans who, now as then, is still employed by Space Models. He acknowledges that the puppet-size model, which preceded the smaller one, was a masterpiece of engineering. So that interior shots could be composed, the car had to come apart at the front and at the rear, as well as at each side. The two sides of the canopy could be lifted off, while the doors could open and slide neatly underneath. The car also had to be able to move, steer and fire off its grille-covered machine-gun in realistic fashion.

With substantial wooden tops for each wing, the car was mainly built from plywood. The wheels, with their wooden disc centres, and the vac-formed tyres were held together with the aid of a black rubber bag. Turned aluminium was employed for the hub-caps. Wag can recall using brass which he then chrome-plated for both the radiator and the miniature Flying Lady mascot, though on completion he was annoyed by the presence of a dull straight line between the wheel arches. Wag spent a great deal of time actually constructing FAB 1 and, bringing the space age down to street-level, he remembers buying its battery-driven headlamps from a bicycle shop. In fact he used only the rim and reflectors.

FAB 1 was only once in need of repair, when the two tubes which held it together at the section joins needed to be replaced. So the puppets could be re-dressed for different scenes, the underside of the car was removable. The larger FAB 1, which was a mobile means of promoting the series, is now kept at the Cars of the Stars Motor Museum in Keswick.

FAB 1, supposedly designed by Brains, who attempted to render it completely indestructible, can also function as a hydrofoil, though Lady P

Hood is speeding through England in her vicinity (she supposedly resides in rural Kent), she is on his tail moments later, heading toward Birmingham on the M1. However, these minor aberrations only ever added to the prevailing spirit of lunacy.

Decked out in unique Penelope fluorescent pink, and with Parker's central driving position and clear roof contributing to its futuristic feel, it contains much to amuse the gadget-happy agent. One of the machine-guns pops out from behind the radiator grille (it zaps and fries The Hood's speeding car in 'Trapped in the Sky'), while missile-launchers, rear-mounted grappling-hooks and oil-slick ejectors are also a great boon.

The design of FAB 1 had to be scrutinised by Rolls-Royce, who offered their keen support. Gerry Anderson recalls that the six-foot Rolls cost about £2,500 (the equivalent of around £30,000 today); while, at £10,000, the full-size working prop cost more then than a real Rolls-Royce. This vehicle made an appearance at the refers her huge luxury yacht, FAB 2, for her aquatic adventures. It features heavily in 'The Man from MI5' where Penelope and Parker are tracking a pack of criminals, only to become trapped and in need of rescuing themselves. Despite also requiring Jeff's help in 'The Perils of Penelope' and 'The Duchess Assignment', his tolerant support means that he has never once complained. Cool even in the heat of danger, Penelope's chief worry when FAB 1 is under attack is: 'I hope they don't scratch the paint, Parker.'

The Anderson effects and writing team knew how to capture the viewers' enthusiasm and imagination by introducing a battery of specialist rescue vehicles, many of whose thuggish industrial appearances contrast convincingly with the space-age streamlining of Thunderbirds 1–5. A dramatic contrast was provided when the smooth slab-sided Thunderbird 2 released a vehicle from its pod, all broken surfaces and jutting hardware.

These vehicles complemented Thunderbirds 1–5 in that they could support walls, fight fires or bore underground. Perhaps the most inspirational of all the machines is the Mole, which, in the manner of a giant drill, can rescue those hapless civilians who are trapped underground.

The cutaway drawing of FAB 1, first seen in the 1965 Summer Extra edition of *TV21* magazine.

FAB 1 Lady Penelope's ROLLS-ROYCE
as seen in 'THUNDERBIRDS'.

Hydraulic platform with fold down safety rails.

Driving position showing the incredibly un-complicated controls for such a complex vehicle.

Swivel laser beam and smoke making apparatus. Set in rear wings.

Gull wing canopy and down-and-under doors.

Laminated, Anti-glare, bullet-proof glass-steel canopy.

Part of the top secret enormously powerful engine

Retro pack air brakes (fitted to both wings — indicated on off-side wing only.)

Rear Hydrofoil.

The hub cap motif extends on rod to form a tyre slasher. (On all wheels — foremost shown in normal position.)

Retractable studs for snow and ice. (Shown on one wheel only—fitted to all six).

Centre pull down arm-rests of back seat have retractable handcuffs and chest band.

Hydrofoils when fully lowered extend below level of wheels thus lifting whole car clear of water when at speed—minimizes resistance. The rear 'foil has a vortex-aquajet powerpack centrally.

FAB 1

FOLLOWING many requests to TV 21 asking for details of Lady Penelope's Rolls-Royce, the Editor has finally secured permission to reveal some of the interesting features which have hitherto remained **top secret**.

The design of FAB 1 has been officially approved by the Rolls-Royce Company but its main power unit must remain on the classified data list. Speeds in excess of 200 m.p.h. have been attained but it is certain that this is only a modest estimate of the engine's real potential.

The four front wheels have been incorporated in the design to support the weight of the power unit and also the heavy machine guns which are retractable and ready for use at the push of a button.

The car has no driving mirror but relies on a small television monitor screen on its dashboard which receives a TV image from the camera concealed in the boot.

Normal television transmitters and receivers, plus UHF and Neutroni radio units are installed within the completely air conditioned car for immediate contact to and from the vehicle.

When FAB 1 parks all six wheels rotate until the car is able to drive into its parking space sideways.

I T C
world wide distribution

The Mole, International Rescue's burrowing machine (left), designed to tunnel through the hardest rock.

Transported to the rescue site by Thunderbird 2 in Pod 4, the Mole travels on its own trolley which, on arrival, tips upwards to near-vertical position; a rocket fires at the rear to activate the Mole, which begins to turn its massive screw and burrow underground. Weighing in at thirty tons and powered by a nuclear reactor, its nose is made from Formula C30/1, a super-strength metal dreamed up by Brains, while the heavy-duty caterpillar tracks enable it to grip the sides of the tunnel it is boring and so return to the surface in safety.

Dramatic participation by the Mole can be seen in 'City of Fire', where a family is trapped by fire in the basement of the world's tallest building, Thompson Tower; while in 'Pit of Peril' it rescues the American army's brand-new Sidewinder from the bowels of a Second World War disposal-pit. Furthermore, it saves the distressed Duchess of Royston from the cellar of an old mansion in 'The Duchess Assignment'.

Derek Meddings generously gives credit for many of these vehicles to a young artist called Michael Trim who, he says, drew excellent storyboards. Busy running three stages with three directors, Derek let Michael, who could be seen drawing at all times of the day, even during his lunch-break, complete many designs. Derek would give him vehicles to design and, although Derek received credit for all of them, there were times when Michael conceived vehicles alone, and others when they were suggested and described in detail by the writers and then discussed with the model makers.

International Rescue's principal fire-extinguisher is the Firefly whose chief skill is to enter the very heart of the blaze and let loose nitro-glycerine shells which cause a blow-out. The nozzle that fires the shells pokes through a heavy-duty plate which can be raised to allow the nozzle a more flexible firing angle. Brain's supermetal, Cahelium Extract X, which was

Thunderbird 2 releases the pod containing Thunderbird 4 into the ocean (right). The front trap opens and the craft moves forward into the sea.

used in the construction of Fireball XL5, can resist the most blistering temperatures and forms the basis of the plate. Just like a giant bulldozer, the plate can shove interfering debris to one side. In 'City of Fire', the Firefly holds the blaze in check, while its plate clears the way so that the Mole can burrow its way to the trapped individuals.

Domo 1 is a brutish demolition machine, which can also move bulky objects from its path; it conceals a powerful nuclear reactor in its rear which powers three linked arms that can exert 64,000 pounds of pressure on any unfortunate object. In order to protect the operator from falling skyscrapers and collapsing mountain-sides, twelve-inch Formula C30/1 has been used for the cabin, with windows made out of nine-inch Visiglaze. Each arm ends in a large suction cup which contains an artificial gravity-field; this enables each cup to glue itself rigidly to any surface. With nuclear reactor going off at full tilt, and supersuction cups firmly in place, Domo 1 has no trouble in dispensing with objects of up to fifty tons.

With such entertaining gadgetry in tow, it is a pity that Domo 1 is only ever seen once when, in 'The Duchess Assignment', it supports a wall that is about to collapse, thus aiding the Mole to reach the cellar below.

Travelling on tracks, like most of the vehicles, to enable it to cope with rough terrain, the IR3 Transmitter Truck displays a giant dish which squats on its rear. The dish emits a beam to any spacecraft in distress and thus immediately assumes complete control of the shaky craft. A great asset in space rescues, IR3 has, like Domo 1, only been seen once in 'Sun Probe'. IR3 here saves Thunderbird 3 during a dual attempt to fire Sun Probe's retro-rockets.

Usually operated by Virgil, the aptly named Thunderiser is essentially a blaster gun that can get rid of bulky objects and slice through doorways. Electrical discharges which are more powerful than lightning enable a cutting laser beam to carve its way quickly to the heart of the rescue. In 'Thirty Minutes after Noon' it frees a British agent from a nuclear plutonium store, while a modified version fires up a rescue pack to the controllers of a television relay tower in 'The Edge of Impact'.

Fitted with eight wheels and caterpillar tracks, the Neutralising Equipment, which can defuse any ticking time-bomb, is operated by Brains. It makes its single appearance in 'Move and You're Dead', when Alan and Grandma are trapped on the San Miguel Bridge where, if either of them moves an inch, a bomb left by rival racing driver Victor Gomez will go off.

The Mobile Crane is possessed of a useful telescopic arm which can extend forty or fifty feet upwards. This it does in 'Path of Destruction', where Virgil and Brains are pushed skywards to rescue the crew of a Crablogger machine which has gone haywire. This was one instance where the machine involved could not be saved, thus embracing Jeff's message of humanity over machines.

The Elevator Cars, which feature dramatically in 'Trapped in the Sky', each have six sets of double wheels and a strong suspension platform to enable sticken aircraft to land on them without recourse to the undercarriage.

Employed in 'The Edge of Impact' and 'Pit of Peril', the remote television camera, which is carried inside a hatch on Thunderbird 1, is like a tiny aircraft which can cover difficult areas that Scott cannot see. It flies out of the hatch at speed to take up the necessary position.

In 'Pit of Peril', the Sidewinder is pulled from a pit by international Rescue's Recovery Vehicles which, by means of steel cables and two large suction missiles, can effect the task in hand. Just as useful is the Hover Bed which, operated by Virgil, emerges from Pod 1 to float on a bed of air on to which a person marooned above can jump with safety. See 'Move and You're Dead' for further details.

Like the Jetmobiles of 'Fireball XL5', the Hover Scooters, a tidy means of transport, are highly flexible ground vehicles. With seat and controls atop the fuselage, they travel down underground corridors in 'City of Fire' and also escape giant alligators in 'Attack of the Alligators'.

Resembling a vast and amusing carnivorous animal in its function, the Excavator, as seen in 'Martian Invasion', eats into impeding rocks and debris which, once clear of its digestive system, emerge via two chutes at the rear as dust and pebbles.

Powered by a radical new fuel called Superon, the Crablogger is more useful than the Junglecat in that, though it yanks trees from the ground, it also processes the wood in the back and offloads neat pieces onto a truck behind. The saws and grabs, meanwhile, adorn the front of a machine which is normally employed to clear the way for new roads.

The crew of the sabotaged Fireflash is picked up from the sea in Thunderbird 2's rescue arm as another mission is successfully completed.

THRILLS AND GASPS IN EVERY EPISODE

1 'Trapped in the Sky'

Endangered by the Hood, who has planted a bomb in its bowels, the superplane Fireflash has to ignore its undercarriage and land instead on three radio-controlled Elevator Cars so the bomb does not explode. Fleeing the airport with photographs of Thunderbird 1, the Hood is hunted down by Lady Penelope on the M1 motorway.

2 'Pit of Peril'

An American army spider-like Sidewinder crashes down into an old landfall which has been transformed into a raging inferno by combustible gases. Even International Rescue, with its state-of-the-art apparatus, has difficulty in winching it up.

3 'City of Fire'

A car crash causes a blaze in an underground carpark and traps a family in the basement of the vast Thompson Tower. Burning rubble thwarts the rescue attempt of Scott and Virgil, who are now forced to use Brains's experimental gas which caused them to pass out during tests.

4 'Sun Probe'

Three astronauts go into orbit to capture a piece of the sun but, when their retro-rockets fail, find themselves on a collision course instead. Thunderbird 3's own retros also fail during the rescue attempt; while, to add even more melodrama to one of the most edge-of-the-sofa episodes, Thunderbird 2 has to endure a whirlwind snowstorm.

5 'The Uninvited'

Like the Hood, the malevolent Zombites operate from a secret temple and here shoot down Scott in Thunderbird 1. He is rescued by two archaeologists who, after being captured themselves by the Zombites, are sprung to safety by Scott.

6 'The Mighty Atom'

The Hood intends to wipe Australia off the map with a nuclear blast but is foiled by the wind, which keeps the radioactive cloud away from densely populated areas. He next causes another fire to draw International Rescue towards his trap; with the help on the Mighty Atom, a mouse-style robot which takes photographs with its eyes, he hopes to film Thunderbird 2 in

rewarding detail. He does not, however, reckon on the presence of Lady Penelope.

7 'Vault of Death'

Lord Sefton is finally convinced by Lady Penelope and Parker to modernise the Bank of England's main vault. Unfortunately, once the task has been completed, a hapless employee called Lambert is locked inside. While Penelope, Parker and Sefton rush to the bank in FAB 1, International Rescue overcomes the fact that Sefton has forgotten the key by tunnelling in via a disused underground railway line.

In their rear-mounted cockpit the crew of the Fireflash (above) looks out along the length of the atomic airliner on its maiden flight in 'Trapped in the Sky'. In 'Vault of Death' Parker demonstrates his safe-cracking skills (below).

THRILLS AND GASPS IN EVERY EPISODE

 8 **'Operation Crash Dive'**

A Fireflash superplane is in trouble once again when it crashes into the sea, from which it is rescued by Thunderbird 4. Scott agrees to co-pilot the next test and, with no mechanical failure located, the plane once again plummets seawards. It is Gordon, winched aboard from Thunderbird 2, who discovers a violent saboteur.

 9 **'Move and You're Dead'**

Hated by rival Victor Gomez when he announces his return to racing, Alan finds himself marooned with Grandma on a lonely Californian mountain bridge, which Gomez' bomb will destroy on detecting the slightest move. If they collapse in the heat, the bomb will surely explode. Will the ever-inventive Brains save the wilting twosome?

 10 **'Martian Invasion'**

The Hood, anxious to deliver details of Thunderbirds 1 and 2 to the enigmatic General Strond, films both craft on a movie set when they arrive to save two actors who, dressed as Martians, are stuck in a cave.

 11 **'Brink of Disaster'**

Pitting global con-man Warren Grafton against the ever-angelic Jeff, who feigns interest in Grafton's rip-off monorail scheme, this episode sends Jeff, Brains and Tin-Tin travelling on a dodgy monorail towards the jaws of a vast canyon. A faulty rail, brought about by Grafton's negligence, causes a disaster. Thunderbirds 1 and 2 come to the rescue, and Grafton is eventually brought to justice.

In 'Martian Invasion' Scott and Virgil are guests of a production crew filming the latest Martian science fiction epic. Could this be the successor to 'Thunderbirds'?

 12 **'The Perils of Penelope'**

eeking out Professor Borender, the inventor of
 formula which converts sea-water into fuel,
ady Penelope and her friend Sir Jeremy Hodge
re threatened in Paris and on a monorail train
y Dr Godber. To prise Borender's secret from
im, Godber places Penelope in the path of a
peeding express train.

 13 **'Terror in New York City'**

Vith mid-town Manhattan now indescribably
habby, an attempt is made to move the Empire
tate Building to pastures clean. It fails, and keen
elevision reporter Ned Cook and his cameramen
re thrown underground where they are trapped
1 a rapidly flooding cavern. With Thunderbird 2
1advertently shot down by a navy warship, will
'hunderbird 4 reach the site in time?

 14 **'End of the Road'**

Constructing a road through a tropical rainforest,
Eddie Houseman, a friend of the Tracys, is
thwarted by landslides and so makes a deter-
minedly crazy bid to save the project. He ends
up teetering on a cliff-edge in his truck, so the
Tracys must approach with caution while also
keeping their identity from their friend Eddie.

 15 **'Day of Disaster'**

A rocket is being transported to its launch site
but, crossing a bridge which has been weakened
by a storm, it plummets into the river and, with
two engineers aboard, activates its own countdown mechanism. Thunderbird 4 must break
through the rubble in time.

The Empire State Building is slowly inched to its new location, but disaster is only moments away in 'Terror in New York City'.

147

'The Edge of Impact'

When General Bron asks him to sabotage the Red Arrow aircraft tests, the Hood cunningly causes a collision between a Red Arrow plane and a tele-relay tower. The tower sways in the breeze, and International Rescue must save the two men trapped above.

'Desperate Intruder'

Travelling to Lake Anasta in the Sahara Desert to locate a submerged temple and its buried treasure, Brains and Tin-Tin have to contend with the Hood, who wants not only the treasure but also access to International Rescue through the twosome.

'30 Minutes after Noon'

Britain's nuclear plutonium store is under threat of destruction by a marauding pack of vicious criminals whose files have been destroyed by fire at the Hudson Building in Spoke City. The gang is thwarted, and a vast nuclear explosion prevented, by the keen assistance provided by Lady Penelope.

'The Imposters'

A gang of criminals, in order to steal papers from an underground vault, stage a fake rescue mission under the convincing guise of International Rescue. An international hunt now begins to discover the Tracys' secret base. Despite being framed, however, they do need to save an astronaut who is floating free in outer space.

'The Man from MI5'

Under the guise of a top fashion model, Lady Penelope sails to the French Riviera in FAB 2 to help the British secret service recover plans for a nuclear device. She is promptly thrown into a boathouse with a time-bomb ticking away at her feet.

'Cry Wolf'

Two young Australian brothers inadvertently call Thunderbird 1 out on a mission by fooling around on their two-way radios. They are, moreover, soon in genuine trouble when the Hood, discovering that their father's weather station is really a space tracking station, traps the boys in an old mine. Will International Rescue take this next call seriously?

'Danger at Ocean Deep'

The mysterious disappearance of Ocean Pioneer 1 means that its special cargo of liquid alsterene will explode if it mixes with OD60, a chemical to be found in the sea where the ship vanished. Ocean Pioneer 2 is now travelling the same route with the same cargo.

'The Duchess Assignment'

The Duchess of Royston, an old friend of Lady Penelope's, has gambled her money away and so, with the help of Penelope, hopes to create income from renting out a valuable painting. Crooks soon lock her in an old house which then catches fire.

'Attack of the Alligators'

A boatman steals a wonderdrug which can cause animals to grow to four times their normal size. He drops some in the Amazon, and giant alligators launch an attack on the beleaguered lab.

One of Tin-Tin's holiday snaps (right) shows Lady Penelope riding by means of quite different transport in the film *Thunderbirds Are Go!*.

In 'Security Hazard' (below) Chip is returned safely to his bed to remember only the most wonderful dream after a visit to Tracy Island.

Playing at International Rescue can lead to disastrous consequences, as this little boy and his brother discovered in the episode 'Cry Wolf'.

Lady Penelope, aka Wanda Lamour, sings 'That Dangerous Game' accompanied by the Cass Carnaby Five. Lady Penelope at her best!

 25 'The Cham Cham'

The Cass Carnaby Five amusingly cause attacks on American space flights every time they perform their number 1 record. Discovering that the group's arranger is up to no good, Lady Penelope and Tin-Tin are soon endangered by a sabotaged cable-car.

 26 'Security Hazard'

An episode which is entirely free of stricken buildings, rampaging fires and bombed bridges, except in flashback, this homes in on a young stowaway who has been found aboard Thunderbird 2. Despite the Tracys' penchant for secrecy, he is treated to a nostalgic canter through the Thunderbirds missions. He falls asleep, awakes at home the next morning and wonders if it was all a dream.

27 'Atlantic Inferno'

With Jeff on holiday on Lady Penelope's Australian ranch, Scott is in charge and has to tackle a nuclear fire which erupts in the ocean near the Seascape oil-rig. The rig is engulfed by fire, as are two men who are trapped underneath in a bathysphere.

 ## 28 'Path of Destruction'

With its crew having fainted from food poisoning, a hulking Crablogger is heading dangerously towards the town of San Martino and a nearby dam. While Lady Penelope attempts to track down the designer, Brains and Virgil must board the rolling metal beast.

 ## 29 'Alias Mr Hackenbacker'

Brains, under the guise of Hiram K. Hackenbacker, joins forces with Lady Penelope when the new Skythrust airliner, which plays host to both Brains's new safety device and Lady Penelope's fashion show, is hijacked by a steward and one of the models who yearn for the secret of a new fabric, reverentially called Penelon.

 ## 30 'Lord's Parker's 'Oliday'

The first place to be powered by solar energy, Monte Bianco, may soon frazzle in the sun after the solar reflector collapses and beams malevolently down on the town. Penelope takes FAB 1 out to sea so as to send a distress call, while Parker and Bruno, the hotel manager, divert the residents from panic by offering homespun entertainment.

 ## 31 'Richochet'

A pirate radio station up in space is sent on a downward spiral by a renegade rocket. A malfunctioning Thunderbird 5 almost misses the distress call, disc jockey Rick O'Shea is afraid to be rescued and Virgil must stop the plummeting radio station colliding with a desert refinery.

 ## 32 'Give or Take a Million'

A New York toy shop is abused by criminals, who are trying to break into the bank next door. Escaping the police, they are finally trapped in a rocket which is ferrying Christmas presents to a children's hospital. The reward for their capture builds a new hospital wing, while one thrilled kid spends his Christmas break on Tracy Island.

The Seascape oil rig faces imminent danger as the World Navy testing of a new rocket goes disastrously wrong in 'Atlantic Inferno'.

BEFORE LIFT-OFF

In an era when big-screen action-thrillers have embraced a seemingly endless conveyor belt of special effects as the norm and, at their worst, have placed imagination on the back burner in so doing, it is heartening to home in on a television series which enthrals a world public.

Still Gerry Anderson's most accomplished creation to date, 'Thunderbirds' not only invented a wealth of special effects in order to realise the far-reaching scripts, but also never swamped credible story-lines, intriguing characters and exhilarating feats of daring with Thunderbirds 1–5 and an arsenal of heavy-duty machinery.

Thunderbird 2 surveys the danger zone around Seascape. Can the cracks in the sea-bed be safely capped?

'Thunderbirds' at once joined the front ranks as a bold vigorous experiment which even now has a sizeable audience of diehards. On 30 September 1965, for an eager audience in Great Britain, Thunderbirds were definitely go, and again in September 1991 for a new BBC2 audience.

Though 'Thunderbirds' creator Gerry Anderson has devised many puppet-based series since his early outings with 'The Adventures of Twizzle' and 'Torchy the Battery Boy', Gerry himself has often claimed that 'Thunderbirds' was the highlight of his career.

It was in fact, cigar-chomping British television mogul Lew Grade who insisted that Gerry make a new series to maintain the audience thrill after thirty-nine successful episodes of 'Stingray'. In the way that newspaper stories often give birth to novels, plays and feature films, Gerry was struck by a German mining disaster of the period and so began thinking about an international rescue team which would rush to the catastrophe but only when conventional methods had failed. Last-minute drama was thus inscribed on every episode.

Yet it was Lew Grade's spontaneous enthusiasm for the pilot episode, 'Trapped in the Sky', which quickly led to a clutch of initial problems. Working by his well-honed instincts, Grade felt that half an hour of space-age thrills was not enough and instantly decreed that each programme was to be one hour long. By the time he saw the pilot and let his exuberance fly, nine entire episodes had been shot, and a further ten scripts written, so Gerry was pleased by Grade's decision yet aware of the complications.

The team was committed to shooting a few more half-hours even after the thunderclap decision, while even later scripts were stretched to make up the full hour. Previously shot half-hours had to be doubled in length, while models which had already been destroyed, since they were deemed unnecessary for future programmes, had to be hastily rebuilt from scratch.

After so many shot nerves and sleepless nights, the final irony of this frenzied escapade – that the Americans finally decided to screen each episode in two half-hour segments – must seem amusing to Gerry and his team only in retrospect. This also meant extra work, since each second half had to be prefaced by a 'story so far' synopsis. Yet their episode-stretching endeavours may well account for the continuing appeal of the series. Extending already filmed episodes like 'The Perils of Penelope' and 'Terror in New York City' inevitably led to a great deal more detail in both character and situation than in any other Anderson series, with the possible exception of 'UFO', which did not emerge until 1970. Viewers thus find it easier to grasp character motivation, empathise with the characters themselves and feel at home on Tracy Island. While Derek Meddings's intoxicating effects and often surreal rescue vehicles would lift the viewer, they would never dwarf the plain humanity of each situation.

Thus, with a slot which followed straight after children's hour, Gerry and his wife Sylvia (who wrote the first script and kept an eye on the various commissioned writers) proceeded to produce at a rate of knots.

Sylvia Anderson's lively imagination ensured constant creative input. She was responsible for character visualisation and paid a great deal of attention to the appearance and sound of each puppet. John Tracy, for example, was initially cast as the dashing hero but, unhappy with his final appearance, Sylvia let Scott fill the lead role instead.

Sylvia decided on individual voices after the completion of each puppet. She provided the voice for Lady Penelope who was conceived by the puppet team with Sylvia in mind.

Born into a poor London family, and with no career plan in mind except a desire to become an architect one day, Gerry emerged from the London Blitz to attend Willesden Polytechnic. Discovering that he was not very gifted at the necessary architectural skill of technical drawing, he fortunately proved dexterous on the practical side and excelled in particular in the plaster shop. Only the film studios had any regular need for skilled plasterers, so he drifted towards the big screen through necessity rather than through any major obsession with film.

Yet Gerry became hooked on film after plaster became his enemy. Taking an examination which involved constructing a sizeable plaster piece, he ran out of plaster and so, mixing some up at great speed, he immediately encased his arm in it. When the plaster was removed, Gerry, owing to the lime in the plaster, lost the skin on both arms right up to the elbow and so developed lasting dermatitis. Strongly advised to move away from a career in plaster, Gerry was by now determined to work in the film business and so, after a period in the plaster shop of Gainsborough Pictures, he headed towards the Ministry of Information.

Gerry eventually secured a job through the Ministry of Information at the Colonial Film Unit which produced newsreels for Africa. This is when the puppet master really cut his teeth. Through spending six-week turns on both switchboard and projector, he also did identical-length stints on camera crew and film editing. It was

schoolmaster-turned-director George Pearson, one of the leading lights of British silent cinema, who pointed Gerry towards the cutting room, insisting that it would give the keen youngster an ideal grounding in all things film.

It was Gainsborough Pictures which gave Gerry his first proper break. Having completed shooting on *The Wicked Lady* (the most successful of the Gainsborough costume dramas),

Christmas at Creighton Manor.

befriended the series cameraman Arthur Povis. Homing in on all kinds of eccentrics, the series sent Gerry and Arthur to film a man who lived in a bottle for a year, to visit a lady who could write simultaneously in three languages scribbling with chalk in both hands, and to witness a fanatic who could propel himself on a bicycle at 109 miles per hour.

Many of Gerry's creative ventures sprang from AP Films, a company jointly launched by Gerry himself and Arthur Povis. They came upon a charming mansion by the Thames with a suitable flat to rent. Particularly keen on the fact that the mansion contained a small ballroom which they could transform into a handy film studio, they also turned the flat into an office and sat and waited, naïvely expecting that film and television moguls would order up films like pizza. With filing cabinet in the corner and notepaper on the desk, the phone was perpetually silent. They eventually ran out of money and so, trained technicians both, employed their skills to keep a non-active company afloat.

Gerry's emergence as a pioneering puppet guru had its origins in these unusual circumstances. Roberta Leigh was a writer who wanted to make a series of puppet films for the tiny budget of £450 a picture. Unsurprisingly spurned by the rest of the British film industry, which presumably could not take her seriously, she received a determined yes from Gerry and Arthur, to whom even £450 must have seemed a major handout from the gods. Gerry himself is even more emphatic: 'It was rather like a man finding a plank in the middle of the Atlantic. It's not the greatest find in the world, but when you're drowning it's a pretty good thing.'

These puppet films were Gerry's first major triumph as a director. 'The Adventures of Twizzle', fifty-two fifteen-minute films made between 1956 and 1957, concerned the antics of a boy doll who could extend both arms and legs and who inhabited Stray Town in the company of other lost toys. With Leigh producing, as well as writing scripts and songs, Gerry was firmly in charge as director.

He progressed both technically and in budget terms with his next series, 'Torchy the Battery Boy', which, as the title may suggest, was a more lavish rerun of 'Twizzle'. Concentrating on a

Gainsborough handed the picture over to an editorial team which included Gerry. The American distributors gasped in horror at Margaret Lockwood's low-cut dress. After taking out the offending close-ups, new footage was shot with Lockwood in a more puritanical state of cover-up.

Next directing a series which Anderson claims is of limited merit, 'You've Never Seen This', he dream paradise called Topsy Turvy Land, Torchy was another boy doll whose magic light lent him a special charisma. Feeling restless at piling invention upon invention in the service of someone else's show, Anderson and Povis decided to make their own programmes.

A huge success which was also translated into strip cartoon form in *TV Comic*, 'Four Feather Falls' took its cue from the popularity of the Western on screens both big and small and was laced with an appealingly lunatic surrealism.

Tex Tucker, sheriff of the town of the title, cares for the son of Indian chief Kalamakooya and so is given four magic feathers in return. While two feathers allow Tex's dog Dusty and his horse Rocky to speak, the other two galvanise Tex's six-shooter into rapid gunfire if the decent sheriff is boxed in by danger. While 'Carry On' regular Kenneth Connor voiced the quaint speech-patterns of both horse and dog, present-day game-show host Nicholas Parsons intoned the voice of Tex, while his wife Denise Bryer and Anderson stalwart David Graham (who later voiced Parker in 'Thunderbirds') supplied back-up.

More important in regard to 'Thunderbirds', and the entire story of Supermarionation, 'Four Feather Falls' ushered in a new wave of technical expertise. The puppets were now controlled by much thinner wires which, carrying an electronic impulse to a solenoid in the head of the puppet, allowed them to open and shut their mouths in time to the prerecorded voices.

With Granada Television lending much-needed financial support to the series, and the problems of puppet realism preoccupying Gerry himself, he took one step nearer the puppet expertise of 'Thunderbirds' with his first space-age series, 'Supercar'.

At a time when science-fiction antics were replacing a waning interest in Westerns, and with Gerry's own admitted interest in aircraft and space travel in tow, he was primarily seeking a solution which would help his puppets walk convincingly from A to B. Though the puppets could pass muster as recognisable humans, their lumbering staccato walk often failed to submerge the viewer completely in a quirky fantasy world.

A set of high-speed wheels provided the answer. Reckoning that a special car which could propel the puppet cast on a series of adventures – be it on roads, in the air or under water – would

Mike Mercury and Professor Popkiss in their Nevada laboratory, Black Rock, with Supercar, 'the marvel of the age'.

mean that the puppets themselves would not actually have to give themselves away with too many gauche movements, Gerry was so pre-occupied with such technical details that he did not even consider it science fiction, in fact, in his own words, he did not even know what science fiction was.

Designed by Reg Hill (who would later re-emerge as associate producer on 'Thunderbirds') and Derek Meddings (supervising SFX director on 'Thunderbirds'), the Supercar itself, with its manifold abilities, was the star of all manner of high-drama escapades. Gerry's new expanded time-limit of thirty minutes per episode meant that plot-lines could be expanded, characters more fully developed and new characters introduced without any risk of cramming.

Aided generously by the puppet creators of the exhilarating super-machine, Professor Popkiss and his willing sidekick Doctor Beaker, the undeniable hero was Supercar pilot Mike Mercury, a man of such thrilling courage that even his name suggests he would have no trouble travelling at the speed of light. Lining up to help Mike were ten-year-old superkid Jimmy Gibson, who had himself been swept from trouble by the Supercar team in the first episode, and Mitch the Monkey who acted as a soft furry antidote to the gleaming hardware and twisted villains.

Chief among these was the mean-minded Masterspy who, much like the Hood in the later 'Thunderbirds', displayed an obsessive determination in his efforts to discover exactly what made Supercar tick.

With AP Films still not awash with money, they sank their entire funds into the 'Supercar' pilot before showing it to their previous backers, Granada, who, purely on budgetary grounds, turned it down flat. Enter television giant Lew Grade who, on a reduced budget, gave the green light for the entire thirty-nine episodes. Giving Gerry a giddy launch into the international market-place, especially the profitable American syndication market, in 1962, 'Supercar' was also notable as the first British television fantasy or science-fiction programme to concentrate on a piece of hardware.

Moving sideways to try his hand with the live-action television cop thriller 'Crossroads to Crime' (which concerns a young policeman who

pretends to take a bribe in order to lay a trap for some hijackers), as well as three prize-winning commercials for Blue Car Holidays, Anderson was soon requested by Lew Grade to follow the global impact of 'Supercar'.

'Fireball XL5', whose spirit of high adventure and constantly improving special effects gives a pointer to the advent of 'Thunderbirds', was the highly successful result. Featuring a more credible streamlined craft, which seemed a more likely contender for space travel than Supercar, and was also a tribute to the ever-expanding talents of Derek Meddings, the series replaced the schoolboy jokiness of 'Supercar' with fast-lane action thrills, though humour was still let in by the back door.

Chief space adventurer this time round was Steve Zodiac, whose fine-boned features were evidence of the continually improving Super-marionation techniques. He was joined in danger by the tempting Venus, whose come-on charisma took its lead from standard-issue Hollywood film stars with Professor Matthew 'Matt' Matic and Robert the Robot as decent support. Zoonie the Lazoon was a futuristic cousin of Mitch the

Colonel Steve Zodiac, hero of *Fireball XL5* stands over uninvited guests in the control room of Space City.

Monkey who balanced the hardware with cute childlike appeal.

With a name inspired by Castrol XL motor oil, and the craft's peculiar launch sequence that prefaced each episode devised by Gerry himself, Anderson also lent his presence to events on screen. Deciding that a strange disembodied voice was required for Robert the Robot, and denied the benefit of the digitally recorded sound of today, Gerry travelled to Edinburgh to investigate the development of an artificial larynx for people who had lost their voice through cancer. To activate the device, it had to be pressed firmly against the jaw, switched on and then words mouthed against its buzzing noise.

'Fireball XL5' became a huge favourite in America on Saturday morning television in 1963, while its theme song, sung by one Don Spencer, became a pop hit; the success of the series even spawned a rival, 'Space Patrol', created by former Anderson associates Roberta Leigh and Arthur Povis.

Yet it was 'Stingray' later that year that began the swell of Anderson-mania which would erupt soon afterwards with 'Thunderbirds'. The first British television series ever to be made in colour (thirty-nine episodes were produced from 1963 to 1964), it centred round the undersea heroics of James Garner look-alike Captain Troy Tempest of the World Aquanaut Security Patrol and his co-pilot George Lee Sheriden, more familiar as 'Phones'. More fully written characters were now appearing, with Commander Sam Shore, the head of WASP, and his daughter Atlanta providing a secure framework for Troy's watery feats. Ray Barrett lent his voice to Sam, while Atlanta's was provided by Lois Maxwell, alias Miss Moneypenny in the James Bond films. The evil Titan was in charge of the undersea tribes, and the mute Marina, whom Troy and Phones rescued from his grasp in the pilot episode, immediately became a useful member of the Stingray team.

With the American market in mind in particular, 'Stingray' was shot in colour (or Videocolor as the technique was called), yet was only able to be seen in Britain in black and white. Technical advances continued apace, so that bigger budgets meant more detailed sets (compare the beautifully crafted interior of Stingray with the spartan flight-deck of XL5), while the puppets themselves could now register a range of expressions. The smile, the frown and the in-between constituted the expressions available on a series of different heads.

Another feature, which became an established convention with 'Thunderbirds', was the inclusion of Christmas specials and flashback episodes. When a character announced, 'I remember when . . .', this took us back to an earlier adventure and also allowed Gerry himself to breathe temporarily in the midst of whirlwind deadlines.

It was at this time, too, January 1965, that *TV Century 21* (more affectionately known as *TV21*) was first produced and eventually became the most widely read British comic since the success of *Eagle*. Drawing upon the established expertise of editor Alan Fennell, who had written the majority of 'Fireball XLS' and 'Stingray' scripts, it was Anderson, who suggested the comic's newspaper format and the items of Twenty-First Century News on the inside. Gerry can still remember the edgy first few days before sales went into overdrive. Striking up conversation with his local newsagent, Gerry learned that of the seventy-eight copies he had bought in, only two sold on the first day, followed by one solitary copy on each of the following two days. Thereafter, it was as if every British child broke free of his or her restraining leash and bought up every copy in the land. *TV21* peaked with a colossal print run of 630,000. The regular imaginative treats in its pages, as well as the relative sophistication of 'Stingray', were moulding enthusiastic British youth in readiness for 'Thunderbirds'.

Alan Fennell, then editor of *TV21*, drew special attention to 'Thunderbirds' in issue 52 which went on sale in January 1966. Previously the assistant editor of *TV Comic*, Alan first met Gerry Anderson when negotiating a comic strip version of 'Four Feather Falls'. When he returned to do the same for 'Supercar' he was invited to write a 'Supercar' script. Alan emerged as a key scriptwriter for AP Films and wrote approximately half of all the scripts from 'Fireball XL5' through to 'Thunderbirds'.

Basking in the cosy warmth of universal success, the team set to work on two 'Thunderbirds' features, *Thunderbirds Are Go* (1966) and

Stingray, pride of the fleet of the World Aquanaut Security Patrol (WASP).

Thunderbird 6 (1967). Despite 'Thunderbirds' director, writer and script editor Alan Pattillo's slight reservation that 'the magic and intimacy of the small screen might be lost on the big', the first feature, in particular, was especially strong – yet both failed dismally at the box-office.

Lew Grade had immediately agreed to Gerry's suggestion of a first feature and to a budget of £250,000. Managers from the Rank Organisation attended a London preview of the film and gleefully cheered at key uplifting moments. How could it fail?

Despite being as convincing, thrilling, characterful and humanitarian as the television series, *Thunderbirds Are Go* took a spectacular nosedive at the box-office. A prime Christmas release-date and a national publicity tour, with Gerry himself as the main star, could not salvage the situation. Although the distributors told Gerry he had a James Bond on his hands in terms of commercial potential, Gerry would not become cash-happy at this stage but instead popped into local cinemas to witness his *Thunderbirds Are Go* entertaining audiences numbering only fifteen.

They were watching a film that exuded the same inventive spark, witty flair and oddball scenarios as the series itself. Multiple plotting, a sprinkling of monsters and a pop fantasy sequence including Cliff Richard and the Shadows (Cliff was once a neighbour of Gerry's in Portugal) were bolted on to the basic story of Zero X, which would propel man to Mars for the very first time.

Pilot Paul Travers, co-pilot Greg Martin and space navigator Brad Newman, as well as space scientists Dr Grant and Dr Pierce, are mastering the awesome technology of Zero X, the most advanced spaceship ever to leave a drawing-board. Glenn Field's understandable tension soon gives way to the spectacular launch of the massive steel hulk. Invisible to the crew, a furtive malcontent is strolling around the belly of the ship, happily taking photographs all the while. With his boot now trapped in the slick gadgetry of the ship, he winces in pain, pulls down his rubber mask and reveals himself as the Hood.

Having caused Zero X to plummet towards the ocean the favourite adversary parachutes clear of the craft, and the disappointed crew are subsequently recovered, thanks to International Rescue and an all-out quick-thinking rescue mission.

Although through this film 'Thunderbirds' enthralled a British audience in colour for the first time, many preferred to watch it in black and white at home. Confused as Gerry by the film's failure, United Artists at once commissioned another film to prove their resolve: *Thunderbird 6*. At least this film offers one comprehensible reason as to why it failed completely.

Teased into guessing the identity of the mysterious Thunderbird 6, the viewer is finally presented with a Tiger Moth as a witty gag. Unfortunately, a simple biplane could never compete with the knockout designs and abilities of Thunderbirds 1–5, while the big screen was an unsuitable place for the gentle irony of steam-age technology scoring triumphantly over an array of fantasy machines.

SUPERMARIONATION AND THE STRINGS BEHIND THE SPELL

A behind-the-scenes shot of the filming of 'Path of Destruction'. Note the attention to detail in the café setting.

All the Thunderbird puppets are still the key symbol of what was, in the mid-sixties, a radical new technique called Supermarionation. The process involved electronic control of realistic figures; yet, unlike the smoother electronic puppets of today, whose free-moving agility has replaced a sense of humanity, the process was not yet advanced enough to control the appealing staccato movements of arms and legs. Lips and eyes, however, did succeed in moving in a way which was marginally less quirky.

It is often wrongly assumed that, in comparison to modern electronic puppetry, Gerry was still a caveman in puppet terms; yet his technique was a breakthrough in its day. Before Gerry kick-started puppet technology and developed lip-sync, it was, for example, only possible to indicate that a puppet was speaking a line of dialogue by nodding its head up and down. Though some puppets of the pre-Anderson era had mouths which could open and close with a pull from the operator's string, their lips had an amusing tendency to develop a life of their own quite separate from the voiceover artist off-camera. Gerry's radical advance involved giving each puppet a flexible mouth and a pivoted tongue and lower lip which was connected to the chin by a flap of supple leather. A solenoid (a wire coil which carries an electro-magnetic field) connected to the puppet wires was secreted under the tongue. With the dialogue for each character carefully pre-recorded, it would then be transmitted to each puppet's wire by way of complex electronic gadgetry. The dialogue would then be played back and send off an immediate impulse which would open the mouth at the start of each word, while a return spring would shut it again at the end of the word.

By the time of Captain Scarlet technology was advancing apace and so the coils employed in the

New puppetry techniques
were initiated during the
filming of 'Thunderbirds';
these led to the type of
animatronics that can be
seen on the screen today.

Captain Scarlet and Blue are briefed by Colonel White aboard Spectrum's Cloud-base headquarters.

mouth movements were becoming ever smaller. It thus became possible to conceal the coil in the chest of the puppet, and consequently puppet heads shrank and became realistically proportionate to the body size. This new realism, though approaching perfection in one sense, ended the surrealism of large heads and tiny bodies which was a much-loved characteristic of 'Thunderbirds'. Paradoxically, the more accurate puppets now became, the more difficult it was to express their feelings and humanity.

The whole process of Supermarionation was unique to Gerry's company, AP Films. Shot in 35 mm colour, 'Thunderbirds' was filmed on complete film stages which were barely a fifth of live-action size. Subtle tricks included back projection and matching live-action drop-in shots with the kind of special effects which would be unthinkable in any standard-issue live-action movie. Gerry also had to grapple with

how to create a sense of depth on stages which, though only eight to ten feet deep, had to play host to often complex action sequences.

The puppets themselves dominated this new search for credibility for which due credit must be paid to Lew Grade and Associated Television, who dug deep to back this radical new process. Such expenditure had already frightened off the art-driven studios of France, Italy and West Germany and even the normally cash-happy moguls in Hollywood.

Christine Glanville, Gerry Anderson's chief puppeteer on 'Thunderbirds', reminisces with affection about puppets which were barely more than twenty-two inches tall: 'There were, you know, only three sizes of body. One size male body for all the boys and Jeff, a smaller body for Brains and Kyrano, and a standard-size female body.'

While the bodies were made by John Blundell,

Christine herself actually constructed the heads for Scott, Alan and Tin-Tin. Sharing puppet tasks with her co-puppeteer, Mary Turner (who created the wonderful Lady Penelope), both ladies would operate all the puppets since 'whichever floor puppeteer was on duty would bring them to the bridge, ready to start.'

Because neither Gerry nor his colleagues could draw, the proposed appearance of each

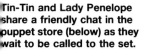

Tin-Tin and Lady Penelope share a friendly chat in the puppet store (below) as they wait to be called to the set.

Hours of work were spent on the detailed preparation before final production of the puppets' heads.

puppet was described in terms of real-life individuals. As Christine herself now explains:

'We had a copy of *Spotlight* [the directory which includes portrait photos of actors] and we would decide on types. Without reference to specific real-life individuals, it would have been hard for Gerry to get his ideas across. For example, Scott was modelled on Sean Connery, the handsome hero-type of the day. Alan looked like the son of a father-and-son lawyer team which was popular on television at the time, while Virgil looked like Alan. In fact Virgil was John Brown's first attempt at creating a puppet, and he ran into difficulties, so I said, "Why don't you copy Alan?", knowing that Virgil would emerge as John's version of Alan and therefore suitably different.'

John, in fact, went on to create Jeff Tracy who, in Christine's view, is one of the finest puppets in the series. Her particular favourite is Scott who, aside from the obvious fact that he was created by Christine, 'looked like James Bond and had lovely dimples'.

Although she believes any more puppet realism

Scott's hands operated the controls of Thunderbird 1 as his elbows were moved from behind by the puppeteers.

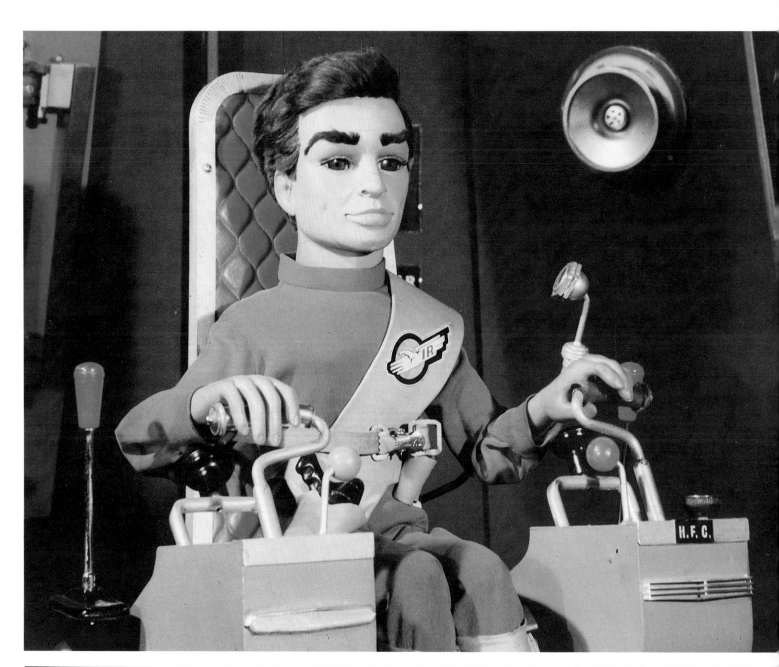

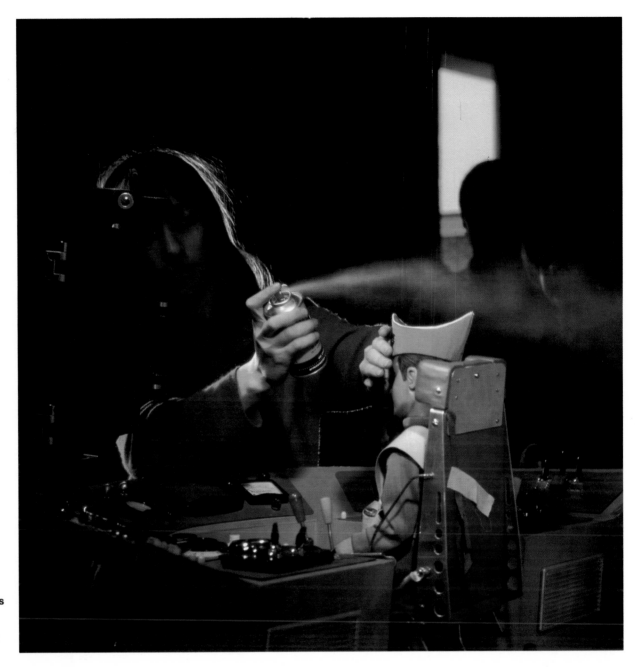

would have removed much of the heart, she stresses the need to accept the limitations of the puppet form: 'In a photograph puppets may look like real men, but it's clear they're not when they try to move.' The balance between realism and artifice was, she admits, about right.

It was the working of the puppets which Christine enjoyed most since she could really bring them to life. While her own puppet operations displayed a great deal of humanity, Mary Turner's, she believes, were more accurate. 'Thunderbirds' writer, script editor and director

Alan Pattillo voices an equal enthusiasm for both puppeteers, contrasting the more 'balletic, natural, graceful' style of Christine with the more angular, experimental interpretations of Mary:

'I remember one scene from "Fireball XL5" in which Venus is hypnotised by a planet outside the window. Christine was the puppeteer on Venus for the first take, and her version was typically graceful. But for some reason we had to do a retake and this time round used Mary. Her interpretation of Venus' reaction was much more strange and disturbing, but equally convincing.'

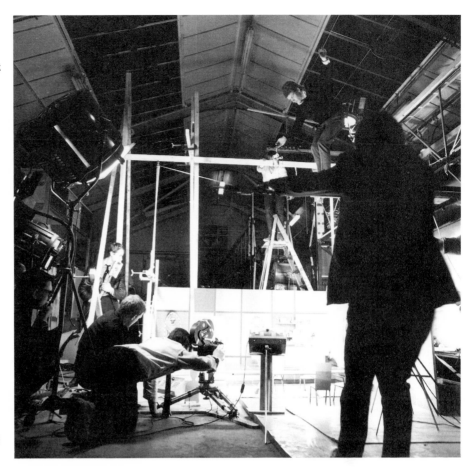

A demonstration of Scott's method of boarding Thunderbird 3 (left); the operator controls the sofa by means of a hydraulic jack beneath the platform.

Lights, camera, action! An excellent example of the film crew at work (right).

All puppets had interchangeable heads, each one of which revealed a different facial expression; yet they never once turned out the same despite being cast in the same mould and finished in exactly the same way. There was constant friendly rivalry between the two units to secure the best heads for their particular set of puppets. (In order to make the transmission deadlines, two units filmed simultaneously, without which each episode would have required four weeks to shoot.

Christine herself confirms the strangeness of one mould giving birth to different bodies and heads: 'Two puppets could share the same body, the same weight, the same hole for the neck and indeed the same neck, yet some would always work better than others. That's always been a mystery to me, even now.'

Still professionally active, Christine has just worked with Gerry on the recent Dire Straits video, *Calling Elvis*, in which puppet versions of band members would pass muster on Tracy Island, while she concocted 'luscious kissing lips

and sniffing noses' for a German detergent ad.

Long before she embarked on her first venture with Gerry in 'The Adventures of Twizzle', she had, when still a young girl, visited a puppet exhibition with her mother. Her mother became intrigued, began to make simple puppets, and consequently both her parents took puppetry up as a hobby. Her mother also became acquainted with someone who had a puppet theatre in Chiswick Mall in West London, and Christine began working there as an operator at weekends. Employing her puppet skills, too, at children's parties, Christine finally moved into variety and cabaret through which she was finally introduced to Gerry.

Despite a tight timetable, no attempt was made to take lazy short-cuts or to spare perfection. It was arduous enough in the first place just creating the puppet characters. Heads were sculpted in clay, then roughly painted so that the final result could be forecast. On a good day, the head would enter the next stage of the process, but more often than not it would be scrapped

and work would start from scratch once again. Heads which could match the proposed visualisation would then be copied in the form of a fibreglass shell.

Puppet bodies were always constructed in plastic and, because of simplification allowed by the three basic body sizes, could be produced in bulk at short notice. Weight, too, was often a problem because if, for example, the puppet was too heavy it would require thick control-wires which would strain the operator and be visible on screen; very light puppets, on the other hand, could not be controlled effectively.

After actual manufacture, puppets were next supplied with operating wires before being dangled from the twelve-foot-high gantry for testing. Even with its puppets fully dressed for work, there was still enough time to make minor adjustments to lip and eye movements. Any alteration could not be made lightly since, because of the constant need for an identical twin to feed the second unit which was working simultaneously, and discrepancy in facial detail, mould or paint finish would be picked up by a probing camera which was sensitive to every detail of a small-scale set.

'You rang, M'Lady?'
(left)

In his temple deep within the Malaysian jungle the Hood plots to infiltrate the network of International Rescue.

Associate producer Reg Hill harks back to terms like 'smilers' and 'scowlers' which they applied to the four or five different heads for each puppet (eight or ten including the duplicate model), according to the prevailing expression on the face. In addition, special effects shooting required single puppets to be re-created to quite different scales.

The entire Tracy clan, as well as Lady Penelope, Parker, Brains, Kyrano and Tin-Tin, were constructed largely from fibreglass, while plastic was deemed sufficient for the so-called 'revamp' puppets which functioned in a cameo or support capacity. Parker, initially envisioned as Penelope's sidekick, soon occupied centre screen and thus made the flattering transition from plastic to fibreglass. Parker himself would undoubtedly have approved of such a promotion.

Taking a cue from the motor industry in its manufacture of glass-fibre car bodies, AP Films took delivery of polyester resin and a special glass-fibre cloth, the latter being judged as smooth enough for modelling. After a plastic mould was completed, the creator of the particular puppet began to laminate, laying on several resin-soaked layers of cloth. Dry to the touch in

A publicity shot of Alan Tracy.

irty minutes, it was fully set in an hour, with a
atural colour of beige and the resin completely
anslucent. Though a fire-resistant resin was
vailable, there was, despite the use of mini-
ockets, no special request for fireproof puppets.
he puppets also benefited from a putty-like
ubstance called Bondapaste, which was used to
ll cracks and add contours, even though it was
ot designed with bonding in mind.

'Fireball XL5' and other Supermarionation
dventures were peppered with coloured puppets,
hiefly because of the difficulty in finding grey,
white and black fabrics which matched the way
ne stories were visualised. Plasticine modelling
lso naturally led to coloured heads. But with
Thunderbirds' now shot in 35 mm Eastman
Kodak, perfect colour-matching was a must.

Typically, nine long wires would operate each
wenty-two-inch puppet from a steel gantry
wenty-five feet wide. The ever-expanding team
f puppeteers (the quaint theatrical term used on
et in preference to the official one, Super-
harionators) would, after carrying out their
hare of puppet construction, split in two; at
east six would work as manipulators, the others
nproving the 'revamps' and constructing
dditional characters.

The wires that moved many, but not all, of the
Thunderbirds' puppets were only occasionally
isible on screen, despite the many jokes made
bout them over the years. The odd unexpected
uest appearance of a stray wire only ever added
o the pleasurable gap between the attempted
ealism and gauche puppetry.

Yet this did not stop the 'Thunderbirds' team
rom regarding intrusive wires with horror.
Associate producer Reg Hill confesses that wire
lways caused a headache since, in order both to
upport and to move the weight of a seven- or
ight-pound puppet, a steel wire had to be 0.005
nches in diameter, although they could get away
vith 0.003 for the arms. Given that a standard
uman hair, which is around 0.002 inches, can
ften be distinguished on a decent television
creen, much thought went into the problem of
isible wires. Of other stronger alloys, only
opper could be reduced to the required thinness;
owever, once it was stretched, it remained in
hat position. The capacity of wire to give off
eflections was minimised in various ways, while

An operator prepares a
puppet for filming.

The Hood's lair, from behind
the camera.

in special-effects sequences, where cameras are often just feet away from the subjects, wires were often painted so as to blend in with the background.

Supervising special effects director Derek Meddings talks amusingly about the transition from television to features in terms of the wires. It was often suggested to Derek that, whereas wires were mostly invisible on the small screen, they would appear large on the big. He always replied to the film executives that he always showed them the rushes for each episode on a cinema screen at Pinewood and, with all wires highly visible, they had never once curled a lip or scoffed in disdain. Derek adds that, although he would blot out a wire that he could see on set, it would still sometimes be picked up by the camera. With a typical insistence on high production values, the team would reshoot an entire sequence whenever an uninvited wire strayed on to the screen. Only on odd occasions was it impossible to reshoot.

Yet moments of fun penetrated intense shooting schedules. Since all the puppets sported artificial human eyes, Gerry once contacted an eye-maker, who knew nothing of his puppet enterprises, to ask for a quote, and the specialist was suitably stunned when Gerry asked for the price of a pair.

A rolling road, in fact, along with a rolling sky was designed by supervising special effects Director Derek Meddings for 'Thunderbirds'. The road, which is still in active use in the Bond films, was employed in conjunction with a smaller road–sky moving model to create a convincing impression of speed. The effect can be seen to best advantage in 'Trapped in the Sky', when the disabled jet airliner comes in to land on three Elevator Cars.

Derek, who not only had a character named after him in the first episode, but also went on to take charge of the effects for the Bond films and *Batman*, can recall showing Gerry a drawing of Thunderbird 2 which bore no resemblance to the script. Much to Derek's surprise, Gerry loved Derek's invention of a giant green bug. Despite being the most difficult Thunderbird to fly, it eventually became Derek's own favourite, and its surreal beauty, which is grandiose and anarchic, has been much adored by artists like

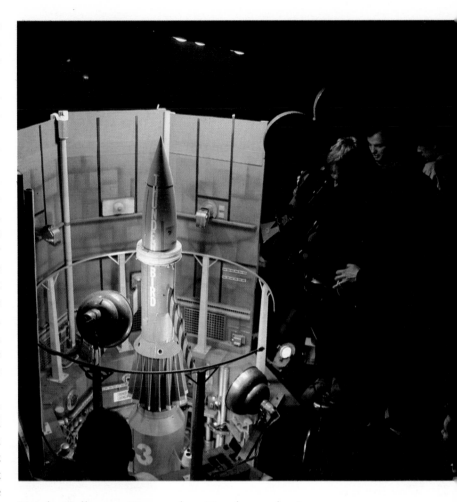

Preparing to film a launch. Models of different sizes were made according to the shots required. This model of Thunderbird 3 was one the largest craft made.

Frank Bellamy. Perversely, Derek made its wings point forward, so placing Thunderbird 2 amusingly at odds with the backward thrust of conventional high-speed craft. Unimpressed by the appearance of Thunderbird 3, Derek least favoured Thunderbird 1, which he found both ugly and dull to film, since it could only be shot from one limiting angle. He adds that Thunderbird 2's size made it difficult to fly, since it had to dwarf the rescue vehicles it was carrying. Had they been any smaller, then they would have been unable to function. This example aside, there was never any conscious attempt to build all the craft in proportion to one another, while the sequence where the sofa speeds through the base of Thunderbird 3 was the only time that Derek constructed a large-scale set-piece.

Of all the set creations, supervising art director Bob Bell's favourite was The Whistle Stop Inn, a station restaurant in *Thunderbird 6*, 'in which trains puff in and out and deliver food to the waiting customers'. He laughs as he admits that 'anything I was asked to do which was a bit dull, I'd pass on to someone else. It was all very hard work, because we had to build all the props from scratch and so create our own props store. It wasn't like a live-action film where you can hire everything.'

Continual fretting with regard to lighting, depth of focus, water scenes and fire was, despite the arm-twisting timetable for each episode, always resolved in some way. Having first toyed with the conventions of dry ice and chemical smoke for full rocket effect, it was then decided to use the real thing. Schermuly Pistol Rocket Apparatus Ltd, which designed Royal Naval and other life-saving rocket devices, dreamed up compressed gunpowder rockets for 'Thunderbirds'. Coupled with an increased camera speed, all jet motors, retro-rockets, explosions and rocket-launches became miniature versions of the real thing.

Running repairs were carried out on the vehicles during production. Here we see Thunderbird 2 receiving some minor attention (above).

Craft control wires also had to be concealed. Here the size of the smaller model of Thunderbird 3 emerging from the Round House can be compared with that on the opposite page.

One potential problem resolved itself in an entertaining way. For 'Attack of the Alligators', it was decided that, since there was no money in the budget to create miniature alligators, real baby crocodiles would be found which would be in scale with the series. Even though water-tanks were set up and heated to the correct temperature, he was paid a surprise visit by an RSPCA inspector who had been told that the crocodiles were being given nasty electric shocks. The inspector was promptly distracted when he realised that it was 'Thunderbirds', his favourite programme, which was being filmed, and after half an hour of wide-eyed enthusiasm he finally tackled Derek Meddings about the purpose of his visit. Because the crocodiles wouldn't move, Derek said, he had touched them with an electrode, to no avail. On learning that Derek was only using twenty volts, the inspector recommended, because of the animals' thick skins, a sixty-volt dose. The exuberant official ended up taking his annual leave to work for Gerry and so applied the electric shocks himself.

While the three-foot crocodiles were mainly functional, except for a particularly docile specimen which loafed all day on the studio floor, a five-foot animal was too vicious to remove from its basket. Derek himself had his own freaky moment when filming that episode. With a non-slip knot around a crocodile's neck, Derek had pulled that animal through and up from the water to make it look as if it was about to snap off the back of a boatful of people. However, for the next shot, where the beast had to open its mouth, Derek, still in the tank in his waders, pulled on the rope to find nothing there. The crocodile had freed itself, and Derek could detect a V-shape rippling through the water; he managed to jump up on to the edge of the tank, leaving his boots in the water.

Penelope (right) remains calm while posing for this publicity shot. Alligators are a girl's best friend!

A production shot of the Seascape oil rig from the episode 'Atlantic Inferno' (left).

Water effect shots had to be taken from the most difficult positions. Cameraman and camera were often balanced at precarious angles (above).

DAZZLING THE EARS AND THE EYES

The composer, arranger and conductor for both films, and indeed for the entire 'Thunderbirds' series, was Barry Gray, who sadly died in 1984 yet is remembered with genuine affection by Gerry and the entire team. A polite and gentle man, he was the musical force behind 'Thunderbirds' and thus a key contributor to the success of the series and Gerry's other early work. Chiefly known as the composer of the rousing 'Thunderbirds' march, which a generation of children would hum for years as they slid down banisters pretending to be Scott or Virgil, he was also responsible for the electronic effects which peppered the series.

Standing apart from the often banal world of television and film music, which regularly appears as an add-on or afterthought, Barry's music for 'Thunderbirds' was an integral part of the drama. Clearly in touch with the characters and their missions, and an obvious fan of the series himself, Barry was paid constant respect by the eighty orchestra members.

A man of small stature, Barry would have no trouble at all in establishing command. One tap of his baton was all that was needed for complete silence. Despite the mighty roar of the 'Thunderbirds' march during the filming of *Thunderbirds Are Go*, Barry would dazzle onlookers with his ability to single out a wrong note from the heat of the musical furnace.

Having made a deep study of the history of music, Barry could play any number of musical instruments and grasp any style of music with ease. Equally *au fait* with recording techniques, he had his own studio and always seemed relaxed and happy when surrounded by banks of state-of-the-art gadgetry.

Barry played a key role in the development of Gerry's own series. For both 'The Adventures of Twizzle' and 'Torchy the Battery Boy', Roberta Leigh, though often credited as composer, had hummed the music into a tape-recorder; and Barry had then arranged it. At this point in his life, Barry was purely an orchestrator and arranger; yet he would secure his first chance as composer with 'Four Feather Falls'.

Gerry, who had yet to attempt to write a script, or indeed create a programme, but was keen to break from Leigh and dream up his own series, told Barry of his intention to do just that. Barry himself was keen to think up an idea, and the result was 'Four Feather Falls', which pushed Gerry, via 'Supercar', 'Fireball XL5' and 'Stingray', towards 'Thunderbirds'. Though Barry made no financial gain from 'Four Feather Falls', he made a strong mark as a composer in his own right.

'Thunderbirds' director, writer and script editor Alan Pattillo has fond memories of Barry:

'So that we could edit, we'd often need a bit of music for our cutting copy. Barry would always be helpful, enthusiastic and creative and record something for us on his synthesiser. It was always fun to pay him a visit. He lived in a little house in Dollis Hill, a 1920s bungalow, with his mother. He had a small studio in the back room. He was also, you know, Vera Lynn's accompanist during the height of her wartime fame.'

**Thunderbird 2 piloted by
Virgil with Brains and
Gordon as crew.**

Despite a continuing successful worldwide career as a film editor, nothing is quite so 'nostalgia-inducing' in Alan's life as 'Thunderbirds' which allowed him to blossom effectively as writer, script editor and director. Through film editor David Elliott, who went on to direct many of the 'Thunderbirds' episodes, Alan met Gerry and was hired at once as an editor, before progressing to director several weeks later. He had, in fact, directed several episodes of 'Supercar', but it was on 'Thunderbirds' that he emerged as writer and script editor.

Pattillo, a pleasantly guarded man who combines precise analytical insights with Aberdonian charm, speaks fondly of his progress through the ranks:

'Everything mushroomed for Gerry so much that he wanted someone to take charge of all the scripts and deal with the other writers, too. So, about two months after we filmed the pilot, "Trapped in the Sky", I became the series script editor. I would discuss story-lines with Gerry and the required special effects with Derek Meddings.'

It seems there was never any problem with ensuring that key writers Alan Fennell and Dennis Spooner, as well as other contributors, were travelling down the same road. Story-lines would be worked out to a high degree and then the writers would meet Gerry and Alan for morning coffee or afternoon tea to discuss the scripts.

Lady Penelope relaxing on her Australian ranch.

The opening caption shots of Lady Penelope and Gordon.

In his multiple roles, Alan was very concerned with the difficulties of puppet filming:

'It was difficult for puppets to get in and out of vehicles without a great deal of trouble. Since we always tried to minimise walking, we'd show the puppets taking one step only, then promptly cut. Through interspersing the programmes with "meanwhile" scenes – that is, showing what else was going on in the story at the same time – we would then cut back to the puppet who was by now already in his craft. But for "Trapped in the Sky" we went to an enormous amount of trouble to show puppets getting in and out of vehicles. These sequences, along with any spare takes, became stock shots which were used time and again.'

Confessing that 'while half of us were trying to make the puppets walk realistically, the other half had accepted that they were just puppets', Alan Pattillo believes that the jump-start walk, the shrugging shoulders and jerky head-movements added to the enormous appeal of the series. The 'Thunderbirds' characters were seen

Wayne Forrester and Paul Kent as Colonel White and Captain Scarlet.

as attractive enough by the team for the addition of a fetching animal, which had characterised 'Supercar' and 'Fireball XL5', and 'Stingray' (Marina had a pet seal called Oink), to be unnecessary.

Alan still holds much affection for a concept which dovetails technical gimmickry with obvious humanity:

'Now electronic puppets, though versatile, can be so cold that you may as well use real actors. It can all be a bit soulless. The family values, in which a father dispatched yet looked after his sons on their various missions, were a big part of our appeal. With all our characters carefully worked on, and with the support of good vocal artists, we had Gerry's best mix so far.'

Gerry, it seems, was excellent at not pressurising the team, despite their frantic two-week deadlines or, as Alan says 'he was good at being uninterfering, and not pushing it too far'. Sometimes, indeed, they even finished ahead of schedule.

Because he wanted to move on, Alan did not script-edit the final six programmes, though he contributed both 'Alias Mr Hackenbacker' and

'Give or Take a Million' as a writer. He declined Gerry's offer to stay on board for *Thunderbirds Are Go*, thinking 'it would be too much hassle on the big screen, with puppet wires showing'. Yet Alan looks back on these years of committed fun with a resonant glow which causes him to discuss single programmes as if they were made yesterday.

It is the limitations of the puppet form which largely contribute to the charisma of *Thunderbirds FAB*, a stage show which is an affectionate parody of Gerry Anderson's creation and has charmed audiences the world over since it began life in 1985 as a small-scale touring production.

In 1989 the show really lifted off. At a time when Batman ruled the world and more than sixty comic-book projects were being put together for both big and small screens, it was unsurprising that two well-known English actors, Andrew Dawson and Gavin Robertson, brought Gerry Anderson's *Thunderbirds FAB* to a West End stage. Once the fodder of dingy pub theatres, the two young men benefited from a soaring interest in comic books and were thus catapulted into the

West End itself. The show, in fact, broke all house records at the Apollo Theatre, London.

Gavin Robertson is still modestly reeling from the shock that the success of *Thunderbirds FAB* has been so colossal: 'We stumbled on "Thunderbirds" in complete naïvety and conceived of it as only a little part of a much bigger show. At Lecoq School in Paris, as well as the Desmond Jones School of Mime, Andy and I had learned the archetypal mime movements of classic marionettes, but we now had to analyse what made the "Thunderbirds" puppets move. It was particularly tough teaching this to the new actors!'

A fan of Lady Penelope in particular ('everyone's waiting for her, and we would be surprised if she didn't appear'), Gavin explains: 'Originally the craft were to be perched on our shoulders,

DAZZLING THE EARS AND THE EYES

but we figured they'd be too small to be seen at the back of the theatre, so we then decided to wear them like huge hats.'

Both a tribute to and a parody of the mid-sixties hit television series, the production was an imaginative showcase for the two talents who delighted both themselves and the audience with those wonderfully staccato limb-movements that have you straining in the dark for giveaway strings. At times, and admirably faithful to the television originals, their hands would dangle pointlessly in mid-air.

A canny mix of schoolboy innocence and arty shrewdness, Dawson was excellent as Scott Tracy, the keen-minded captain of Thunderbird 1, while Robertson was equally adapt as the hapless Virgil living in the shadow of his brother and only allowed to pilot Thunderbird 2. When not acting out the cockpit antics of the two superheroes, both artists were able to stage spectacular nose-dives and heady acts of lunacy with only a few deft hand-movements and some telling squints of the face. Dawson's face, in particular, looked as if it were being pulled in all directions at once by invisible fingers.

Precision timing, simple lighting and elements of pantomime also enabled Robertson to turn Lady Penelope into an exercise in camp, while Dawson's sprawling limbs were ideal for his version of Captain Scarlet. The spoof was completed when both actors reappeared to let Thunderbirds 1 and 2 take the stage as fetching headgear.

A more solemn Space Panorama, which served as an opening act to the show, was designed as an affectionate satire of Neil Armstrong and chums landing on the moon. Noisy levity and quiet melodrama both found their place in a piece which parodied both bland news-speak and our uncritical devotion to technology.

The recent version of the stage show, which last year returned to London's theatreland in celebratory style, was now directed by its creators, Gavin Robertson and Andrew Dawson. Actors Paul Kent and Wayne Forester were in the cockpit this time round and amusingly fleshed out twelve Anderson creations, including Scott and Virgil Tracy, Brains, Parker and Lady Penelope. Any casual theatregoer who had never immersed himself in the specialist universe of the 'Thunderbirds' fan would blink twice before grasping that mirror-image versions of the characters on stage were liberally sprinkled throughout the auditorium.

Wayne and Paul perform a spectacular launch sequence during their performance of *Thunderbirds FAB: the Next Generation*.

SPELL UNBROKEN

Certainly 'Thunderbirds' has sparked the imagination of a world public like no other puppet series before or since. Yet its influence, extending beyond millions of eager viewers, has also been both technical and ideological.

Back in the mid-sixties, an established British film studio was facing problems as it grappled with the task of filming a live-action air crash in open countryside. For three weeks they strived to squeeze credibility from a balsa-wood model crashing on to pylon wires. Unhappy with the resulting lame effect, they requested assistance from AP Films and, having seen AP's own crashing sequence for 'Thunderbirds', had their own shot in the can in just one afternoon.

Amongst all the rumours about the influence of 'Thunderbirds', Gerry himself believes that, although it may not be true that American air force designers were inspired by the series, it did excite a future generation of scientists and engineers, whose ideas have been shaped by the craft and their capabilities. Meanwhile, charities and the Government (through their public safety films) have often employed International Rescue. And thus the dynamism of the characters, the breezy confidence with which they reacted and the ease with which they handled their freshly minted machinery drew a deceptive cloak over the full-tilt effort which Anderson and many others lavished on this complicated series.

Still creating ever more inventive rescue operations, Gerry had intended to go out on a high after the first exhilarating batch of twenty-six

episodes and move on to a new project, most likely with Zero X as the starring machine. However, the enthusiastic support from his world-wide public led to a further six episodes, which were first broadcast in autumn 1966.

To the avid 'Thunderbirds' *aficionado*, the final six programmes were markedly different, even though only a handful of small details tilt the scales. 'Atlantic Inferno', 'Path of Destruc-

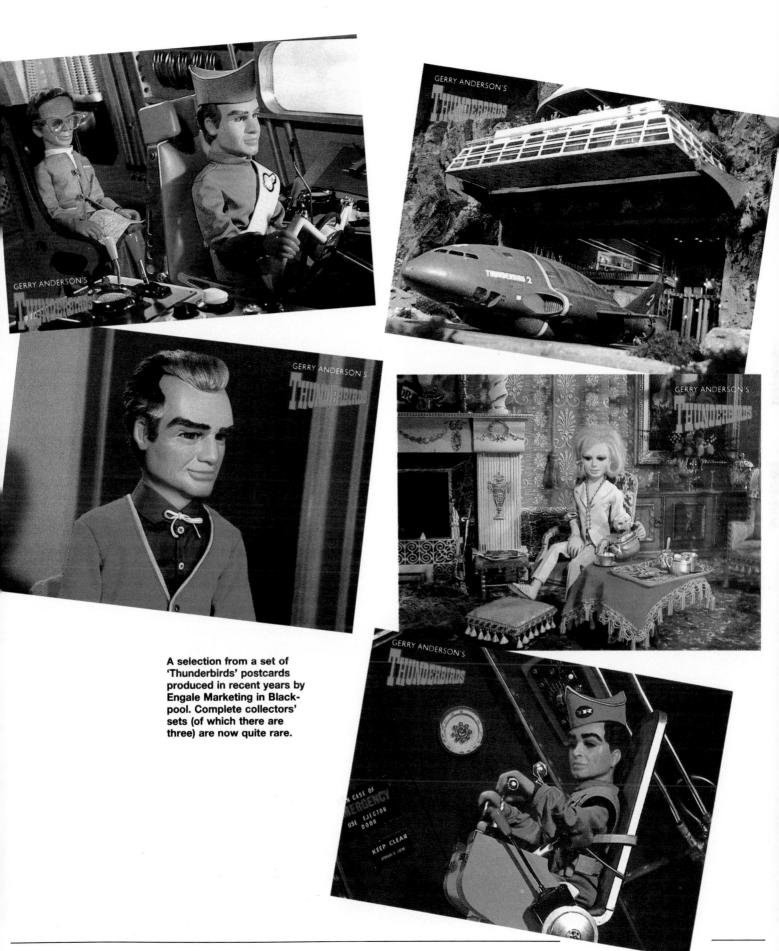

A selection from a set of
'Thunderbirds' postcards
produced in recent years by
Engale Marketing in Blackpool. Complete collectors'
sets (of which there are
three) are now quite rare.

tion', 'Alias Mr Hackenbacker', 'Lord Parker's 'Oliday', 'Ricochet' and 'Give or Take a Million', constitute the six shows.

Like the twenty-six previous shows, each episode cost around £22,000 (roughly what Anderson's more recent 'Terrahawks' cost in equivalent terms). Keen eyes will pick up on the fact that, in the final six, the Thunderbirds logo carries the date 1966 instead of 1964, while the puppets themselves, all of which edge away from caricature and move towards realism, sport an array of minor, and barely perceptible, differences. The only vocal difference was that David Holliday, who originally supplied the tones of Virgil Tracy, was not available in time, so Jeremy Wilkin replaced him.

Despite our ability now to view the 'Thunderbirds' series in colour, in Britain it was only possible to watch the programmes initially in black and white, though Gerry had made the entire series, like 'Stingray' before it, in a splash of wonderfully contrasting colours. For quite some years, British fans could only enjoy the brightly coloured craft on the big screen and through the popular pages of *TV21*.

The most recent ideological impact of 'Thunderbirds' led to the creation of a real-life International Rescue in the early-eighties: a team of roughly seventy highly skilled operational volunteers which flies in, courtesy of free British Airways seats, to the scene of a disaster. In the manner of Scott Tracy, but with staccato body-movements nowhere in sight, they arrive at the zone with talking rope, thermal-imaging cameras and other pieces of advanced rescue equipment, pinpoint the requirements and move on quickly to the next spot. The honorary president of International Rescue Corps, by the way, is Gerry Anderson himself.

Gerry has thought at times of reviving his International Rescue as a live-action show or a new puppet production, while allowing himself to change a number of details. Lady Penelope, who would now drive a Porsche, would also, as a concession to the times, have given up smoking; while Brains would be relieved of his thick-lensed glasses and Scott of his simple Boy Scout persona. Though this has never occurred, the series has recently been repeated on BBC2 in its thirty-two component parts to over six million

(Opposite) From left to right: Reg Hill, Sylvia and Gerry Anderson and John Read at the Slough Studio at the height of 'Thunderbirds' original success.

A publicity shot (above) of Lady Penelope and Jeff reading a preview copy of the novelisation of their adventure *Thunderbirds are Go!*.

viewers, while 'Thunderbirds 2086', a Japanese television cartoon series with new characters and craft, (and no connection with Gerry Anderson) has recently been relaunched on video. The affectionate parody of the original series, *Thunderbirds FAB: The Next Generation* continues to attract theatre crowds and Thunderbirds fans across the world.

One such 'Thunderbirds' devotee is Lorraine Malby, a twenty-eight-year-old East Ender whose chief fancy is dressing up like Virgil Tracy. A ten-inch yellow sash and seemingly shrunken peaked cap sit strangely on an otherwise respectable insurance clerk. It calls to mind Clark Kent, who, gauche, bespectacled grey suit in his day job, would vanish into a callbox and re-emerge only moments later as Superman.

Unusual in that she has a tolerant mother who sees nothing odd in all this, Lorraine confesses that: 'My mum understands, because she's a Trekkie, but Dad can't understand it. He's into model railways, you see.' Lorraine even bought her mother a blue uniform which is a quality match for Mr Spock's in *Star Trek*.

Ralph Titterton, who is in charge of merchandising and liaison for Fanderson (the Gerry Anderson appreciation society), is clearly in no danger of becoming Scott Tracy. Initiating a range of products which are available exclusively to Fanderson members, he has been 'totally hooked throughout the years' since he first saw 'Fireball XL5' in 1961. Despite his avid worship of all things Anderson, and impressive rooms full of neatly stacked books and videos, as well as assorted rare memorabilia, he realises he is not living in 2026 but in present-day Ashford, Kent: 'For certain fans, "Thunderbirds" has become a religion, yet I've never lost sight of the fact that it's just a television programme, albeit an excellent one, made to make money for its backers.'

A charge nurse at an intensive and coronary care unit in Dover, he shares both his house and his enthusiasm, the reasons for which he finds 'difficult to describe', with his girlfriend Cathy Ford to whom he presented a raffle prize at a Fanderson convention long before they became co-pilots. Combining an open-hearted delight in Gerry Anderson's puppet universe with a charming ability to smile wryly at their joint fascination, they are unlikely to emulate the

Any Thunderbirds collector would be envious of this display of original 1960s merchandise.

Tracy brothers' staccato puppet walk as they stroll round the town of Ashford.

The products offshoots of 'Thunderbirds' were tremendously varied. Alan Fennell was assisted in the creation of *TV21* by Keith Shackleton, managing director of AP Films Merchandising, which, in early 1966, went on to become Century 21, the products offshoot of 'Thunderbirds'. Shackleton not only introduced a sister comic, *Lady Penelope*, after the success of 'Thunderbirds', but also the Rosenthal range of Thunderbirds toys at Harrogate Toy Fair in 1965. His subsequent sales drives took him to both the United States and Hong Kong. Shackleton, having travelled yet another century through time, now heads Century 22 Merchandising which is partially responsible for the current popularity of world wrestling.

Merchandising products include annuals, puppets and dolls, models of the Thunderbirds craft, dressing-up costumes and Lady Penelope accessories such as the hairband and, a real collector's item, the charm bracelet.

These souvenirs of an era are treasured and exhibited. There are dedicated collectors of Thunderbirds memorabilia as well as those who keep their single items in pride of place as a reminder of their favourite childhood series. With the revival of the Thunderbirds series, the associated publishing comes full circle. The first issue, in October 1991, of *Thunderbirds – the Comic* sold exceptionally well and the circulation continued to rise steadily with each issue.

Until the juggernaut-style merchandising campaigns of *Star Wars* and *Batman: The Movie*, no film or television merchandising operation had been as colossal or as successful as 'Thunderbirds'. With a new series of products recently launched, and likely to sell out rapidly, fans can also enjoy the recent Dire Straits video, *Calling Elvis*, to which collector-turned-modelmaker Philip Rae lent his assistance. Also involving the full participation of Gerry himself, it features 'Thunderbirds'-style puppet versions of band members whose bodies, along with those of certain 'Thunderbirds' characters who also appear, were based on Philip's Alan Tracy master-body. Philip also supplied the studio with photographs which enabled the re-creation of 'Thunderbirds' sets.

Thunderbirds – the Comic – the first issue. Within weeks of release Issue No. 1 has become a rare collectors' item – an excellent example of the continuing popularity of Thunderbirds merchandise.

INTERNATIONAL RESCUE CALLING
THUNDERBIRDS ™

65p

THE COMIC

October 19th - November 1st 1991   No.1

© 1991 ITC
Entertainment
Group Ltd by

THUNDERBIRDS

FREE THUNDERBIRDS ARE GO! BADGE

3 GREAT THUNDERBIRDS ADVENTURES IN GLORIOUS COLOUR

INSIDE

4 PAGE PULL-OUT WALL-CHART FEATURING TB1

ISSN 0963-9047

SUPER COMPETITION THUNDERBIRDS T-SHIRTS TO BE WON

STARRING

CAPTAIN SCARLET

DESTINY ANGEL

CAPTAIN BLUE

SYMPHONY,
MELODY,

RHAPSODY
AND
HARMONY ANGELS

COLONEL
WHITE

MYSTERON
AGENT

CAPTAIN
BLACK

CONTENTS

THE FINGER IS ON THE TRIGGER

Fear rules the twenty-first Century! The Mysterons of the planet Mars have declared war on Earth. Cold as silicon, merciless as an electric shock, the Mysterons have conquered death itself. They can create an exact copy of a human being and turn him against his family and friends. Bullets can't stop him and bombs will only slow him down, because Mysteron agents are indestructible.

Only one man can defeat the Mysterons. One man with the strength to fight off the Mysteron influence and regain control of his body. Captain Scarlet is that man – loyal to Earth but now completely indestructible. Brave as any hero that ever lived, Captain Scarlet has one big advantage; when his luck runs out, he can repair his wounds and return from the dead.

Captain Scarlet is the creation of Gerry Anderson, the man who gave *Stingray* and *Thunderbirds* to a worldwide TV audience. Captain Scarlet is radically different from any other puppet-hero Gerry Anderson produced in the 1960s, not least because he was born out of what seemed like disaster.

For Gerry Anderson, *Captain Scarlet and the Mysterons* began one morning in 1966 when ATV's Lew Grade told him that he didn't want another series of *Thunderbirds*. In the years since ATV had bought Anderson's struggling AP Films company, they'd produced *Supercar*, *Fireball XL5* and *Stingray*. *Thunderbirds* had been the biggest hit of all. Under the new name of *Century 21*, Anderson's company was creating comics, records and toys based on *Thunderbirds*. United

Artists had financed a movie called *Thunderbirds Are Go!* Lew Grade had even commissioned a further six episodes of the *Thunderbirds* TV series. So it was even more amazing, that late summer morning in 1966, when Grade decided that he wanted a totally new TV series. Even today, Anderson sounds surprised: 'because of the merchandising and because of the huge success, I wrongly assumed that he would continue with *Thunderbirds*. And he didn't.'

Tricolour: Captains Scarlet, Ochre and Blue unwind in the Cloudbase lounge.

Courageous, determined, indestructible. The man they call Captain Scarlet!

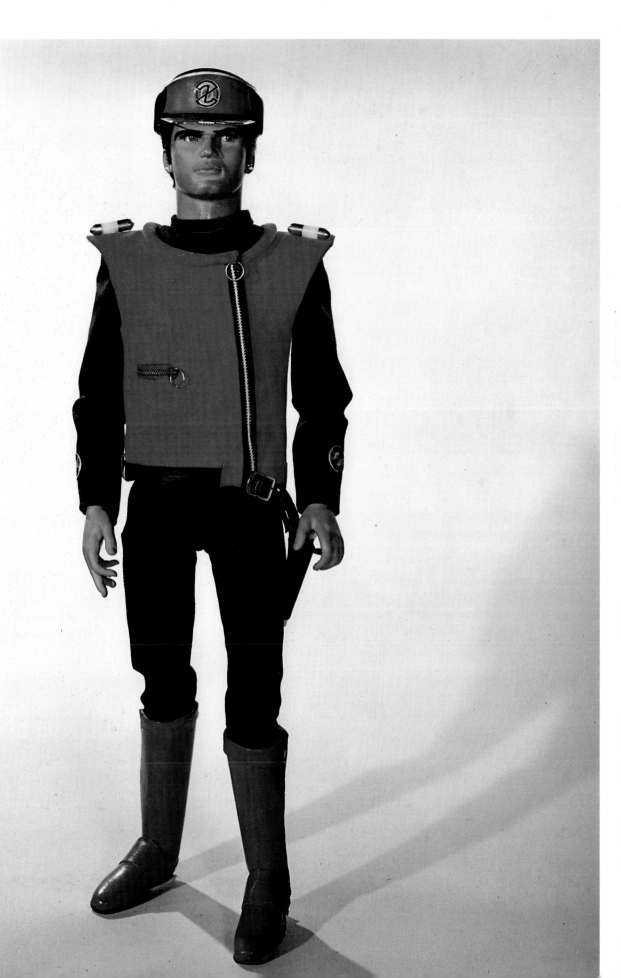

Just like the Spanish Inquisition: human actors have to stand on their marks for lighting purposes, but the puppets are simply clamped into position.

One thing was certain: Lew Grade was nobody's fool. In the ten years since Independent Television had begun in Britain, Grade had turned Associated Television into ITV's biggest money-maker. ATV ran stations in London and Birmingham, but most of the money was made by selling film series to America through ATV's Independent Television Corporation. As Gerry Anderson explains, 'These programmes were very expensive to make. To get that money back you'd have to sell to 80 countries individually, but if you take that total amount of world sales, 60 per cent of that global sum came from the States.' Even in America, the bullseye for which Grade aimed was the network sale. In one deal, Grade could sell *Fireball XL5* to the National Broad-

casting Company, and the show would go out to hundreds of 'affiliated' stations across America. If a series didn't sell to the networks, the only alternative was to try and sell the show to each of the individual stations, one by one.

Thunderbirds was a massive success in Britain, but it did not get a network sale in America. To Lew Grade it must have been sense to forget *Thunderbirds* and channel the money into something new and better that he could sell to the American networks.

One of the biggest obstacles for *Thunderbirds* in America had been the lack of hour-long time slots. Consequently Gerry Anderson knew that his next show had to be fast, exciting and only half-an-hour long. As he drew up the pilot script

A woman of substance: *Captain Scarlet* was the first ITC series to feature black co-stars such as Melody Angel.

– the blue-print for the series – Anderson was aware that the puppets were better than ever. Mary Turner and 'Plugg' Shutt had built stringless puppets which could be controlled from the waist up, while John Read and Reg Hill had struggled tirelessly to reduce the size of the mouth control mechanism. With the smaller device lodged in the chest rather than the head, the size of the heads could be cut down so that they were in proportion with the bodies. Inspired both by the less-caricatured puppets and the success of Cliff Richard Junior in *Thunderbirds Are Go!*, Anderson saw a chance to get Hollywood 'guest-stars' for his new show. As he explained in the pilot script, an actor such as Dick Bogarde or Efrem Zimbalist Junior (then starring in *The FBI*) would lay down a voice track in the recording studio and then, 'a replica of his face would be made to appear in the film as a puppet.' The pilot script offers the example of *Dangerman*'s Patrick McGoohan playing the part of the World President. Unfortunately, time and money meant that the 'guest-puppet' idea had to be scrapped, but the concept of character-based storylines had already worked through into the pilot script.

In fact, Gerry Anderson was still so excited about his improved, life-like puppets that he dubbed Captain Scarlet, 'the Mechanical Man'. In the development script, the Mysterons kill the real Captain Scarlet and create an exact copy. This 'booby-trap' is captured at the end of the story and Spectrum's Doctor Fawn concludes that, 'with a specially designed computer it would be possible to bring him under our control.' The closing titles of the show would have underlined the 'mechanical' nature of Captain Scarlet by showing pictures of him in 'association with computers, printed circuits and electrodes'. Somewhere along the line, however, Gerry Anderson realised that viewers might find it hard to sympathise with what was basically a robot. Gradually, Captain Scarlet regained his flesh and soul and became the Indestructible Man.

Gerry Anderson had another reason for playing down the mechanical man angle. He'd realised that his puppets weren't quite as lifelike as he'd thought. 'Suddenly, all the movements had to be as realistic as the puppets and that made it difficult for the puppeteers to animate them.' Chief Puppeteer Christine Glanville explains that, 'when you see a puppet walk on film, the camera is so exacting that it exaggerates every movement, and they look as if they're skating!' Rather than show Captain Scarlet walking, the directors often used moving shots from the puppets' point of view, or even cut to another character as the puppets' footsteps were heard.

One landmark for the series was that Lieutenant Green and Melody Angel were the first black characters to star in an ITC series. This was a deliberate move on Gerry Anderson's part. 'When I made *Supercar* for ATV, we put quite a number of black characters in an episode because the story demanded it. ATV had an American advisor at that time, and he made us take out every black character and replace them with white characters and white voices. He said he would not be able to sell it to stations in the South because of the black characters. By the time *Captain Scarlet* came along, we had got to the point where American distributors were now prepared to accept black actors. I was always very anxious to promote racial harmony, so as soon as people had become more sensible I took advantage of it.'

As filming began, Anderson turned his attention to the merchandising. 'I knew only too well that if our shows didn't make a profit that would be the end of the studio and the end of me as a producer. Now the merchandise was extremely important, not only because it made a lot of money in its own right. A show creates a strong desire for a child to buy the toys, and when they get the toys and play with them, that in turn creates a desire to see the films again.' Keith Shackleton, the head of Century 21 Merchandising, had bounced back from the loss of *Thunderbirds* by spearheading the biggest TV-tie-in Britain had ever seen. Toys, sweets, and even clothes were busily being blazoned with the Spectrum symbol or Captain Scarlet's face. Aware of the success of Pye Records' *Thunderbirds* mini-albums, Gerry Anderson even assembled a pop group called The Spectrum to sing the *Captain Scarlet* theme over the end-titles. As Gerry himself admits, 'it soon became clear that they weren't going to be the next Beatles,' although the drummer, Keith Forsey, did go on to a successful career as a producer for performers like Billy Idol and such films as

Captain Scarlet and Dr. Kurnitz en route to Clondbase, secure within Spectrum's disguised VIP Transporter.

The Breakfast Club (he even wrote the Simple Minds hit, 'Don't You Forget About Me').

Century 21 also published its own range of comics, which generated pre-publicity for each new Anderson series. *TV Century 21* had given Lady Penelope her own picture strip months before *Thunderbirds* hit the TV screens, because the head of Century 21 Publications was Alan Fennell, who had written almost half the episodes of *Fireball XL5*, *Stingray* and *Thunderbirds*. Unfortunately, the success of *Thunderbirds* had helped to weaken the links between the comics and the studio. Century 21 now published *Lady Penelope, Candy* and *Solo* (starring *The Man from UNCLE*) in addition to *TV21* and a score of annuals and paperbacks. Fennell didn't have time to write episodes for *Captain Scarlet*, while Anderson's increased workload forced him to turn over his seat on the Century 21 Publishing board to Louis Benjamin of Pye Records.

The result was that Alan Fennell was almost as bewildered as his readers when the time came to create pre-publicity for *Captain Scarlet*. The format of the series was still being revised during filming, and the background to the series was quite complex. Fennell also found Scarlet himself quite perplexing: 'What works in film doesn't always work in comics. An indestructible hero presents problems in comics because there is nothing that can threaten him and therefore there is no drama.' The writers of *Superman* had been able to introduce Kryptonite to weaken their hero, but for *TV21* the format of *Captain Scarlet* was unalterable.

Months before the series had even finished filming, Fennell and his team got together around a table to create a background for *Captain Scarlet*. Starting with the most human characters, they introduced a strip called *The Angels* on the back page of *Lady Penelope*. Drawn by Jon Davis, the story began with five women pilots being called to a lonely Italian airfield and offered the chance to pilot unmarked white interceptors for an unseen master. Readers were soon curious to know the identity of the 'voice from the loud-speaker' which gave the Angels their orders, but one reader discovered the answer by a strange twist of fate. On Saturday 29 April 1967, Milton Finesilver was watching a comedy show which had been slotted into the end of BBC 1's transmission

Scarlet Lady: Rhapsody Angel first appeared in the *Lady Penelope* comic, but kept the truth about Spectrum under her hat.

after it had won the Golden Rose of Montreux. 'After it finished, I was flicking around the channels, even though the scheduled programmes had finished, and there on ATV London was the first episode of *Captain Scarlet*.' This was long before the advent of all-night television, so it is likely that Milton had stumbled upon an engineer's transmission test. Yet by another quirk of fate, Milton had already applied for a job at Century 21 Publications, and managed to astound office manager Tod Sullivan at his interview by relating details of a programme that only the upper rank of insiders were supposed to have seen.

By this time, Century 21 was blazing a trail for *Captain Scarlet* in almost all of the comics. *Solo* printed articles credited to Alan Fennell in which he warned of a malevolent force using strange powers to cause disasters across the globe. The force was eventually tracked down to the Mysterons, and *Solo* began running a feature called 'Spectrum News' ('so called because we believe the Mysterons cannot see colour'). Because the Mysterons were at the very heart of the new series, it would have been difficult to release much information about them without spoiling the surprises in *Captain Scarlet*'s first episode. For this reason, *Solo* began running a strip called 'The Mark of the Mysterons'. Drawn by ex-*Dan Dare* artist Don Harley, it was set in 1967, and followed *Solo* reporter John Marsh as he tried to warn a disbelieving world that alien bodysnatchers were invading Earth.

Over on the newspaper-style front page of *TV21*, Captain Black's Martian Excursion Vehicle was reported missing as it tried to trace the source of enigmatic radio signals in the Rock Snake Hills of Mars. As the editor of *TV21* asked which secret organisation had sent Captain Black to Mars, he had little idea just how lucky Black had been. Christine Glanville recalls that, as the first Mysteron victim, Captain Black was originally supposed to die at the end of the pilot episode. As a human, Captain Black looked quite bland, 'but once I'd painted him up to look gaunt and pallid, Gerry took one look and decided to keep him on as a regular.'

Back in *TV21*, a strip drawn by *Modesty Blaise* artist John Burns showed two journalists investigating a mysterious UFO hovering over Nice. The UFO was Cloudbase, speeding to intercept

Once a top Spectrum agent, Captain Black now obeys new masters.

Captain Black's Zero X ship on its return from Mars. In a stunning cliffhanger, the journalists flew directly into Captain Black's re-entry path, and although they avoided a collision, Captain Black was able to escape from Spectrum in the confusion. In the pages of *Lady Penelope*, Lieutenant Green was revealed as the voice behind the loudspeaker and the Angels were admitted into Spectrum. In the same week, the final issue of *Solo* climaxed with the first instalment of a comic strip about the history of the Mysterons. The story would continue in another comic.

On Friday 29th September, *Captain Scarlet and the Mysterons* premiered on ATV Midlands, closely followed by ATV London and Scottish

'I'll string along with you': Captain Blue tends to a wounded Symphony Angel. A romance between the two characters bubbled sedately beneath the surface.

TV on Sunday 1st October. It would take a few weeks for the series to appear on the rest of the ITV stations, but until that time, the eager public could feast their eyes on the first part of *TV21*'s new *Captain Scarlet* strip. For the first time a Spectrum Pursuit Vehicle was seen charging across the landscape as Captain Scarlet raced to keep an appointment with destruction. In every home across the country, eager fingers flicked the TV switch to ITV. As the sky grew dark, anxious eyes fastened on shimmering blue screen, waiting for Captain Scarlet to take his first fateful walk down that mean dark alley.

One Man Fate has made Indestructible

Captain Scarlet is like no Supermarionation hero that has gone before. Scott Tracy and Troy Tempest are both brave and intelligent but the success of their missions depends on the superior technology of the machines they pilot. Captain Scarlet succeeds, not because of his Spectrum Pursuit Vehicle or Spectrum Passenger Jet, but because the Mysterons have made him indestructible. Yet even before he joined Spectrum, Captain Scarlet was unique. Under his real name of Paul Metcalfe, he was the youngest Colonel in the World Army Air Force, trained to pilot a variety of aircraft and expert with hundreds of weapons, from the latest Ultrasonic Bazooka to the ancient Bundi dagger. Drilled to survive in the toughest of conditions, Metcalfe demonstrated a mental resilience which coupled with his humour and concern for others made him a prime candidate for Spectrum.

Under his codename of Captain Scarlet, Paul Metcalfe is Spectrum's top agent. In 'The Launching', Colonel White obviously feels that Scarlet can be the most diplomatic of the Captains, as he is sent to convince America's President Roberts of the danger of the Mysteron threat. However, 'Lunarville 7' shows that Scarlet's single-mindedness can sometimes override his subtlety, when he makes it very clear to the Lunar Controller's assistant that he is interested in the mysterious Humboldt Sea.

In 'White As Snow', and 'Treble Cross', Colonel White offers Scarlet the chance to command Spectrum in his absence. In Colonel White's eyes, Scarlet has only one great failing,

underlined in 'Flight to Atlantica' when he says, 'As usual, Captain, you were too impetuous.' Evidence for White's assessment is seen in 'Treble Cross' when he pre-empts the Colonel's order and announces that he and Blue will fly to Slaton air base, while in 'White As Snow' he is openly critical of White's decision to destroy the incoming satellite and makes no attempt to disguise his distaste. However, he is prepared to admit that he was wrong and risks his career in order to make amends. But whatever his personality may be it was the Mysterons who changed Captain Scarlet

Captain Scarlet may be wounded, but even as the SPJ ejector seat floats to earth, his body is rapidly repairing itself.

From behind his computerised desk, Colonel White briefs his two top agents.

and inadvertently made him more than human; a weapon every bit as powerful as the Thunderbird machines or Stingray!

The origin and powers of the Mysterons are still unknown. The first Captain Scarlet annual, written while the series was in production, speculates that the Mysterons were actually a 'strange race of people from an unknown galaxy' who landed upon Mars, and settled there, with computers 'planning constructing and running their city for them'. The annual continues to speculate that the Mysterons eventually tired of Mars and took off again in their spaceships, leaving their city of computers behind them. This intriguing scenario is slightly contradicted by *The Mysterons*, a comic strip published in *TV Tornado* from September 1967 onwards. To make the job of the

Red planet Mars: home of the Mysteron menace.

illustrator easier, the comic strip implies that the Mysterons are actually formless beings controlled by a giant computer, who rapidly take on their 'ancient, Mysteron shape' when exposed to alien atmospheres and environments.

These two contrasting theories highlight the fact that no one was completely certain what the Mysterons were. However, the evidence of the TV series suggests that intelligences on Mars were actually called the Mysterons. The pilot episode opens on a Martian Excursion Vehicle crewed by World Space Patrol officers under the command of Spectrum's Captain Black. His mission is to find the source of strange radio signals detected on Earth, and in an ancient valley it is revealed: a shimmering, opalescent city which glows against the rocks like a giant pinball machine. Inside the

Mysteron moonbase: built by robots, it showed no signs of life.

city, lights pulsate behind the walls as a sleek, piston-like device pumps rhythmically up and down. A deep, unearthly voice echoes around the complex: 'The first of the Earth travellers have arrived. Like us they have a curiosity about the Universe in which we live. We must take a closer look at them.'

If the Mysterons purposely transmitted the signals in order to lure intelligent life to Mars, they obviously underestimated man's capacity for trust. As the Mysterons take that 'closer look' at the MEV, the crew mistake the panning cameras for weapons and assume that they're about to be attacked. Captain Black gives the order to open fire, and whether through an extremely destructive missile, or a direct hit on a power source, the city is turned into a wasteland within seconds.

As the dust clears, an automatic device grinds into action, shining a glittering green light over the wreckage. Before the eyes of the astonished Earthmen, the complex re-materialises. The Mysteron voice vows revenge for this act of aggression and announces that one of the MEV crew will become their agent. The cameras close in on Captain Black, his eyes now dark and lifeless.

This opening sequence suggests that the Mysterons cannot or will not move outside their city. Although the Mysterons employ robot vehicles to build and defend their moonbase in 'Lunarville 7' and 'Crater 101', the pre-programmed vehicles are easily outwitted by electronics genius Lieutenant Green. Since the completed Mysteron moonbase shows no signs of intelligence this raises the question of why the Mysterons should physically build a city on the Moon when they had already taken control of Lunarville 7. The Mysteron complex displays a number of features (such as an hypnotic screen and an anti-gravity shaft) designed for humans plus a power source which is easily identified and removed. This suggests that the entire moonbase was just a giant 'rat trap' designed to test the intelligence and ingenuity of the Spectrum personnel.

The answers are never revealed in the TV series, but it seems most likely that the Mysterons are a form of Artificial Intelligence which has evolved into something more than mechanical yet less than human. This would explain the apparent petulance of their decision to exterminate an entire race in return for an attack by three men.

Blue and Green watch
Captain Scarlet remove the
power source of the
Mysteron's lunar complex.

As for the powers of the Mysterons, these are graphically demonstrated in the pilot episode as Captain Brown and Captain Scarlet speed to the defence of the World President. The Mysterons can transmit raw energy across space, using this energy to manipulate the timing mechanism of a nuclear bomb, take control of a speeding lorry or, in the pilot episode, blow out the tyre of Scarlet and Brown's saloon car.

In the crash which follows, the two green haloes which will become the Mysteron signature drift across the bloodied bodies of Captains Brown and Scarlet. Just as the beam of light from a photocopier passes over a picture, registering the different light and dark areas of the image, so the Mysteron scanners probe deep into the microscopic structure of the two men. Every twist and turn of their molecular structure is transmitted back to Mars and translated into the bio-mechanical code of the Mysterons. Just as computers can add colour to black and white movies, or reconstruct photographs that have been blemished by age, the Mysterons can piece together the molecular structure of people and objects, even if they have been destroyed.

In less time than it takes to blink an eye, the Mysterons have changed the molecular structure of Scarlet and Brown, and transmitted the information back to Earth. Just as a photocopier needs paper and ink to print out an image, the Mysterons use the raw energy they can transmit to create duplicates of Scarlet and Brown.

These doppelgangers are identical in appearance to Scarlet and Brown, and like spies who have learned the life-story of a close friend, they can imitate the original exactly. However, their minds are activated by a Mysteron control signal, carrying operating instructions for the body and a fanatical devotion to the cause of the Mysterons. This control signal also enables the fake Scarlet to decode the extra-sensory communications signal radiated by his fellow Mysterons, making it possible for Scarlet to receive instructions from Captain Black many miles away.

When the Mysterons create a duplicate, they give him, her or it the power of retro-metabolism. All living beings have the power to grow new skin or mend broken bones over a period of time, but Mysteron duplicates can quickly repair any damage or wounds, even ones which would be fatal in a human. The energy needed to repair the wounds is collected through the skin of the Mysteron and stored within its cells in much the same way that a plant collects the energy from sunlight and converts it into a more useful form. Unlike a plant, the Mysteron doppelgangers can release this stored energy in a single violent burst, as Captain Brown demonstrates when he literally explodes beside the World President. In the pilot episode, Colonel White assumes that Brown was carrying a bomb, but by 'Point 783' Spectrum have deduced that the Mysterons can literally self-destruct.

The duplicate Captain Scarlet manages to kidnap the World President just before the body of the original Captain Scarlet is discovered. This untidy habit of leaving bodies and wreckage

Every move you make: Captain Black co-ordinates another mission for his Mysteron masters.

behind becomes such an Achilles' heel for the Mysterons that it is easy to suspect that the Mysterons are simply playing with the Earthmen by leaving clues behind. Yet the fact that Captain Scarlet's body is found so quickly also underlines the question of what happened to Captain Black's earthly remains.

Captain Black was taken over by the Mysterons as he sat in the control cabin of the MEV. Yet Black was not apparently duplicated. Subsequent episodes reveal that he stayed with the Zero X ship until it reached Earth. The next time he is seen in the pilot episode, Black is pallid and unshaven and his American accent has been replaced by the uninflected tones of the Mysterons. Could Captain Black still be alive under Mysteron control? Certainly, when Lieutenant Dean suggests a quick escape after destroying the Mysteron City, the real Captain Black insists that they go down and survey the ruins. Wouldn't it be a monumental punishment for someone with such assurance and self-control to be conscious but unable to stop his body from carrying out the misdeeds of the Mysterons?

It seems clear, in episodes such as 'Fire at Rig 15', that Black's body has been altered in some way; he acts as a conduit for the ultrasonic rays which knock out Jason Smith, and also displays a phosphorescent effect when the lights are turned out. Yet in most episodes, Captain Black is simply carrying out the assassinations which create new Mysteron slaves (usually by shooting or causing car accidents) and then 'relaying the instructions of the Mysterons'. Significantly, though, Black never puts himself in physical danger. On the rare occasions when he is about to be captured, ('Model Spy' and 'Heart of New York') the Mysterons simply teleport him and his automobile out of the scene. Could it be that Captain Black, alone among the Mysteron agents, is not indestructible? Perhaps the reason that no body was found in the MEV is that this is still the original Captain Black.

In theory then, all Mysterons are indestructible. So why do they always die when their missions fail? The explanation seems to be that the Mysterons shut off their control signal. If the duplicate is of a car or helicopter, it simply rolls to a halt or crashes. Subsequent episodes establish that electricity is the only sure way to kill a

Mysteron. 'Flight 104' shows Scarlet and Blue gaining control of a Mysteron-controlled jet when an electric power station cuts off the control signal from Mars. Of course, an electric pulse can damage a Mysteron just as it would (fatally) damage a human, but electricity will also block the control signal of the Mysteron. The importance of Spectrum's Electron Gun, therefore, lies not in its capacity to kill a Mysteron, but in its ability to prevent the dead Mysteron from being regenerated. Without the control signal, the Mysteron dies, unable to activate its fantastic powers of retro-metabolism. So it seems that, if a duplicate fails in its mission, its Mysteron masters simply abandon it. They turn off the control signal and leave it to die.

Yet Captain Scarlet was different. As he failed in his mission and fell 800 feet from the Car-Vu Tower, the Mysterons cut his control signal. Any other duplicate would have fallen to the ground and been instantly killed. Captain Scarlet did not, and the reason for this seems to lie in an oversight by the Mysterons.

Can electricity kill a Mysteron? Spectrum's Intelligence Agency devised this electron gun in *Spectrum Strikes Back* but for the rest of the series, bullets worked just as well.

Black's cat: Mysteronised fashion model Helga is a perfect duplicate of the original. Even during a kidnap she keeps her best side to the camera.

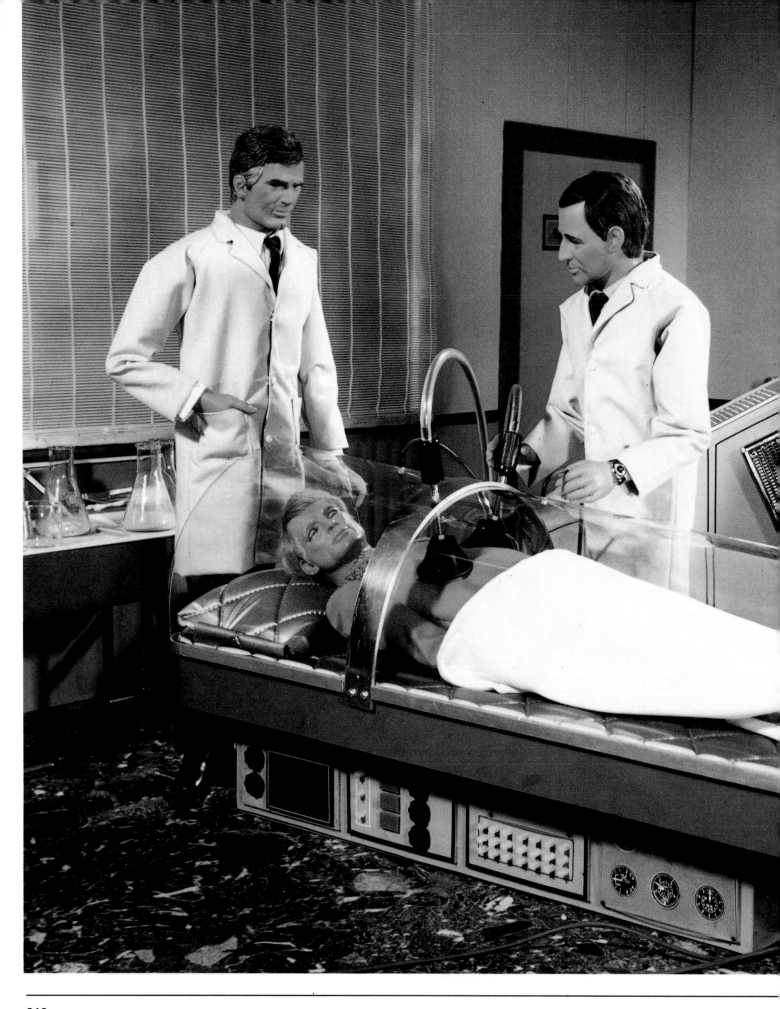

A resuscitation machine preserves a fragment of Major Gravener's consciousness in *Treble Cross*.

The 'Treble Cross' episode demonstrates that it is not necessary for the human to be dead when he is scanned by the Mysterons. (Although Major Gravener is comatose, and referred to as 'dead' in the episode, it is obvious that he has not actually died. Even a few seconds without oxygen will damage the human brain forever, but there are several recorded instances of people who 'drowned', like Major Gravener, but were saved by the Mammalian Diving Response, which automatically slows down the heartbeat and channels oxygen to the brain. One woman even recovered in a mortuary after having been pronounced 'dead' on the slab.)

What the Mysterons need is a person who is unconscious and unable to think. Captain Scarlet illustrates the problems the Mysterons face when they do duplicate someone who is not dead or unconscious. As Scarlet tells Doctor Fawn in 'Winged Assassin', his final memories after the car crash are of the flames closing in on his body as he lay beside the wreckage. To be precise, those are the final memories of the original Captain Scarlet. As the Mysterons scanned his body, Scarlet was still struggling to survive, deep within the recesses of his mind. Because his mind was still active, that struggle was part of the information copied by the Mysterons. Although they altered the physical structure of the new Captain Scarlet, they failed to notice that the original mind was being copied along with the memories and personality. Just as computers can create a default program which takes over the machine when no other program is running, so Scarlet's mind lay dormant within the brain of the Mysteron doppelganger, waiting to be awoken.

As the duplicate lay shattered on the ground after the fall from the Car-Vu, the real Captain Scarlet's will took over where it had left off, desperately trying to survive and activating the regenerative powers of its strange new body.

Captain Scarlet is indestructible, but this does not make him a superman. It's not surprising that he still sounds uncertain as he and Blue debate ramming the wheels of a speeding jet with the SPV (Spectrum Pursuit Vehicle), in 'Winged Assassin'. 'That'd be suicide!' rasps Blue. 'For you, yes,' says Scarlet, 'For me . . .?' Still only half convinced of his powers, he pulls the switch which will eject Blue from the SPV. It's a measure of his bravery that Scarlet is willing to gamble his life on the basis of one diagnosis from Doctor Fawn. Even when he knows that he is indestructible, he is not immune to pain and feels every cut, graze and bullet wound. Of course, even though it seems likely that electricity would not kill Captain Scarlet (because he does not need the Mysteron control signal to keep him alive) he is understandably wary of putting this theory to the test. In 'Noose of Ice', when told that the Eskimo Booster station churns out 100,000 volts, Scarlet muses 'dangerously high'. He does, none the less, chase the Mysteron saboteur into the Booster station, thus 'endangering' himself.

Despite the gifts that the Mysterons have inadvertently given him, Captain Scarlet is still the hero because of the way he uses those gifts. Each episode of the series reveals a little more about the physiology of the Mysterons. Scarlet's body can hold energy in reserve for mending wounds, so it comes as little surprise that he also needs very little sleep, prowling the night-time corridors in 'Lunarville 7', 'Inferno' and 'Shadow of Fear'.

More perplexing is the Mysteron reaction to X-rays revealed in 'Operation Time'. Obviously the process referred to as 'X-raying' is far in advance of even today's science because in 'Spectrum Strikes Back' this 'X-ray Camera' is used in much the same way as a conventional Polaroid (to take an X-ray picture, the subject must be placed between the film and the radiation source since the X-rays have to pass through the subject). It appears that the 'X-ray machines' are actually an improvement on today's process of Nuclear Magnetic Resonance, which causes the molecules of the body to emit radiation.

Like a walking solar battery, Captain Scarlet is constantly recharging himself from the sun's rays, ready for his next duel with death.

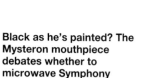

Black as he's painted? The Mysteron mouthpiece debates whether to microwave Symphony Angel.

Whatever the physics behind it, this 'X-ray machine' is used to take pictures of a human skull prior to brain surgery. When a Mysteron accidentally places his hand on the patient, some side-effect of the retro-metabolic process causes the picture of his hand to gradually turn positive. In 'Spectrum Strikes Back', a Mysteron Detector is developed which takes an 'X-ray' picture of humans and a positive picture of Mysterons – including Captain Scarlet. Bizarre as it may sound, Captain Scarlet is also able to 'fog' a conventional camera in 'Flight 104', even though Captain Black is photographed without any strange side-effects in 'Manhunt'.

Disassociated from Mysteron control, Captain Scarlet is now unable to decipher the radiation from other Mysterons. Just as an ordinary phone receiver will pick up an unintelligible squawk from a Fax machine, the physical effect of the Mysteron radiation confuses Scarlet's body, creating a sensation similar to car sickness. It appears that some Mysterons are able to retune the frequency of their personal radiation, since Scarlet's 'sixth sense' doesn't always warn him of a Mysteron presence. Strangely though, Captain

Black appears unwilling to face Captain Scarlet, talking to him from behind a closed door in 'Special Assignment'.

It is noticeable that, although Captain Black often assassinates on the orders of the Mysterons, he refrains from killing when it is not entirely necessary. In 'Big Ben Strikes Again', for instance, he knocks out Macey, the driver of the nuclear transporter, even though this means the man is soon at large and able to give Spectrum a valuable lead. An apparently sensitive aspect of his nature is shown in the episode 'Manhunt' when, having forced Symphony Angel into a radiation chamber, he apologises for what he has to do and assures her that the radiation will kill her within three minutes. Having set the process in motion, he seems uneasy as he watches the girl weaken, and turns the machine on to maximum output, as if to speed up the process. A few moments later, he shuts the machine off, explaining that 'Mysterons also have compassion'. An interesting revelation and, unless Black is trying to cover for some surviving human trait, a strong indication that the Mysterons are anything but the cold and pernicious minds they seem to be.

Spectrum is Green

Colonel White briefs Spectrum's elite of colour-coded officers in the Cloudbase conference room.

Cloudbase: Spectrum's solitary sentinel of the stratosphere.

Captain Scarlet may be Spectrum's top agent, but just what is Spectrum and why was it formed? The name of Spectrum was chosen to signify the fact that its agents are not limited to one area of operation (such as the sea or space) but instead cover the entire range of World Security just as the light spectrum spans the complete range of colours.

Spectrum answers only to the World President, James Younger, who is the head of the World Government. Although the nations of 21st-century Earth still have their own national leaders such as President Roberts of America, they are united by the World Senate, which sits at Unity City. Spanning the coral reefs of Bermuda, Unity City is a fusion-powered zone of such complexity that it is dubbed 'Futura City' by the locals.

Yet the world is not at peace. To the East of Europe lies Bereznik, a small but predatory state whose battalions of robot tanks present a constant menace to its neighbours. Below the pacific Ocean, Titan and his Aquaphibian hordes continue to threaten the surface world.

To combat these threats, the World Government has established Supreme Headquarters Earth Forces, which from its New York base controls four unique defence agencies around the globe. The World Navy and World Aquanaut Security Patrol protect the oceans, while the World Army Air Force co-ordinates the air and land defences of member nations.

The World Space Patrol is responsible for the defence and exploration of Earth's borders, and controls several specialised divisions. The XK

Fleet provides a shuttle service to the commercial Moonbases, while for longer journeys the WSP turns to its nuclear-powered Zero-X craft which have the extensive life-support systems needed for long-distance missions. The WSP also maintains the XL squadron based at Space City Atoll in the Pacific. Because the faster-than-light engines of the XL ships are extremely expensive to operate the ships are mainly used for emergencies and journeys to the edge of Earth's solar system, beyond the range of virtually all XK and Zero-X ships.

Unfortunately, these agencies, together with the World Police Corps and Universal Secret Service, were and are hampered by legal and diplomatic regulations. At a meeting of the World Security Council in January 2065, the Supreme Commander of Earth Forces put forward the idea of a new organisation. Capable of swift intelligence gathering and even faster reaction, the unnamed agency would have full police powers, both on Earth and in space. As the World President began preparing the authorisation for this unnamed organisation, a committee was appointed to bring it to life. Working from an empty office above the Dewar-Elf shopping mall in Unity City, the seven men and women, whose identities are hidden to this day, spent months on end sifting through personnel files to locate the ideal candidates.

By the autumn of 2065, the committee had selected Charles Gray, a former admiral in the World Navy, as leader of the new organisation. Working from plans drawn up by a civilian

engineering genius, the committee used several anonymous 'shell' companies to commission the individual components of Cloudbase, the unique floating headquarters of the new agency. The finished parts were then secretly shuttled out to an abandoned Weather Satellite where engineers from the WSP and WAAF were waiting to assemble the pre-fabricated sections. Supervising the construction was Conrad Turner, a WSP Colonel who had been one of the unnamed organisation's first recruits – and one of their best. Working in the zero gravity of space, Turner pushed his crew to finish Cloudbase in record time. All that was needed now was to move Cloudbase down into Earth's atmosphere.

As Colonel Turner triggered the chemical rockets Cloudbase blasted free from the weather satellite. The forces of gravity quickly began to rattle and shake the massive structure as it plummeted towards the Pacific Ocean. Finally, the hurricane force of the Hover Combine engines began to slow Cloudbase's fall until it stabilised at forty thousand feet.

During 2066 Cloudbase was equipped, the prototype Angel Interceptors were delivered, and the five women pilots chosen to fly them were

selected and trained. By the summer of 2067, Spectrum was fully manned, fully equipped and ready to roll. Finally, after long negotiations with his fellow politicians, the World President was able to sign the Charter which gave Spectrum official recognition.

Most of Spectrum's agents work, undercover, at the worldwide network of camouflaged Spectrum Ground Bases. Occasionally a Cloudbase officer will come to collect a Spectrum Pursuit Vehicle, and when the agent is satisfied with their identification, he or she will push the button which unveils the SPV. Whether hidden behind the sliding wall of a casino, or inside an oil storage tank, the SPV is soon hurtling into action.

Developed from the Zeus Combat Tank, the SPV is Spectrum's most remarkable and vital piece of land-based hardware. For use in cases of extreme emergency, the SPV provides Spectrum agents with a fast and virtually unstoppable means of transport. With its roof-mounted dorsal-fin and sleek, streamlined body, the SPV resembles a bizarre, road-travelling shark. Armed to the teeth and with a top speed of 200 mph, it is a fearsome adversary; just like a Rottweiler never letting go of its prey.

Spectrum is environmentally friendly: even when converted to a jet-pack, the SPV power unit works on hydrogen and oxygen and produces no harmful emissions.

As its name and design imply, the SPV comes into its own when used in the pursuit of an otherwise unstoppable quarry. In 'Winged Assassin', for example, Captain Scarlet chases the Mysteronised DT19 Stratojet along the runway at London Airport, before ramming his SPV into the plane's undercarriage. A slower vehicle would have been unable to match the aircraft's speed; while anything less durable could not have withstood the incredible friction generated as it chafed against the jet's rapidly spinning tyres.

Another example of the SPV's structural strength can be seen in 'Point 783' when, during a clash with the Unitron Combat Tank, both vehicles plummet over the edge of a desert canyon, crashing on to the rocky ground hundreds of feet below. Considered by the army to be their ultimate weapon, the Unitron it totally destroyed by the impact, whilst the SPV remains virtually unscratched and undamaged.

Should a more conventional form of attack be required a powerful retractable cannon is housed beneath a sliding hatch, located in the nose of the vehicle. Capable of delivering explosive missiles with computer-guided accuracy, the awesome destructive power of this weapon can be seen during the closing moments of 'The Trap', when Captain Blue unleashes a volley of shots which completely destroy Glengarry Castle.

Access to the SPV is gained through two hermetically sealed hatches, which slide outwards and inwards on a telescopic ram. Once inside, the most incredible feature of the SPV's design becomes apparent. For extra safety during a crash, both the driver's and co-driver's seats face towards the rear of the vehicle; forward visibility is gained by means of a high-definition television monitor. This unique set-up is shown to have just one major drawback, when, in 'Codename Europa', a Mysteron agent causes an SPV to crash by disrupting the TV signal with an electronic jamming device. In an emergency both seats, fitted with rockets, can be ejected through the roof of the vehicle. Once a safe height has been achieved, in-built parachutes are deployed.

Situated in the floor, between the two seats, is a sliding hatch giving access to the SPV's portable hydrogenic power unit. As soon as the power pack is removed, the main six-wheel drive shuts down, and the four smaller wheels (powered by an emergency battery) take over. The driver then selects an option from the keyboard situated beside the steering console. Easily removed, the power unit can be adapted quickly into anything from a sea-sled to a power-drill. Whatever option is chosen, the on-board computer quickly delivers the components needed to adapt the power pack. The most frequently used option is the one-man jet-thruster pack, which is put to good use firstly by Captain Blue in 'The Mysterons' and then by Captain Scarlet in such episodes as 'The Trap' and 'Expo 2068'. It should be noted that each SPV carries five different helmets corresponding to the colours of the five Spectrum Cap-

tains. Since the on-board computer demands an identification code from the officer who keys in a selection, it is immediately able to deliver a Scarlet helmet to Captain Scarlet or a Blue helmet to Captain Blue.

One intriguing feature of the SPV was the set of rear-mounted caterpillar tracks which, according to the 1967 annual, allowed it to climb mountains by tilting back into a vertical position. Anyone sitting inside would have literally hung from their rear facing seat if this manoeuvre had been attempted, and Derek Meddings, who designed the SPV, has recently confirmed that the tracks were intended to flip down for extra traction.

Piloted by Melody Angel, a Spectrum helicopter tracks a Mysteron agent across the Himalaya.

Whether inside or outside the SPV, each Spectrum officer is in constant contact with Cloudbase through the personal computer stored in the epaulettes of his or her uniform. If the officer receives a message from Colonel White, the epaulettes flash on and off, at the same time emitting an infra-red beam which activates the microphone and speakers situated in the officer's cap. The other standard item of equipment is the Spectrum blaster, carried in the waist holster. This Combustion Augmented Plasma gun carries a magazine of sixteen shots. Each cartridge is packed with liquid propellant and is fired by an electronic pulse from the battery in the handle.

If the Spectrum agent is out of bullets and his SPV has crashed, he can still call upon the Spectrum Auxiliary. From Maximum Security Centres such as Vandon Base, they can despatch a battalion of armed guards or Radar Tracking Vans manned by trained operators. The Spectrum Auxiliary also maintains a fleet of fast-moving vehicles for the use of Spectrum agents. To provide Spectrum agents with a fast, efficient means of transport for use during routine operations, Spectrum developed the unique, wedge-shaped Spectrum Saloon Car. Fitted with racing tyres and a roof-mounted stabilising fin, the cars are capable of speeds in excess of 150 miles per hour and incorporate a sturdy roll cage, the central rib of which runs the entire length of the car, dividing the windscreen and ending in a strengthened nose buffer, which can be used to ram enemy vehicles.

The five-seater Saloon Car is used frequently during the series, both as a patrol car and an

Spectrum saloon car: overhead shot highlights the liquid crystal windscreens which can turn opaque at the touch of a button.

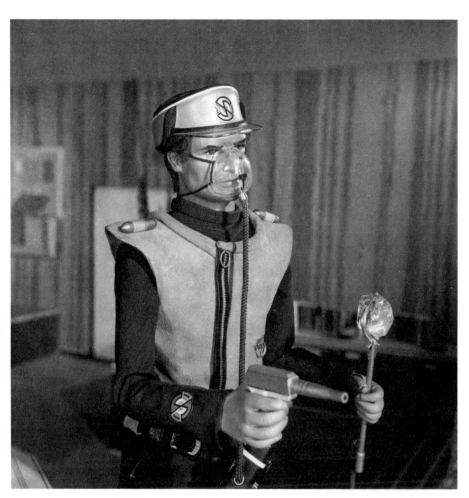

Under pressure: Captain Ochre grabs a respirator before blasting open one of the protective portholes in Cloudbase. Decompression could kill him before the bomb in his hand explodes!

passenger cabin is virtually indestructible, the truck section is not. Due to the hazardous nature of this assignment, the VIPC is usually driven by an experienced officer such as Captain Ochre.

Finally, from the roof-top hangars of the Maximum Security Centres, the Spectrum Auxiliary can launch their purpose-built helicopters. Although primarily used for transport, the Spectrum helicopter is equipped with a rapid-fire 20mm cannon at the front of the cockpit. The tough Maylon skids are capable of landing in any land or sea conditions, while the ring-shaped tail gives stability at speeds of up to 302 miles per hour. The tremendous power of its twin-turbo jets gives the Spectrum helicopter the lift it needs to reach Cloudbase.

Floating seven miles above sea level, Cloudbase is the nerve centre of Spectrum. It functions around the clock, with its crew of six hundred working constant four-hour shifts. To combat fatigue, Cloudbase employs the Room of Sleep, an hypnotic chamber with diffused lighting and 'weightless' gimbal-slung couches which make it possible for Cloudbase operatives to cram eight hours sleep into thirty minutes.

Being so close to the Sun, Cloudbase is ideally located for solar power. Most of Cloudbase's surface area is covered by non-reflective photovoltaic cells which capture the Sun's rays and convert them into electricity. This is directed to the twenty liquid Cahelium engines which power the four hover-combines. The combines keep Cloudbase afloat by sucking air in through the horizontal ducts and then circulating it at great pressure. The air is then blown out an an angle, creating a cushion of air upon which Cloudbase rests. Although this must seem an astounding achievement to 20th-century eyes, the combines are still not operating at their full capacity. Extra reserves of power can be called upon to generate horizontal jets. Working in conjunction with the fan-rudder located on the stern, these jets can move Cloudbase's position above the Earth.

Despite being inside the Earth's atmosphere, Cloudbase is built on similar principles to a space station, since it must operate within extremes of low temperature, low air pressure and high cosmic radiation. Cloudbase is pressurised and can only be entered through air locks. If a hole was knocked in the hull of Cloudbase, the air would

integral part of any Spectrum roadblock or Motorcade. Easily identifiable, the car bears the distinctive Spectrum emblem on both doors and, like the Ferrari, is available exclusively in a startling shade of red.

When Spectrum has advance warning of an attack, however, they roll out the Maximum Security Vehicle. This grey, armadillo-shaped vehicle is pressurised with its own internal life-support system. Designed to survive the toughest assault, the MSV has bullet-proof twin tyres and a shell which sandwiches a radiation-damping alloy between a steel interior and an armour plate exterior. Although its portholes may appear to offer a tempting target for a Mysteron sniper, they are actually made from high-density boro-silicate which is impervious to both bullets and radiation.

Despite the strength of the MSV it is often used for decoy duties to draw attention away from the Very Important Personnel Carrier. Disguised as a petrol tanker, the VIPC is equipped with a luxurious, bomb-proof passenger cabin, Although this

quickly rush out, carrying people and furniture with it. For this reason, most of the rooms in Cloudbase are windowless. Those areas which do contain windows, such as the rooftop promenade deck, employ a toughened glass which is also designed to filter out ultraviolet rays. In addition, face mask respirators are stored within recesses at regular intervals throughout the base. If Cloudbase should be damaged beyond repair, every crew member is within sixty seconds' sprinting distance of one of the many gyroscopic escape capsules which are clamped on to all the emergency exits.

Cloudbase is constantly patrolled by small, tracked robots which both clean and inspect every inch of its interior. Even the flight deck is regularly swabbed by the robots in order to remove potentially hazardous oil leaks and vented jet fuel. Signals from the robots are relayed back to the control centre, just behind the observation tubes in the bridge section.

The control room is entered through a green sliding door, beneath which is a moving walkway that leads directly to Colonel White's desk. Beside the walkway is Lieutenant Green's control console, a glass display screen at least fifteen feet long. All incoming information is assessed by the console before being passed to the Spectrum Information Centre for recording. A digest of this information can be read direct from the light pattern display or paper print-outs. Diagrams and video pictures can also be displayed on the colour liquid crystal display screen behind Colonel White's desk.

Mounted on a steam-powered rotating platform (steam is another cheap source of energy on Cloudbase due to direct solar heating of water pipes) Colonel White's desk is a compact supercomputer running a program tailored to White's own personality. In any one minute, the desk can assess the hundreds of reports being relayed by Lieutenant Green's communications console and highlight those of special interest to the Colonel. By pressing the appropriate coloured button on his desk, Colonel White can instantly contact the

View into Cloudbase control room, as Colonel White surveys the observation tube.

As Cloudbase reels from the Mysteron attack, Colonel White prepares to go down with his command.

corresponding Spectrum Captain anywhere in the world. Voice recognition circuits within the computer react to Colonel White's verbal commands by instantly withdrawing information stored at the Spectrum Information Centre and displaying it, either as a diagram or moving pictures, on the screen behind him.

Next door to the control room is the Spectrum Information Centre. Painted in warm pastel tones, this air-conditioned room is actually maintained at a constant chill to keep its complex of Seventh Generation computers from overheating. Although slower in operation than the control room computers, these 'super brains' are infinitely more powerful. Where most computers, however fast, can only work on the information they receive, the Seventh Generation computer is capable of intuitive thought based on incomplete information. Primitive in comparison to the Mysterons, these digital detectives are still a vital asset in Spectrum's attempts to outguess the enemy.

The far wall of the Spectrum Information Centre is a swirling, pulsating sea of colour – in fact, this wall-to-wall plastic shield contains the liquid plasma that is the physical store of verbal, digital and video reports transmitted by Spectrum ground stations.

Behind the Spectrum Information Centre is the Observation Room, a mass of telescanners, lasers, multi-spectral scanners and return-beam vidicons monitoring outer space and planet Earth. Radio altimeters keep a constant check on Cloudbase's height while the spectral irradiance monitor measures the intensity of solar radiation hitting Cloudbase. Information from the Observation Room is relayed back to Spectrum Information Centre and Lieutenant Green's control console.

Beneath the control deck is level C, which contains an Auxiliary Generator, the Circular Conference Room and the Sick Bay. The domain of Doctor Fawn is in effect a miniature hospital. Chemical analysers can perform complex blood tests within seconds, while the Auto-Pharmacist can synthesise anything from headache pills to a cure for snake-bites within fifteen minutes. Apart from the consulting room, the Sick Bay contains a fully equipped operating theatre, intensive care module, isolation ward and an electronics lab in which Doctor Fawn experiments on his development of robot surgeons.

Lieutenant Green controls Cloudbase and much of Spectrum from this one communications computer.

Below the bridge the two hollow support struts contain ventilated escalator units which carry Spectrum staff down into the flight deck. The escalators terminate inside the two nearest hover-combines, which are insulated against the tremendous noise of the engines. Here the staff must transfer to another of the moving walkways which criss-cross Cloudbase. At the far end of Deck E is the Amber Room, duty station for the Angels. Like the recreation room that is shared by both the Angels and Spectrum Captains, the Amber Room contains a mass of entertainment equipment which helps pass the hours in between alerts. As Spectrum's first line of defence, the five pilots work continuous four-hour shifts. Each Angel takes her turn as Angel leader, stationed permanently in Angel One, ready for immediate take-off. During change-overs, a red light flashes on Lieutenant Green's console if Angel One is unmanned for more than sixty seconds.

A launch alert automatically fires up the engines of Angel One, and the jet is hurled forward by a steam catapult running below the surface of the flight deck. Down below in the Amber Room, the two remaining Angels take their seats in the recessed elevator. The opaque glass shield slides shut forming a pressure seal, and the elevator rides up towards an airlock on the next level. At this point, a computerised switch-back takes over, moving the Angels sideways to positions beneath the two remaining aircraft (a third track leads forwards towards the position of Angel One, which is boarded by the same elevator). Here, they enter pressurised glass chutes which extend up through the flight deck and lock on to the entrance hatches located in the base of the Angel jets. As the air pressure within the chutes and jets is equalised, the pilots are raised up and locked into position within the cockpit. The chutes retract and the jet engines fire automatically as the catapults launch the Angels forward into space.

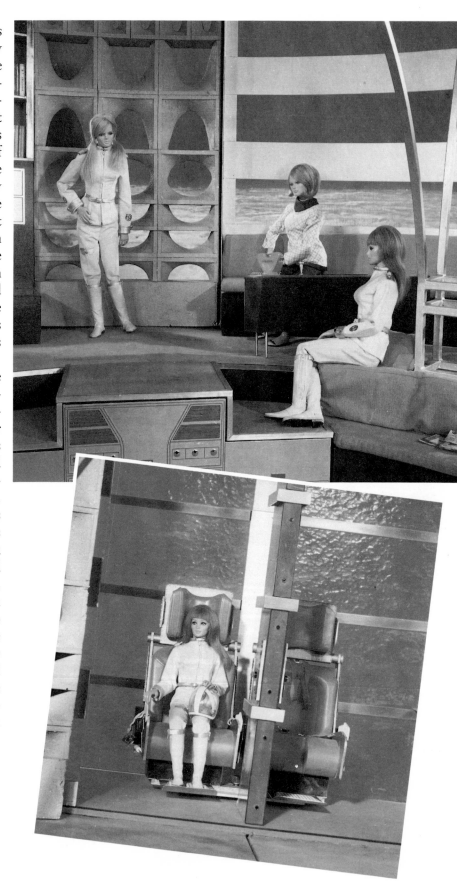

The Amber Room: Destiny, Symphony and Rhapsody Angels relax.

Rhapsody Angel in the elevator seat, ready to begin her four hours stand-by duty in Angel One.

Based on the World Army Air Force Viper Jet, the Angel interceptors are designed for supersonic combat. The needle-sharp nose contains sophisticated proton navigation systems which are linked to the on-board computer. Flight information is projected on to a transparent green screen facing the pilot. Armed with a 9mm cannon and five Seraph missiles, the Angels fly on JP12 fuel, processed exclusively by Spectrum's refinery at Bensheba. Launched horizontally for speed, the Angels are also equipped with Vertical Take Off and Landing jets which are vital to the Cloudbase landing procedure.

Locking on to a microwave beam projected from Cloudbase, the Angel 'rides' the beam down towards the flight deck. At the rear of the deck is a magnetic 'trap' raised hydraulically into a vertical position (this should not be confused with the large directional fan at the other end of Cloudbase). Guided by her on-board computer, the pilot triggers her landing jets and steers towards the 'trap'. As the jet is magnetically captured, the platform quickly lowers into a horizontal position. From here, magnetic pulleys drag the ship forward as the trap rises to receive the next incoming Angel.

Elevators can carry the Angel ship down into the maintenance hangar where each jet has its own individual team of 'whitejackets' – technicians and robots who carry out regular 24-hour checks. Replacement Angel interceptors are also stored and maintained in this hanger, so that Cloudbase always has at least three Angels ready to launch. Beyond the maintenance hanger is the insulated fuel dump, where the highly combustible JP12 is stored. Regular supplies are ferried in from Bensheba by a conventional WAAF tanker, and fed in through a pump nozzle in the hangar wall.

Beyond the fuel dump is the duty hangur, which acts as a base for the Spectrum Passenger Jet. Based on an original design by Universal Aerospace, the SPJ, with a range of twelve thousand miles, is the main method of transport to and from Cloudbase. When Captains Scarlet and Blue must leave on an urgent mission, they taxi the SPJ out of the duty hangar and through an airlock on to the main flight deck. Up above, Angels Two and Three may still be taking off from their own flight deck. Once the Angels have cleared Spectrum air-space, the pilot triggers the twin reheat engines of the Spectrum Passenger Jet. As the jet moves forward, the nose-wheel prop is caught by the shuttle of a steam catapult which compresses the strut into a 'kneeling' position. As the jet engines fire, the catapult hurls the plane forward and the energy in the compressed nose strut is released, guiding the nose of the SPJ up into the correct take-off position.

As the SPJ flies up and away from Cloudbase, the pilot signs off in Spectrum Code: Spectrum Is Red, if something has gone wrong, or more usually, when everything is proceeding according to plan, Spectrum is Green. SIG!

Mysteronised Angel jets dive over French fields.

THE UNITED COLOURS

OF ANDERSON

With attention shifted away from space-craft and onto characters, *Captain Scarlet and the Mysterons* had the largest regular cast of any Supermarionation series. The characters were not given a complex history, even though the series was the first to be tied in with the 'Anderson world' devised by *TV21*. As Alan Fennell explains, it was left to Angus Allan, Tod Sullivan and other staff working on the annuals to devise a past for the Spectrum agents. 'The film people were more concerned with the visual side, so they didn't have time to produce character profiles. Instead we'd get together round a table and decide where each character should come from.'

Captain Scarlet

Captain Scarlet was born with the name Paul Metcalfe in Winchester in 2036. Metcalfe took degrees in Technology, History and Pure Mathematics at Winchester University before transferring to West Point Military Academy. He joined the World Army Air Force, where he quickly rose to the rank of Colonel. Metcalfe was headhunted by the committee assembling Spectrum in 2066, and assigned the codename of Captain Scarlet. The Captain Scarlet who stars in the TV series is a duplicate of the original, possessing his mind and memory but also indestructible. Scarlet is essentially an easy-going character, always a gentleman when informing the enemy that their plans have failed.

Captain Scarlet relaxes off-set.

Captain Blue

Scarlet's best friend in Spectrum is Captain Blue, whose real name is Adam Svenson. Born August 26th 2035 in Boston, Massachusetts, he is the eldest son of a wealthy financier. After winning a scholarship to Harvard University he disappointed his father by joining the World Aeronautic Society instead of the family firm. After progressing from Test Pilot to Security Officer, he volunteered to join Spectrum. Probably the most quick-witted of Spectrum's agents he is also the most cautious.

Bostonian Adam Svenson, Captain Blue to his workmates, is not only Captain Scarlet's partner, but also his best friend. He also has something of a soft spot for Symphony Angel.

Colonel White

Colonel White is the commander of Spectrum. A former admiral in the World Navy, his real name is Charles Gray. Born in London on July 14th 2017, Colonel White has an almost religious devotion to rules and procedure. Where the other puppets have individual 'smiling' heads, Colonel White has a 'slightly curling lip' head.

Lieutenant Green

Seymour Griffiths, better known as Lieutenant Green, the Cloudbase controller, was born in Trinidad on January 18th 2041. With degrees in Music, Telecommunications and Electrical Engineering, Griffiths joined the World Aquanaut Security Patrol as a hydrophones operator, before being promoted to Marineville's Control Centre. As the man who designed Cloudbase's communication systems, Lieutenant Green is normally too valuable to be assigned field duty. So when a case such as 'Lunarville 7' demands his acknowledged electronics expertise, Lieutenant Green is eager to volunteer.

Colonel White delivers another stirring monologue to Spectrum agents throughout the world from his computerised control desk.

Lieutenant Green (Seymour Griffiths) takes advantage of Colonel White's absence from the Control Room!

Rhapsody Angel

Although there are no female Captains in Spectrum, Cloudbase is protected by its team of women pilots – the Angels. Rather than colours, the Angels are codenamed by 'classical' or 'artistic' codenames. Rhapsody Angel is Dianne Simms. Born in Chelsea on April 20th 2043, she studied Law and Sociology at London University. After working for a solicitor in Manchester she joined Airways Light Freight Agency in Norfolk as a pilot. According to the Angels strip in *Lady Penelope* comic, ALFA went bust and Dianne's last job was to deliver a package to a deserted airfield in Italy. There she meets girl pilots from all over the globe. A voice on a loudspeaker (later revealed to be Lieutenant Green) offers the pilots the chance to train as part of the Angels Air Display Team in their unmarked interceptors. They all accept because, as Dianne says, 'Even in the 21st Century, the best jobs still go to male pilots'.

Symphony Angel

Symphony Angel is Karen Wainwright. Born on January 6th 2042 in Cedar Rapids, Iowa, she joined the Universal Secret Service after graduating early from Yale University. After seven years' service, she resigned to join a small air charter company, from where Spectrum recruited her. As the most impulsive of the Angels, she is taken hostage during an attempt to capture Captain Black in 'Manhunt'. A romantic involvement with Captain Blue is hinted at once or twice during the series.

Destiny Angel

Destiny Angel – Juliette Pointon – was born in Paris on August 23rd 2040. Educated in Rome she later joined the World Army Air Force Intelligence Corps. After three years she resigned to set up her own firm of air freight contractors. Destiny is the most ruthless of the Angels, but the fact that she is called to make a formal identification of Captain Scarlet's body in the first episode suggests that they share a close relationship.

Harmony Angel

Harmony Angel (real name Chan Kwan) was born in Tokyo on June 19th 2042 to Chinese parents. After putting her degrees in Physics and Aerodynamics to practical use by establishing a world record for endurance flying, she took over her father's Air Taxi business.

Melody Angel

Melody Angel is Magnolia Jones. Born on January 10th 2043 in Atlanta, Georgia, she is one of the first black Supermarionation characters. An ex-World Army Air Force pilot, it is her insistence that she saw Goddard's plane hit by lightning that alerts Colonel White to the possibility of Mysteron activity.

Rhapsody Angel (Dianne Simms) relaxes with her fellow Angels in the Amber room. Hailing from 'swinging London' Rhapsody is, of course, sporting the latest Carnaby Street fashions.

Symphony Angel – American Karen Wainwright – is a cool and versatile pilot. Her impetuous nature, however, lands her in trouble on more than one occasion.

Melody Angel: Hailing from America's deep south, Magnolia Jones is a confident and meticulous pilot.

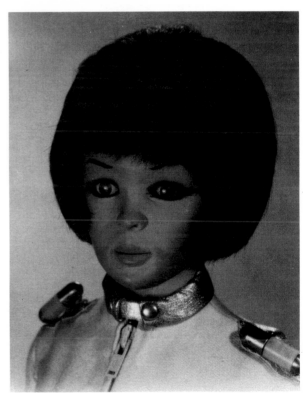

Parisian beauty Juliette Pointon (better known as Destiny Angel) displays a lust for adventure and often acts as Angel leader.

Harmony Angel – Oriental beauty Chan Kwan – is a Judo black belt, as well as being one of Spectrum's most accomplished pilots.

Captain Ochre

Captain Ochre was born Richard Fraser in Detroit on February 23rd 2035. The only Spectrum agent not to attend university, Fraser was turned down by the World Army Air Force because of his lack of formal qualifications. Joining the World Police Corps, Fraser learned to fly in his own time and also carved out a career as a crimebuster. Captain Ochre is more often in charge of personal protection, guarding Conrad Olafsson in 'Codename: Europa' and driving the VIP transporter in 'Dangerous Rendezvous'.

Captain Grey

Captain Grey is the oldest of the Spectrum agents. Born Bradley Holden in Chicago on March 4th 2033, he trained in the World Navy before joining the fledgling World Aquanaut Security Patrol as a Security Commander. Captain Grey is usually seen providing back-up in a variety of Spectrum vehicles, but in 'Winged Assassin' Grey takes centre stage when he saves the Director General of the United Asian Republic from a stealthy Mysteron sniper.

As Captain Ochre, former police chief Richard Fraser specialises in personal security.

Sean Connery lookalike Bradley Holden is better known to his Spectrum colleagues as Captain Grey.

Captain Magenta

Captain Magenta was born in Dublin in 2034 as Patrick Donaghue. His parents emigrated to a tough district of New York when he was only three but despite great poverty he eventually won a scholarship to Yale University. As a student he was briefly jailed for his part in a riot against the totalitarian state of Bereznik, but managed to graduate with degrees in Physics, Electrical Engineering and Information Technology. His first job as a computer programmer offered few challenges and Donaghue turned to crime. However, the Committee which created Spectrum recognised his essential strength of character and offered him the chance to redeem himself. So far, he seems to have justified their gamble. In 'Operation Time' it is Magenta who deciphers the cryptic Mysteron riddle, while in 'Lunarville 7' and 'Crater 101' he replaces the electronics genius, Lieutenant Green, as communications controller.

Doctor Fawn

Whilst on Cloudbase, Edward Wilkie is better known as Doctor Fawn – Spectrum's chief medical officer. Born in Yalumba, Australia on July 10th 2031, he is the son of a famous specialist. After studying medicine at Brisbane University he joined the World Medical Organisation, where he developed the Autonurses seen in *Stingray* episodes.

Captain Black

Officially listed as absent without leave from Spectrum, Captain Black's official file gives his identity as that of Manchester-born orphan Conrad Turner. The biography states that he was raised by a distant relative and received little affection as a child. Despite excelling at college and university, Turner never learned how to display emotion. In 2047 Turner was seriously disfigured by a bomb explosion, while trying to save a British WAAF base from a booby-trap. After his face was reconstructed by plastic surgeons, Turner transferred to the World Space Patrol, where he rose to command Fireball XL3. Yet Spectrum appears to be concealing a deeper mystery about Captain Black; despite being raised in Lancashire, Black's voice in the pilot episode is clearly that of an American.

A graduate of Yale University, Patrick Donaghue joined the Spectrum ranks as Captain Magenta.

Man or Mysteron? As one of Spectrum's top agents, Captain Black (Conrad Turner) was chosen to lead the doomed Zero X mission to Mars.

As the puppets were less caricatured in this series, the tendency was also towards more realistic voice portrayals. To play Captain Scarlet, Gerry Anderson chose Francis Matthews, who had recently played the hero of Hammer Films' *Dracula Prince of Darkness* (1966). Born in York, Francis Matthews had a well-established stage and TV career before Captain Scarlet. He starred as Ranjit Kasel opposite Ava Gardner in MGM's *Bhowani Junction* (1956) and played Peter Cushing's apprentice, Hans Kleve, in *The Revenge of Frankenstein* (1957).

Francis Matthews was not auditioned for the role of Scarlet. 'Gerry Anderson had heard me at some time doing an impersonation of Cary Grant and decided that was the voice he wanted for his new hero.' He recalls that although Gerry Anderson didn't move heaven and earth to get him he certainly came close to it. 'At the time of the first two recording sessions I had to be flown up and down to Manchester where I was appearing in Coward's *Private Lives*.' Presumably, this provoked Captain Scarlet's quip that, 'I wouldn't exactly call Manchester the Place of the Angels.'

Following Captain Scarlet, Francis Matthews played the BBC detective Paul Temple for four seasons. Although subsequently offered more action-adventure roles he turned them down, finally accepting 'with relief' a multiple role in Alan Plater's *Trinity Tales*, an update of the

When Cloudbase receives a glamorous guest, Scarlet, Blue and Symphony Angel find themselves entertaining one of their biggest fans!

Canterbury Tales for BBC 2. Since then, Francis Matthews has appeared in over 40 films, countless plays and the most recent series of Scottish Television's *Taggart*.

Captain Blue's voice was provided by New York-born Ed Bishop, whose first film role was opposite Steve McQueen in *The War Lover*. This was followed by two astronaut roles in *2001: A Space Odyssey* and *Mouse on the Moon*. Following *Captain Scarlet*, Ed Bishop went on to star as Commander Straker in Anderson's first live action series *UFO* (1970). Still much in demand as an actor, Ed Bishop has appeared in *The Mad Death* (BBC Scotland), *The Professionals* (LWT) and *Canned Carrott* (BBC), as well as playing Raymond Chandler's *Philip Marlowe* for BBC radio.

Donald Grey was the voice of Colonel White – and also the voice of Captain Black and the Mysterons. Born Eldred Tilbury in 1914, Donald Grey starred in the 1939 version of *The Four Feathers*, as one of the blood-and-thunder buddies who present John Clements with the white feathers of the title. In 1957, he began starring as one-armed detective *Mark Saber* in the long-running Danziger production. Having lost an arm during the war, his voice was arguably Grey's greatest asset: he was able to suggest the essential good nature behind Colonel White's bureaucratic and crusty exterior.

Cy Grant, who voiced Lieutenant Green, had his first starring role in John Elliott's *Man From the Sun*, a BBC play about West Indian immigrants in England. He later achieved fame as a calypso singer in the BBC's magazine programme *Tonight*. Following Captain Scarlet, he appeared as a head of state in *The Persuaders!*, Dayna's father in *Blake's Seven* and a Pellucidan leader in *At The Earth's Core*.

Elizabeth Morgan voiced both Destiny and Rhapsody Angels. At the time she was best known for presenting a schools programme called *Finding Out*. She recalls that acting for puppet voice-overs was more challenging than ordinary radio work because the puppets themselves were restricted in their display of emotions. 'During one session, Rhapsody Angel was worrying about some life or death situation that was threatening Captain Scarlet. I was close to tears and I was told, "Puppets can't cry Liz . . . do it

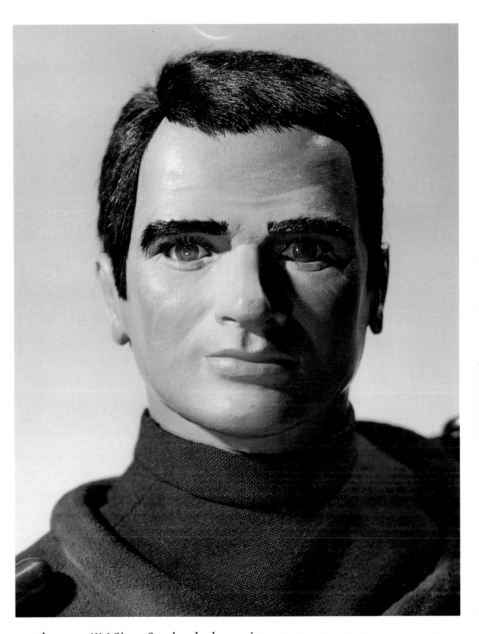

Captain Brown – one of Spectrum's leading agents until the Mysterons turned him into a living bomb.

another way!".' Since Scarlet she has written over 24 plays for BBC Radio 4 and has taken her one-woman shows to America and the National Theatre. She appeared in *The Old Devils* for BBC Wales and was Joanna the District Nurse in both series of HTV's *We Are Seven*.

Captain Ochre's voice was furnished by Jeremy Wilkin who succeeded David Holliday as Virgil Tracy in the last six episodes of *Thunderbirds* and the two feature films. In 1965 Jeremy Wilkin had starred as Drewe Herriot in the ABC fantasy thriller, *Undermind*. He stayed with Century 21 Productions for *Joe 90* and *The Secret Service* (in which he played The Bishop), whilst in 1970 he donned a green string vest to become a

Jason Smith, Mysteronised firefighter, prepares to destroy Spectrum's oil refinery. He was one of the characters voiced by David Healy.

Skydiver navigator in *UFO*. Apart from guest starring in *Doctor Who* and *The New Avengers*, Wilkin returned to voice-over work for Halas and Batchelor's RAI cartoon series, *The Count of Monte Cristo*. Wilkin also provided the voice of the human Captain Black, during the opening scenes of 'The Mysterons'.

Paul Maxwell provided the voice of Captain Grey, the World President and several 'guest-stars' in the series. A naturalised American, Paul Maxwell was actually born in Canada and first came to Britain with the Commonwealth forces during World War Two. Maxwell's rich expansive tones will probably always be associated with Colonel Steve Zodiac of *Fireball XL5* but he also provided the voice of Paul Travers, the Zero X commander in *Thunderbirds Are Go!* By co-incidence, Paul Maxwell was also appearing in *Coronation Street* during the summer of 1967. As Steve Tanner he was brought into the show specifically to marry Elsie Tanner (Pat Phoenix). Their TV wedding, drawing a massive audience, took place on September 4th 1967, only a month before Scarlet's TV premiere. Subsequently, Paul Maxwell played Lt. Lewis, a Skydiver crewman, in the *UFO* episode 'Sub-Smash'. He continued to work in film and TV, appearing as the Man with the White Hat in the opening sequence of *Indiana Jones And The Last Crusade*.

Playing Captain Magenta was Gary Files. Australian born, but a naturalised Canadian, Files had appeared in *The Spies* and *Softly Softly* for the BBC before landing the role of Captain Magenta. He also substituted for Ray Barrett in the role of John Tracy in the film *Thunderbird Six*. Subsequently, he played Matthew, the six-inch spy in *The Secret Service*, character voices in *Joe 90* and Phil Wade in the first episode of *UFO*. Since returning to Australia, Gary Files has played a variety of stage roles from the manic DJ Leonard Brasil in *City Sugar* to the Joe McCarthy figure in *Insignificance*. He appeared alongside Charles Tingwell in *The Money Movers* (1978), but to *Neighbours* fans Gary Files will be best known for his rare appearances as Tom Ramsey.

The voice of Doctor Fawn and the ill-fated Captain Brown was Charles Tingwell, star of ATV's *Emergency Ward Ten* from 1957 to 1968. Tingwell appeared as Inspector Craddock in the Miss Marple movies (including *Murder Ahoy* in 1964, with Francis Matthews) and also played the brother of Francis Matthews in *Dracula Prince of Darkness* (1966). Despite an extremely busy schedule, Tingwell had found the time to record character voices for the last six episodes of *Thunderbirds* and the movie, *Thunderbirds Are Go!* Tingwell later starred in *Catweazle* and the 'Mindbender' episode of *UFO*. In the 1970s he returned to Australia, where as Charles 'Bud' Tingwell he appeared in many movie roles including

Rod Dexter: Hollywood stars were too expensive for *Captain Scarlet*, even as puppets, but this Robert Mitchum lookalike played support in several episodes such as *The Trap* and *Fire at Rig 15*.

gang leader Jack Henderson in Bruce Beresford's *The Money Movers* (1978).

Although each regular character had his own voice artiste, (with Janna Hill playing Symphony Angel, Sylvia Anderson playing Melody and Lian-Shin performing some of Harmony's lines) the 'supporting players' were voiced either by the 'second leads', such as Tingwell and Maxwell, or specially drafted actors. Shane Rimmer can be heard providing uncredited voices in 'Special Assignment' and 'Flight to Atlantica' while Martin King and David Healy played the 'guest-stars'. Healy in particular leapt on the opportunity to step outside the casting restrictions which usually applied to American actors in ITC series. His roles range from the Australian fire-fighter Jason Smith in 'Fire At Rig 15' to the bull-headed President Roberts in 'The Launching'. Following Captain Scarlet, Healy played the dead gangster Bugsy Spanio in *Randall and Hopkirk (Deceased)*, Nicely Nicely in the National Theatre's *Guys and Dolls*, the voice of Shane Weston in *Joe 90*, and even an English mercenary in an episode of *Charlie's Angels*.

'WE WILL BE AVENGED . . .'

Captain Scarlet's fight against the Mysterons was to last for thirty-two episodes, each with an on-screen running time of approximately twenty-five minutes. The structure of the episodes is notable for the fact that, with the exception of the pilot story, they each boast two opening title sequences.

The opening titles are seen over an eerie and largely symbolic sequence, in which Captain Scarlet is introduced and his indestructible nature established. Early versions of this sequence were mainly silent, whilst the majority featured an introductory voice-over by Ed Bishop.

The secondary title sequence (over which the voice of the Mysterons issued its weekly threat) followed the episode's 'teaser' and introduced the viewer to Captain Blue, Colonel White and the five Angels. The omnipotent nature of the Mysterons is stressed, as the familiar twin circles drift over the oblivious Spectrum personnel. The sequence ends with another largely symbolic shot, this time of a uniformed Captain Black standing in a mist-shrouded graveyard.

Each episode ended with the Captain Scarlet theme, composed by Barry Gray. Early episodes of the series featured a predominantly instrumental version: the words 'Captain Scarlet' repeated at regular intervals in an unearthly, electronic voice, which was produced by Barry Gray using a ring-modulator (a device which imposes complex patterns on any sound which passes through it). Most of the episodes, however, closed with the well-remembered vocal arrangement of the theme, performed by The Spectrum, the group

formed by Gerry Anderson purely as a marketing exercise. Both versions of the theme were accompanied by excellent colour paintings by *TV21* artist Ron Embleton, showing a grim-faced Captain Scarlet in a number of spectacular and seemingly fatal situations.

The following chapter covers all thirty-two episodes of the series, presented in their original order of transmission. The episode title is followed by the often cryptic Mysteron threat-of-the-week.

Lurking doom: Scarlet suspects a Mysteron ambush.

Death hides in the shadows as Captain Black sets his sights on another unfortunate victim.

 The Mysterons

'**Our first act of retaliation will be to assassinate your World President.**'

It is the year 2068 and, following what they mistakenly believe to be an attack on their Martian city, the Mysterons declare war on mankind. As Earth's first line of defence, the Spectrum organisation swings into action, but not before Captains Scarlet and Brown are killed and their Mysteron duplicates dispatched on a mission of death. Surviving an attempt on his life by Captain Brown exploding beside him the World President is placed under the protection of Captain Scarlet – who proceeds to kidnap him and take him to the top of the 800-foot high London Car-Vu. Pursued and eventually shot by Captain Blue, Scarlet falls to his death but, upon recovery of the body, Spectrum make a startling discovery! Scarlet is mysteriously able to regenerate himself and live to continue Spectrum's fight against the Mysterons – unwittingly the Mysterons have created Spectrum's most important weapon.

One of the many points of interest in this episode is the unusual shot of Harmony Angel preparing to board her aircraft. Following Lieutenant Green's order for immediate launch, Harmony is seen moving towards her chair, located behind the double glass doors in the amber room. The stringless puppet is then viewed from behind and shown to sit down in the chair, which then slides back into the elevator-shaft. An effective shot which was never re-used. Also worth mentioning is the 'grimacing' Captain Scarlet who is seen to fall from the London Car-Vu, having been shot by Captain Blue during the episode's climactic battle. By using a highly detailed landscape, an amazing sense of perspective is achieved for the shot in which Scarlet is seen to plummet towards the ground!

Teleplay by Gerry & Sylvia Anderson
Directed by Desmond Saunders

2 Winged Assassin

'We will assassinate the Director General of the United Asian Republic.'

As the elected leader of two hundred million people, the life of the Mysterons' latest target has to be safeguarded at all costs. Following an unsuccessful attempt by an agile sniper, Spectrum make arrangements to transfer the Director General of the United Asian Republic from his London hotel to his private jet at London International Airport. On Cloudbase, Captain Scarlet makes a full recovery after his fall from the London Car-Vu and, together with Captain Blue, is sent back to the city to take part in the operation. Despite elaborate precautions, the Mysterons are one step ahead and, as Scarlet, Blue and the Control Tower staff look on, a Mysteronised Stratojet breaks away from its terminal and heads on a collision course with the Director General's plane. Scarlet must prove he is invincible and save the Director General.

Continuity buffs will no doubt make much of this episode's July 10th dateline, as it is also the date given during the much later 'Treble Cross'.

Teleplay by Tony Barwick
Directed by David Lane

3 Big Ben Strikes Again

'Our next act of retaliation will be to destroy the city of London.'

It is almost midnight and a high destruction-ratio atomic device is being transported through London; its destination, an underground construction site ten miles outside of the city. At the wheel of the huge transporter, the driver, Macey, can only watch helplessly as his vehicle seems to take on a life of its own, careering madly through the streets, before coming to a sudden stop in an underground car park. Finding himself sealed in, Macey switches on his radio and is baffled to hear Big Ben strike thirteen times! Suddenly aware that he is no longer alone, Macey is struck from behind and knocked unconscious, but not before he has seen the atomic device become fully armed – turning it into a bomb of devastating power. Naturally, Captain Scarlet is the only hope to deal with the deadly situation.

Teleplay by Tony Barwick
Directed by Brian Burgess

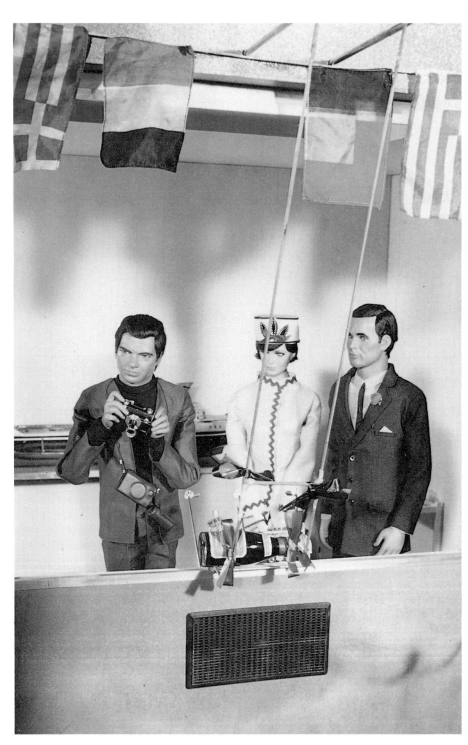

Mysteron Mervin Brand (with the camera) made an earlier appearance as Macey in the episode *Big Ben Strikes Again*.

 **4 Manhunt**

 5 Avalanche

A Mysteron scheme is foiled when, having broken into the Culver Atomic Centre, Captain Black is discovered and forced to beat a hasty retreat. On Cloudbase, Colonel White reveals that, during his escape, Captain Black exposed himself to a short-life atomic isotope, meaning that, for the next 48 hours the Mysteron agent will be a source of radioactivity. Using special detector trucks, equipped with directional, long-range Geiger Counters, Spectrum closes the net around the fleeing Black, but not before he steals an SPV and takes Symphony Angel as a hostage!

It is unclear exactly what Captain Black hoped to achieve by breaking into the Culver Atomic Centre as, unlike every other episode in the series, 'Manhunt' didn't feature a specific Mysteron threat or announcement; instead, the secondary title sequence was accompanied only by a re-iterated promise that the Mysteron retaliation would be '. . . slow, but none the less effective.'

Also worth noting are the frequent requests by Lieutenant Green that he be allowed to join in the manhunt. Colonel White refuses, but eventually relents, as the following episode shows.

Teleplay by Tony Barwick
Directed by Alan Perry

'**We will destroy key-links in your Frost Line Outer Space Defence System.**'

When the Mysterons threaten the Alaskan chain of missile complexes and observation posts, the Frost Line commander, General Ward, promises massive retaliation if any of his installations are attacked. Concerned about the consequences should Ward launch a strike against Mars, Colonel White sends Captain Scarlet and Lieutenant Green to investigate, when contact with one of the missile bases is suddenly lost. Arriving at the base, the Spectrum men discover that a Mysteron agent has sabotaged the air-conditioning system. As Lieutenant Green repairs the damage, Captain Scarlet must prevent the saboteur from reaching the Command Base.

A notable episode, in that while Captain Blue remains on Cloudbase at the communications console, Lieutenant Green accompanies Scarlet on his mission. No on-screen reason for this is given, although it is safe to assume that Colonel White sent him along in response to his requests during the previous story.

Teleplay by Shane Rimmer
Directed by Brian Burgess

Rolling thunder: the virtually indestructible Spectrum Pursuit Vehicle.

White As Snow

'Our next act of retaliation will be to kill the Commander in Chief of Spectrum, Colonel White.'

Following an unsuccessful attempt to destroy Cloudbase – the Mysterons having set a communications satellite on a collision course – Colonel White announces that, in order to safeguard the lives of everyone else on the base, he is to leave for a secret destination. The Mysterons, as ever, prove difficult to thwart and, no sooner has Colonel White made contact with a World Navy submarine than one of the crew dies in an accident – his Mysteron duplicate being assigned to look after the Colonel during the voyage!

An amusing episode in which Captain Blue is given the opportunity of commanding Cloudbase in Colonel White's absence. No doubt aware that his newly-acquired status will be short-lived, the Captain clearly enjoys himself by organising unpopular lectures and repeatedly sending the Angels to carry out target practice.

Teleplay by Peter Curran & David Williams
Directed by Robert Lynn

Colonel Whites takes to the sea in an attempt to elude the Mysterons.

 **The Trap**

'At the appointed hour, as the clock is chiming, the wings of the world will be clipped.'

Spectrum is assigned to provide the security for an international air conference, at which all the high ranking officers of the World Airforce are to discuss methods for dealing with the Mysteron menace. En route to Cloudbase, the plane carrying Air Commodore Goddard crashes, having been struck by lightning, and it is a Mysteron duplicate which eventually completes the journey. Colonel White is surprised when Goddard announces that he has changed the location of the conference to the isolated Glengarry Castle in Scotland, but accepts the decision and sends Captain Scarlet to the castle with Goddard to check security. Making a search of the Banqueting Hall, Scarlet discovers a heavy-duty machine gun concealed behind a huge painting; manned by Holte (Goddard's pilot) the weapon is trained on the table at which the delegates are due to meet. Bound and gagged, Scarlet is helpless as, using his voice, the Mysteronised Air Commodore contacts Cloudbase and informs Colonel White that it is safe for the conference to begin.

Making its one and only appearance in this story is the Magnacopter. Looking more like a submarine than an aircraft, the incredible machine clearly belongs to the World Airforce, although Symphony Angel is given the sought-after job of piloting it to and from the conference.

Worth noting is a mix of live action and puppetry in order to create the illusion of great depth for the scene in which Captain Scarlet and Symphony are discovered in the castle dungeon.

Teleplay by Alan Pattillo
Directed by Alan Perry

Imprisoned within the dungeon of Glengarry Castle, Scarlet and Symphony must warn the conference delegates that they have walked into a trap.

 Operation Time

'Our next act of retaliation will be to kill time.'

In an exclusive London clinic, General Tiempo, Commander of the Western Region World Defence, is due to undergo a brain operation, under the supervision of Professor Magnus, a pioneering surgeon who has developed a revolutionary piece of apparatus known as the Cerebral Pulsator. Night falls and tragedy strikes, as, driving home, Professor Magnus dies when his car is forced off the road by Captain Black. Now merely a soulless puppet, the Mysteronised Magnus returns to the clinic with one purpose only – to kill General Tiempo.

A 'key' episode of the series, in which we discover the Mysterons' Achilles' heel – they are impervious to X-rays and can easily be killed by a high voltage electric current. The episode is also notable for those with a particular interest in the layout of Cloudbase, as it reveals that both the Sick Bay and Generator Room are on deck C.

Teleplay by Richard Conway
& Stephen J. Mattick
Directed by Ken Turner

9 Spectrum Strikes Back

'You will never solve the mystery of the Mysterons.'

Colonel White, Captain Scarlet and Captain Blue travel to the secret headquarters of the Spectrum Intelligence Agency, where Dr Giardello demonstrates two new advances in the fight against the Mysterons: the portable Mysteron Detector and the Anti-Mysteron Electron Gun. As the assembled delegates watch the demonstration, Captain Black arrives and kills Captain Indigo and it's not long before the new devices are put to the test.

Intended as a sequel to 'Operation Time', Spectrum's newly developed Anti-Mysteron devices make their first (and in the case of the Electron Gun, only) appearance. 'This is the only gun that kills a Mysteron,' announces Scarlet, as he zaps Captain Indigo. Strange, then, that it is never seen again – conventional bullets proving to be adequate for the remainder of the series.

Teleplay by Tony Barwick
Directed by Ken Turner

10 Special Assignment

'We intend to obliterate the sub-continent of North America.'

Spectrum personnel are expressly forbidden to gamble, so when Captain Scarlet loses $5,000 at the Dice Club casino, Colonel White has no choice but to ask for his resignation. Destitute and with nowhere to go, Scarlet returns to the scene of his downfall and, at the seedy Gregory hotel, meets a couple of racketeers who promise to cancel his debts in return for an SPV. Accompanying the villains to a remote ranch house, Scarlet discovers that they are Mysterons and is informed, by Captain Black, that they intend to use the stolen SPV to destroy Nuclear City. But the jigsaw is not yet complete . . .

An unusual episode which contains more than one red herring. For example, how did Spectrum know in advance that the two racketeers running

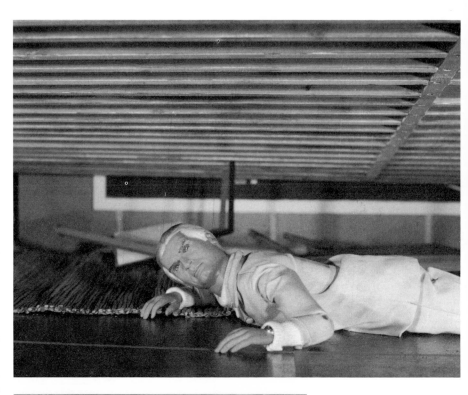

A pressing engagement for Colonel White when a Mysteron agent brings the house down.

Unable to watch, Captain Blue turns away as Scarlet loses everything on the roulette wheel.

the casino were Mysterons? The answer is that a Spectrum Intelligence agent is working undercover at the drab Vincent Bar, so obviously he overheard the two Mysterons plotting!

Teleplay by Tony Barwick
Directed by Robert Lynn

11 The Heart of New York

'We've seen the greed and corruption of the world in which you live and will take our revenge upon it.'

When three crooks break into the Spectrum Security Vault, they come away with nothing but microfilm and classified documents. Their haul seems useless, until their leader discovers that it contains detailed information about the Mysterons and their powers of reconstruction. The Mysterons, meanwhile, announce that they are to attack New York – the city is evacuated and Spectrum personnel sent in to patrol the deserted streets. Using their newly-acquired information, the crooks convince Spectrum that the Mysterons' target is the Second National Bank. Colonel White is unwilling to risk Spectrum lives to protect a bank and so orders his agents to withdraw. With nothing to stand in their way, the crooks enter the unguarded bank and prepare to make off with a fortune in gold ...

The Spectrum personal radio receiver makes its one and only appearance in this episode. Manning a road block on the outskirts of New York, Captain Magenta dons a pair of sporty sunglasses, the arms of which contain tiny speakers which allow him to hear the voice of Captain Ochre, who is concealed nearby.

Teleplay by Tony Barwick
Directed by Alan Perry

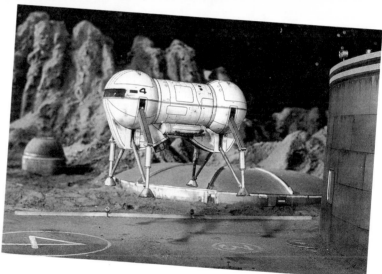

12 Lunarville 7

'We have no quarrel with the moon and we accept their offer of friendship.'

Together with Lieutenant Green, Captains Scarlet and Blue are sent to the moon to investigate claims by the Lunar Controller that he has established contact with the Mysterons and succeeded in coming to a peaceful agreement. As night falls, the three Spectrum men steal a moon mobile and head for an area on the dark side of the moon, known as the Humboldt Sea, as it is from here

that strange signals have been detected. As the moon mobile reaches the edge of a huge crater, the earthmen are unable to believe their eyes. Within the crater, moving with an ominous sense of purpose, bizarre machines are seen scuttling about, engrossed in their task – the construction of a new Mysteron city!

A good episode and the first of three ('Crater 101' and 'Dangerous Rendezvous' being the others), 'Lunarville 7' features the voice of Gerry Anderson himself as the Lunarville computer, SID!

Teleplay by Tony Barwick
Directed by Robert Lynn

When they break into the Second National Bank, this trio of crooks discover that impersonating Mysterons carries a high price.

A bug-like moon mobile – ideal for lunar tours and unofficial excursions to the Humboldt Sea.

Fashion designer André Verdain entertains two of his favourite models.

 13 Point 783

'We shall destroy the Supreme Commander of Earth Forces within the next twenty-four hours.'

In order to counter the latest Mysteron threat, Captains Scarlet and Blue are assigned to protect the endangered Commander. Travelling with Captain Blue to Point 783, a remote Command Post in the Sahara Desert, the Supreme Commander watches as the new Unitron tank is put through its paces. Unmanned and completely impervious to attack, the Unitron is the ultimate weapon of war. What chance do the observers have, therefore, when the tank veers off course and opens fire on the unprotected bunker . . .

A point of note: doesn't the Command Post interior look like *UFO*'s SHADO control room? Clearly Supervising Art Director Bob Bell was pleased with his own work and decided that a full-sized version of the design was just the place to base Ed Straker and his underground defence force.

Teleplay by Peter Curran & David Williams
Directed by Robert Lynn

 14 Model Spy

'We are about to attack the House of Verdain.'

Why should the Mysterons wish to kill top fashion designer André Verdain? Perhaps it's because he is a spy for the European Area Intelligence Agency and has been trailing Captain Black for months. Going undercover, Captains Scarlet and Blue, together with Destiny and Symphony Angels, travel to sunny Monte Carlo, where Verdain is putting on a fashion show. Unbeknown to everyone, two of Verdain's top models are now in the hands of the Mysterons and waste no time in acting upon the instructions of their new masters . . .

A *Man from UNCLE*-type episode in which Scarlet and Blue don their civvies for an unusual assignment on the French Riviera. A nice break from the routine and some convincing antics from a couple of stringless puppets towards the end.

Teleplay by Bill Hedley
Directed by Ken Turner

Ditched! Scarlet, Blue and Destiny Angel come under fire from Mysteronised Angel aircraft.

. . . and this is how it was done! Dry-ice and powerful lights are used to create an explosive effect.

Designed to overcome all forms of defence, a Mysteron-controlled Variable Geometry Rocket homes in on its own base.

 15 Seek and Destroy

'We intend to kill one of the Spectrum Angels.'

Unaware that three unfinished Angel Aircraft have been destroyed in a fire, Colonel White sends Captains Scarlet and Blue to Paris, to pick up a holidaying Destiny Angel and return her to the safety of Cloudbase. En route to the airport, Scarlet and his colleagues are attacked by the Mysteronised aircraft and, from the safety of a roadside ditch, they watch as the real Spectrum Angels are engaged in a deadly battle with three perfectly matched opponents.

Featuring plenty of spectacular aerial sequences, this episode turns out to be an excellent showcase for the Angel Aircraft, as well as providing the small 'Flying Unit' of Century 21 with an opportunity to express themselves in full.

Teleplay by Peter Curran & David Williams
Directed by Alan Perry

 16 Renegade Rocket

'We are going to launch one of your own incendiary rockets and you will have no way of knowing its target.'

On his way to Base Concorde, an island-based rocket installation, Space Major Reeves is killed by Captain Black – a Mysteron duplicate immediately taking his place. Once in the Rocket Control Room, he launches a Variable Geometry Rocket: a missile designed to overcome all forms of defence in order to reach its target. Arriving at the base, Captains Scarlet and Blue are on hand as the rocket suddenly reappears on the radar and it is discovered that Base Concorde is its target.

Having gained access to the Control Room at Base Concorde, Major Reeves is seen to shoot the missile technician with Captain Scarlet's colour-coded pistol. Strange – these personalised guns are never supposed to leave the side of their owner!

Teleplay by Ralph Hart
Directed by Brian Burgess

On Lunarville 6 Linda Nolan points the way as the Spectrum trio plan to infiltrate the Mysteron's moon city.

17 Crater 101

'Although you have discovered our complex on the moon, it will never reveal its secrets.'

Returning to the moon, Captain Scarlet, Captain Blue and Lieutenant Green set off from Lunarville 6 to penetrate the newly discovered Mysteron complex. Once inside, they have to find and remove the power source before the installation can be destroyed by an atomic device. Unbeknown to the three agents, the driver of the Lunar Tank is a Mysteron and the bomb which he is bringing has been set to explode one hour ahead of schedule.

The sequel to 'Lunarville 7', this episode carries a couple of interesting technical points. First, the interior of the moon mobile seen in this episode differs slightly from the one used before. Where the Lunarville 7 mobile was controlled by twin joy-sticks, this one features two steering columns. Second, the scene in which the Mysteronised Frazer departs the moonbase in a Lunar Tank is also technically noteworthy, as the domed building glimpsed in the background is, in fact, the camera-housing of the Mini-Sat which would be featured in the following story.

Teleplay by Tony Barwick
Directed by Ken Turner

Inside the Mysteron complex, Lieutenant Green stands transfixed by a hypnotic screen.

Astronomer Doctor Breck takes a close look at Mars. Nothing can prepare him for what he is about to see.

 18 Shadow of Fear

'You will never discover the secret of the Mysterons.'

In order to obtain close-up pictures of Mars, astronomers soft-land a mini satellite on the Martian moon Phobos. At an isolated observatory, high in the Himalayan Mountains, Captains Scarlet and Blue keep watch and wait for the revealing pictures to be transmitted back to Earth. When one of the astronomers disappears, Captain Scarlet suspects it to be the work of the Mysterons and sets out to find him before he can sabotage the whole operation.

A pioneer in the use of electronic music and effects, composer Barry Gray produced an eerie score for this episode which adds considerably to the space sequences. Not surprisingly, much of this score is used later in *UFO*.

Teleplay by Tony Barwick
Directed by Robert Lynn

19 Dangerous Rendezvous

'Spectrum Headquarters Cloudbase will be destroyed at midnight.'

By using the diamond pulsator power-source taken from the Mysterons' lunar complex, Colonel White succeeds in communicating with the inhabitants of Mars. In replying to his offer of friendship, the Mysterons insist that a lone, unarmed member of Spectrum meets their representative at a location of their choice. Aware that he could be walking into a trap, Captain Scarlet volunteers for the crucial assignment.

This is an interesting episode as it features a detailed explanation and demonstration of the unique cap-mike communications system. The recipient of this demonstration, the scientist Dr Kurnitz, is also treated to a specially arranged Angel launch, which, bearing in mind that Cloudbase has just been threatened, seems a fairly unwise thing to do!

With the help of Doctor Kurnitz, Colonel White prepares to communicate with the Mysterons.

Teleplay by Tony Barwick
Directed by Brian Burgess

 20 Fire at Rig 15

'We intend to immobilise the whole of Spectrum.'

In order to carry out their latest threat, the Mysterons cause a fire at Spectrum's Bensheba Oil Refinery. Arriving at the rig, Captains Scarlet and Blue watch as ace fire-fighter Jason Smith succeeds in blowing the fire out with high explosives. Unbeknown to them, however, it is a Mysteronised Smith who walks away from the now safely gushing oil well, the real fire-fighter having fallen under the influence of Captain Black and perished in the explosion.

A good example of deceptive model work can be seen near the beginning of this episode, when Captains Scarlet and Blue leave Cloudbase in a Spectrum Passenger Jet, escorted by an Angel flight. As the Angels close in around the jet, Captain Blue watches Angel 2 glide into view, apparently several yards from the plane. In fact, what the viewer is seeing is a scale model, no larger than Captain Blue himself, being suspended only inches from the cockpit set.

Teleplay by Bryan Cooper
Directed by Ken Turner

 21 Treble Cross

'We will destroy the world capital – Futura City.'

When Captain Black attempts to kill ace test-pilot Major Gravener, he reckons without two pioneering doctors, who pull the comatose man from his watery grave and bring him back to life. Unaware that his human counterpart is alive, the Mysteronised Gravener returns to Slaton airbase and requisitions an XK107 bomber – complete with armed nuclear warhead. When the real Major Gravener turns up, he joins Spectrum in a daring plan to deceive the Mysterons.

Realism was important to Gerry Anderson and his team and, during the making of this series, efforts were made to ensure that the puppets were

as believable as possible. A good example of this is the puppet of Major Gravener which, thanks to a small air-bag hidden beneath his bedclothes, is seen to breathe deeply as he lies within the hospital Recovery Unit.

Teleplay by Tony Barwick
Directed by Alan Perry

 Flight 104

'The conference at Lake Toma will be sabotaged.'

Captains Scarlet and Blue are assigned to escort the leading astrophysicist Dr Conrad to a special conference in Switzerland – the purpose of the conference, to decide the method and purpose of man's return to Mars. On the way to Geneva airport, Scarlet makes a startling discovery: the flightdeck of the plane in which they are travelling is empty. As Scarlet and Blue wrestle with the controls, a hazardous mountain range looms into sight and they realise that there is nothing they can do to prevent a crash.

A point worth noting is that this episode features a small amount of footage from *Thunderbirds* when, towards the end fire tenders are seen rushing to aid the imperilled airliner.

Teleplay by Tony Barwick
Directed by Robert Lynn

Captain Scarlet, following his attempt to land the Mysteron-controlled airliner in *Flight 104*.

Laboratory assistant Judy Chapman gets to grips with a deadly man-made virus.

Kitted out in a thermal pressure suit, Captain Scarlet goes after the Mysteron saboteur who has imperilled the Hot Spot Tower.

 23 Place of Angels

'We will destroy the place of the Angels.'

Judy Chapman, laboratory assistant at a bacteriological research centre, falls under Mysteron control and steals a phial of K14 – a newly developed culture, capable of causing death on a massive scale. Throwing off her pursuers, Chapman arrives at the Boulder Dam on the Colorado river and, as a wounded Captain Scarlet parachutes on to the scene, she prepares to contaminate the entire water supply of Los Angeles.

Composer Barry Gray produced some extremely effective music for the series, but time was always tight and, occasionally, it would be necessary to use appropriate pieces of earlier scores. The dramatic music which can be heard as Dr Denton mixes the K14 virus will be familiar to fans of *Stingray* as one of the earlier series' recurring themes.

Teleplay by Leo Eaton
Directed by Leo Eaton

 24 Noose of Ice

'We will make sure that you never return to our planet, Mars.'

Deep below the polar ice cap, scientists are drilling for Tritonium alloy – a rare metal essential for the new space fleet bound for Mars. Massive heating elements keep the surrounding water at a constant 60 degrees, thus preventing the ice from closing in and crushing the installation. When a Mysteron saboteur cuts off the power supply, Captain Scarlet must race against the forces of nature in order to avert disaster.

With a limited amount of space in which to build sets, the series' principal vehicles and buildings were modelled in a variety of different sizes and used depending upon the requirements of any particular scene.

Teleplay by Tony Barwick
Directed by Ken Turner

As a nuclear device approaches, Captain Scarlet jets on to the scene – ready to save the situation.

25 Expo 2068

'Disaster will strike the Atlantic seaboard of North America. We will deal a heavy blow to the prestige of the world.'

When a nuclear reactor disappears during transit, Spectrum suspect it to be the work of the Mysterons. Tracing the stolen device to the site of Expo 2068 – a massive world trade fair – Captain Scarlet must gain entry to a hovering cargo-copter and defuse the potentially explosive situation.

This episode is significant as being the only one in which real black and white television screens are used as monitors, instead of the usual mock-up flat-screens, brought to life by convincing visual trickery.

Teleplay by Shane Rimmer
Directed by Leo Eaton

26 The Launching

'We will destroy President Roberts within the next twelve hours.'

Assuming that the Mysterons intend to assassinate the head of state, Colonel White dispatches Captains Scarlet and Blue to throw a security cordon around his residence. As Scarlet tries to convince the President that he is in mortal danger, little does he know that a Mysteron agent is already in the area – his sights set on a far bigger target.

Whilst it was usual for model aircraft to be suspended from wires in order to simulate flight, this episode contains a scene which suggests that this wasn't always so. As Rhapsody and Destiny fly past Mysteron Brand's jet, it is apparent that the Angel aircraft are attached as a suitably clever alternative to the rapidly moving backdrop.

Teleplay by Peter Curran & David Williams
Directed by Brian Burgess

Electronics genius and
Mysteron agent Gabriel
Carney cuts his way into a
Spectrum Security Centre.
Can Scarlet and Blue stop
him wiping out the
Triumvirate of Europe?

27 Codename Europa

'The triumvirate of Europe will be destroyed.'

John L. Henderson, Conrad Olafsson and Joseph Maccini; after the World President, the most powerful men on earth – and now marked for death. Concealing the men in separate security establishments, Spectrum are confident of beating the latest Mysteron threat. But they have reckoned without the skills of an electronics genius, Gabriel Carney, now on the side of the Mysterons, who soon turns out to be a formidable opponent.

In order to add that extra touch of authenticity, small figures were often used on the model set, which would have been far too small to accommodate full-sized puppets. A swivelling model of Captain Magenta is put to good use during the scene in which the Mysteronised Professor Carney spectacularly crashes his car through a Spectrum road block.

Teleplay by David Lee
Directed by Alan Perry

Inferno

'Our next act of retaliation will be to destroy the complex at Najama.'

When the Mysterons threaten a desalination plant in the Andean foothills, Captains Scarlet and Blue set up camp in an old Aztec temple and mount a round-the-clock vigil. In space, a Mysteronised recovery vehicle plummets towards the earth – its re-entry computer homing in on a transmitting device which Captain Black has concealed in a very unusual place.

Obviously keen to establish the existence of a European space operation in addition to the obvious American space programme, the writers of this episode placed the SKR4 recovery vehicle firmly under the control of an agency known as Euro-Space.

Teleplay by Tony Barwick & Shane Rimmer
Directed by Alan Perry

29 Traitor

'The Spectrum organisation will be torn apart from within.'

When the Mysterons announce that a traitor will create havoc for Spectrum, Colonel White sends Captains Scarlet and Blue to Koala Base, Australia, where a number of mysterious hovercraft accidents have resulted in the deaths of several men. Joining the crew of hovercraft number 4, the Spectrum captains travel deep into the Australian outback, recreating the exact conditions surrounding the previous crash. It is then that disaster strikes.

The superbly designed blue-and-white hovercraft were an impressive addition to the Spectrum fleet; although their role within the organisation is never made entirely clear.

'Traitor' was also the first episode to incorporate a lengthy flashback scene – in this case, no doubt for the benefit of viewers new to the series, Captain Blue explains how Captain Scarlet became indestructible in the first place.

Teleplay by Tony Barwick
Directed by Alan Perry

As Captain Blue sleeps, Captain Black stealthily prepares his rude awakening.

30 **Flight to Atlantica**

'We intend to destroy the World Navy complex at Atlantica.'

Assigned to destroy a dangerous drifting wreck, Captains Blue and Ochre succumb to the effects of some Mysteronised champagne and, having had their flight-plan switched by Captain Black, attack the World Navy's Atlantica complex. Incapable of rational thought, the two men are unaware that they are being pursued by Captain Scarlet and Colonel White and plan a repeat attack. But the Spectrum chief determines to stop them, even if it means shooting them out of the sky!

An amusing episode and one which will be of particular interest to *Thunderbirds* fans, as it features an instrumental version of the song 'The Dangerous Game', which was sung by Lady Penelope in the story 'The Cham Cham'.

Teleplay by Tony Barwick
Directed by Leo Eaton

A fleet of flying saucers surrounds Cloudbase. Have the Mysterons finally come to Earth?

Dazed and confused, Captain Blue finds himself in an apparently deserted Cloudbase.

High on Mysteronised champagne, Captains Blue and Ochre prepare to bomb the Atlantica missile complex.

31 **Attack on Cloudbase**

'We will destroy Cloudbase.'

When Symphony Angel is shot down over the desert, it seems that the Mysterons have finally launched an all-out attack on Spectrum's headquarters. Saucer-like space craft appear out of nowhere and, as Cloudbase is mercilessly blitzed, Captain Scarlet tries to take off in the only surviving Angel aircraft.

A tense and exciting episode which is guaranteed to keep the viewer guessing. As the story draws to a close, it appears that the Mysterons have won the war. The denouement, however, reveals that this is not the case!

Teleplay by Tony Barwick
Directed by Ken Turner

 32 **The Inquisition**

'One of the members of Spectrum will betray you all.'

Having drunk some drugged coffee, Captain Blue awakes in what appears to be a deserted Cloudbase control room. Colonel White is nowhere to be seen and, sitting at his desk, is a man named Colgan, who claims to be from Spectrum Intelligence. Colgan informs Captain Blue that he has been missing for three months and, in order to prove his identity, demands the secret Spectrum cypher codes.

An unusual final episode which relies heavily upon flashbacks to earlier episodes – in particular, an eight-minute long sequence from 'Crater 101'. Rather intriguing, however, is the scene in which, to escape his captors, Blue leaps through a glass portal, and the viewer is afforded a brief glimpse of what must be the back of the control room set.

Teleplay by Tony Barwick
Directed by Ken Turner

'HOLD ON, I CAN SEE SOME WIRES!'

'The Magnacopter's clear, let him have it.'

A sudden burst of machine-gun fire reminded Captain Scarlet that, although Symphony Angel and the conference delegates were now safe, he himself was still within range of Goddard and the armour-piercing shells that had threatened to cut the aircraft to pieces on take-off.

Twisting the directional control of his jet-pack, Scarlet moved forwards at full speed. Behind the machine gun, Goddard spotted him and brought the great weapon to bear. Desperately Scarlet loosed off a couple of shots, but they went wide and he knew that it was hopeless.

The machine gun spat fire in his direction, and he felt the impact and searing pain as a volley of cahelium-tipped bullets tore into his body. Agonised, he released his grip on the jet-pack controls and, like a broken doll, crashed to the floor. The last thing he saw, before unconsciousness claimed him, was the turret of Glengarry Castle erupting like a volcano and hurling shattered blocks of masonry into the sky.

That was how it appeared on November 10th 1967 when the episode 'The Trap' had its TV premiere. But how did 'The Trap' come into being? For the answer, we must journey back to January 1967 when Tony Barwick was assembling the scripts for the series. Barwick, a former computer programmer who had script-edited the last six episodes of *Thunderbirds*, had a small office at the studios of Century 21 and it was here that most of his work was done; meeting and briefing potential writers, editing their finished scripts and writing episodes of his own.

Barwick needed writers who understood the technicalities of writing for puppets, as opposed to flesh and blood actors, and was particularly keen to employ Alan Pattillo, who had acted as script-editor on the first 26 episodes of *Thunderbirds*. Although he was now working on other projects as film-editor, Pattillo was happy to get involved, even though he could only spare enough time to write one script.

With the format of the series already well established, Pattillo was simply given a location and

A jet-propelled Captain Scarlet prepares to shoot it out with Goddard.

asked to write a script around it. The setting for the story, the remote Glengarry Castle, didn't come as a surprise to him because, as he remembers today, 'Gerry always liked to have a Scottish subject in his series!'

Once Pattillo had delivered the finished script, Tony Barwick discussed it with Producer Reg Hill and the various department heads. As Gerry Anderson describes it, 'the whole thing is done with military precision'; therefore, in order to locate and iron out any potential difficulties, each department head looked at the script from their own point of view.

Supervising Art Director Bob Bell defines his job as, 'visualising the backgrounds against which the characters perform. I supervised the working drawings of the interiors which went to the Construction Manager, and then watched the set construction, working with my assistants on the details of the interior design and furnishings.'

Puppet Co-ordinator Mary Turner was responsible for 'casting' the puppets who would

The delegates congregate in the Banquetting Hall of Glengarry Castle. With ten working puppets all in the same shot, this was a time-consuming and difficult scene to film.

play Morton (the caretaker of Glengarry Castle) and the two Mysteron villains: Air Commodore Goddard and his pilot, Holt. For the part of Morton, Mary chose to use a puppet whose face was based on that of Robert Mitchum. As one of the more successful 'guest players', this rugged-faced puppet can be seen, re-costumed, in several episodes, including 'Fire at Rig 15' as the Rig foreman, and 'Spectrum Strikes Back' as Dr Giardelo.

This script provided an additional complication with scenes which called for the ten members of the World Air Conference to be seen in shot at the same time. Since the series was filming two episodes at once on separate stages, duplicate puppets of Captain Scarlet and Captain Blue were kept on both stages, but the supporting players (known as revamps) had to be juggled carefully between both stages. Quite apart from the large number of puppets, these crowd scenes would call for several new military uniforms to be designed, or adapted from others, by Wardrobe Mistress Iris Richens.

At the same time, Production Manager Frank Hollands was checking over the script to see what equipment would be needed for which scenes on which particular stage. Although comparing film production with a factory production line sounds unglamorous, Gerry Anderson points out that 'you could hardly come into a studio of a hundred technicians and say, 'I'm sorry guys but we haven't got the next set ready so can you all go home for a week.'

That weekend, Reg Hill would meet up with the small cast of voice actors at Anvil Films Recording Studio in Denham. Liz Morgan recalls that 'Cy Grant used to pick me up *very* early in the morning, since we both lived in Notting Hill at the time, and we'd drive out to Denham.' With the technical side of the recordings supervised by Anvil's Douglas Hurring, the Century 21 crew would record several episodes in one day.

Because the voices were just one element of what would eventually be a very visual production, this meant that the recording sessions were quite different from an ordinary radio play and the actors needed quite a lot of guidance from Hill or Gerry Anderson. Gerry Anderson explains: 'If you are making a normal feature film or television programme, then the actor knows: "I am running up the stairs, therefore I am out of breath. I am

Captain Scarlet, Goddard and Morton in the Banquetting Hall of Glengarry Castle.

projecting my voice sixty yards across a courtyard. I am falling out of a plane while I am screaming" – he knows the situation. But, of course, when you pre-record the dialogue for a programme, they don't necessarily know how it is going to be filmed. So, for that reason, I always made sure that I was in attendance.'

Actor Ed Bishop, who gave voice to Captain Blue, remembers the sessions well. 'It was very interesting to watch the five or six permanent members of the cast because, after a while, we began to take them very seriously and we'd argue among ourselves and say "Well, my character would never say that!" and often we would have to remind ourselves that we were just recording a children's programme!'

Day one of filming at the Century 21 studio in Slough, and the small army of technicians start work on the 'teaser' – the short scene before the main titles designed to excite the interest of the viewer and make him watch on.

Escorted by Melody Angel, a World Airforce jet flies across a stormy night sky. Lightning illuminates the scene and, as the storm worsens, a fierce bolt of lightning forks from the heavens, striking the aircraft and causing a dramatic explosion. Out of control, the blazing aircraft plummets from the sky, hits the rugged, wooded terrain and explodes. As torrential rain sweeps the smouldering wreckage, the familiar Mysteron circles appear and drift slowly across the bloodied bodies of Goddard and Holt.

Working on a small, dimly-lit set, the equally small 'Flying Unit' take care of the shots of Melody Angel's aircraft and the XQR jet. Attached to thin but strong wires, the two aircraft are suspended in front of a painted backdrop. By rolling the scenery back, the illusion of forward motion is achieved, without having to move either plane so much as an inch. The effect is further enhanced by technicians who stand just out of shot, spraying water and wafting clouds of smoke on to the set from a smoke gun.

Satisfied that the results look convincing, the director moves on to the next shot; that of the lightning strike. Although distant lightning is simulated by the flashing of an arc welder, forked lightning is a different matter altogether. A realistic effect would be impossible to create live in the studio so the lightning will have to be superimposed over the shot by a process known as optical printing.

On the director's cue, a small explosive charge attached to the hidden side of the plane is detonated. Smoke and flames billow from a tube of Jetex fuel pellets fastened to the side of the model. As the smoke is blown backwards by an out of shot fan, the camera is tilted at a steep angle to give the impression that the aircraft is diving towards the ground.

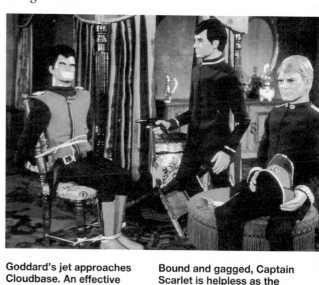

Goddard's jet approaches Cloudbase. An effective shot, achieved by the Flying Unit, unfortunately cut from the finished episode.

Bound and gagged, Captain Scarlet is helpless as the Mysteronized Goddard contacts Cloudbase – using Scarlet's voice!

An unusual publicity shot of Melody Angel, but it does illustrate the unique mechanism which allowed the puppet to be controlled from below.

On the model stage, the sequence is completed by the special effects unit, under the direction of Shaun Whitaker-Cooke. Again trailing fire and smoke, the XQR aircraft slides down a wire towards the rocky mountainside, which is the floor of the set. Although not apparent from the camera's point of view, the foreground is actually separate from the background, leaving a gap between the two just large enough for the plane to fall into. As soon as the plane disappears from sight, carefully positioned petrol gel explosives on the foreground set are ignited. It requires precision timing, but it means that the aircraft can be 'destroyed', whilst, in fact, it remains undamaged. An expensive and highly detailed prop can then be modified and re-used in a later episode.

No sooner has the explosion been captured on film than Whitaker-Cooke shouts 'cut!' and, almost immediately, a couple of technicians rush on to the set with fire extinguishers, to stop the whole thing going up in flames! As the smoke clears, the unit begin to prepare for the next shot – the sequence in which Melody Angel, flying low over the trees, spots the wreckage of the crashed jet. Before any more filming can take place, however, the camera must be carefully dusted down, in order to remove any dust particles thrown up by the explosion, and lubricated, in order to stop the works from seizing up during the high speeds at which it must operate whilst recording special effects shots.

On one of the two puppet stages, a stringless Melody Angel sits in the cockpit of her aircraft, while puppeteer Judith Morgan operates her from below. The unique under-puppet mechanism allows Melody to move convincingly, whilst enclosed within her cockpit. Without this device, such close-up shots as this would have been impossible, as a hole would have to have been made in the roof of the cockpit for the strings to pass through – a hole which would have been difficult to hide from the all-seeing lens of the camera. As director Alan Perry announces a 'wrap', work on the 'teaser' is complete.

Eight thirty the following morning and everyone is preparing for another hard day. On the main puppet stage, a large and well-lit set has been erected – the main control room of Cloudbase. On a raised section of the stage, Colonel White sits behind his circular desk. Below him, sitting before his intricate control console, is Lieutenant Green. The scene being shot requires Green to report to the Colonel whilst moving towards him in his special travelling chair. Hidden from view, just behind Colonel White's desk, a technician slowly pulls the moving walkway to which the Lieutenant's chair is attached. On the overhead bridge, puppet operator Peter Johns matches the Lieutenant's speed, whilst carefully pulling the strings which will give movement to the puppet's arms and head.

An amusing sight, unseen by the programme's viewers, is the caps usually worn by Captains Scarlet and Blue, seeming to hover a couple of feet above their heads. As Puppet Supervisor Christine Glanville explains: 'The caps had to be threaded on to the wires, which were then attached to the puppeteers' hand controls. It would have been a complicated process to have removed the caps completely, when they weren't required, so instead, we simply moved them up out of shot and used insulating tape to hold them in place!'

With the bridge puppeteers positioned eight feet above their respective puppets, the task of making the various characters appear to look at each other during conversation is not an easy one. However, much of the hit-and-miss element of the early shows has been ironed out, thanks to the development of a system known as 'Add-a-Vision'. A very small, closed-circuit view-finder is attached to the camera, allowing everyone on the set, including the bridge puppeteers, to enjoy a 'camera-eye view' of the proceedings.

As the Cloudbase scenes are being shot, the set of the castle interior is being lit on the other puppet stage, under the supervision of Lighting Cameraman Paddy Seal whose job it is to deceive the camera, with careful positioning of lights, to produce a sense of depth and realism. Christine Glanville recalls that 'Gerry always insisted that the eyes of the puppets should be lit to make them look alive. So the lighting cameraman had to position his little key lights in front of them, and of course, if we moved the heads too far to one side, one of the eyes would "go out".'

Several 1000-watt lights hang from the gantry; each one is carefully trained on a different part of the set; this has the effect of producing 'real' shadows, thus exaggerating the natural perspective of the scene. Wall-paintings, suits of armour, the main banqueting table, they all have to be carefully and individually lit – there's even a smaller 120-watt Fresnel behind the window,

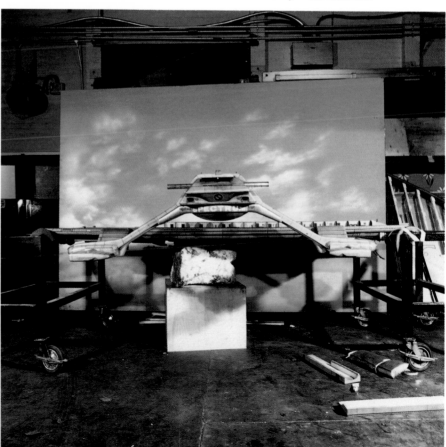

The massive and highly detailed model of Cloudbase stands ready for the cameras.

creating the illusion of daylight. The process can take hours; far too long for the puppeteers to hold Captain Scarlet and the others in position, so wooden cut-outs, with the puppet's image painted on, are placed in the relevant positions.

Setting up each shot is a lengthy and meticulous process, as one problem after another arises and has to be solved. Gerry Anderson remembers one problem in particular. 'Imagine a shot with, say, five puppets. You've got everything set up and you're about to go for a take. The puppeteers take up all the slack in the wires and then the camera operator would say, "Hold on, I can see some wires". In would go a guy with a palette of colours and a very fine brush, he would put the brush into shot and the camera operator would literally say "left, left, left – that one there. It's glinting against green." So you'd paint that little bit green, then: "Oh, now the next bit's glinting against black", so you would have to paint the next bit black and this would take forever.'

At last they are ready to go. Surely nothing else can go wrong now. Oh yes it can, as Gerry points out. 'The director would say, "Right, turn over and action", and then an eye-string would break. So, after all that, the whole set-up would have to be canned for twenty minutes to repair the wire. Believe me, it was absolute hell making some of these pictures.'

While all this is happening on the shooting stages, the processed film from previous episodes is being assembled in Century 21's editing suites. Positive black & white 'slash prints' are taken from the negatives and spliced together by the film editor. It is here that the episode really takes shape, as footage from all the different units is cut together to create a smooth-running, 25-minute programme. Once the finished episode has been assembled, the slash print is sent back to the labs where a copy of each selected scene is taken from the original negative.

Once the finished episode has been assembled, the soundtrack has to be added. Together with Music Editor George Randall, Composer Barry Gray views the two separate reels of film which make up the completed episode through a moviola. Using a stopwatch, they decide exactly where each passage of music should begin and end. Working from his home studio in Esher, Surrey, Gray creates the unusual electronic sound

effects and music using such instruments as the Baldwin electronic harpsichord and the Ondes Martenot (an electronic device which produces high-pitched wails similar to that on The Beach Boys' hit 'Good Vibrations'). Together with tape recorders, which can slow down or reverse these noises, Barry is able to create the bizarre oscillating sounds associated with the Mysterons. Having already recorded the theme music at two earlier sessions, Barry will then travel to Anvil Studios in Denham where, with a small orchestra, he will record much of the incidental music for the episode. Recorded on to ¼-inch tape, the music and sound effects are taken back to Anvil Studios and, under the careful control of Anvil's Ken Scrivener, mixed with the dialogue track and transferred to the finished film.

The final day's shooting and all that remains is the episode's climax, a dramatic scene in which Captain Scarlet confronts Goddard amid the battlements of Glengarry Castle. A highly

Close-ups of real hands were inserted at key points in the programme for added realism. Here, stand-ins act out the scene in which Captain Scarlet is surprised by Goddard.

High on the battlements, Goddard has the Magnacopter pinned down. Can Captain Scarlet distract his attention for long enough to allow the delegates to escape?

detailed set has been built, which incorporates a battlement wall, a rough, earth-strewn floor and a curved and windowed turret. Positioned at one end of the set is the Mysteronised Goddard, his face set, gripping the handles of a powerful, heavy-duty machine gun. At the other end of the set, strapped into his jet-pack, is Captain Scarlet.

As well as his supporting wires, Captain Scarlet has now been fitted with an additional wire and thin rubber pipe which will allow his hand-held gun to fire. The carefully concealed rubber pipe carries a supply of gas to the nozzle of the gun. An electric impulse is generated and travels down the wire, igniting the gas and making the gun appear to fire. The machine gun works on a similar principle, although obviously uses a much larger gas jet.

With Special Effects Director Derek Meddings busy on the model stage, Special Effects Assistant Ian Wingrove attaches a strip of Cortex explosive to the mock granite wall, behind which Captain Scarlet is seen to hide. As Director Alan Perry shouts 'Action!', Goddard opens fire and, as Scarlet is pulled back by his operator, the strip of Cortex is ignited, giving the impression of a line of bullet holes suddenly appearing in the wall. Moving back into the open and returning fire, Scarlet orders Captain Blue to open up with the SPV rocket. It is then that his luck seems to run out. Hovering a few feet off the ground, Scarlet is without cover and, as Goddard opens fire, the Spectrum agent is caught in a stream of bullets. Now wearing the 'grimacing head' first seen in 'The Mysterons', Scarlet is seen to clutch his bleeding stomach, before crashing to the floor. To achieve the effect, Floor Puppeteer Rowena White takes hold of Scarlet, his strings now slack, and, upon the director's command, throws him to the floor. The puppet is sturdy enough to withstand the fall without any damage and Alan Perry is satisfied that he has got the result he wants.

On the model stage, meanwhile, Derek Meddings and his assistant Ian Wingrove are wiring up the scale-model of Glengarry Castle for what will be a truly explosive climax! Having packed the tower with petrol gel, Meddings and his assistant don protective helmets and retreat to a safe distance. Then the high-speed camera rolls and the firing button is depressed. All at once the tower of Glengarry Castle explodes brilliantly, balsa wood and chunks of polystyrene masonry being thrown in all directions. It takes only a couple of seconds and in the studio it looks spectacular enough but when slowed down and combined with the appropriate sound effects, it will look just like the real thing!

7

'THIS INDESTRUCTIBLE MAN WILL SHOW WHAT HE'S WORTH.'

Captain Scarlet premiered in the days before home video recorders. Fans had just half an hour to see the show before it was over for the rest of the week. There was only one way in which a truly dedicated fan could fill the hours until the following week's thrilling episode, and that was to collect the merchandise. Captain Scarlet was created with merchandising potential very much in mind. 'Make it a Captain Scarlet Christmas' was Century 21's slogan and the British toy industry responded with enthusiasm.

Lines Brothers, the massive combine responsible for a third of British toys, led the stampede with their Dinky subsidiary. One of the best-selling Dinkys of all time was their metallic blue SPV. Boasting an intricate door mechanism which opened sideways to lower Captain Scarlet to the ground, the 16-cm-long model was almost completely faithful to the TV original. Despite its many working parts (such as a missile-launcher) the SPV was robust enough to survive the toughest playtime crash. Dinky had enough pride in the SPV to put it on the cover of their 1968 catalogue – itself a collector's item today.

Dinky's 14-cm MSV was an attractive as the SPV but offered less in the way of entertainment. Once the owner had flipped up the cream 'gull-wing' doors and pulled down the red plastic ramps, there was little to do except ponder over the plastic crate of 'radioactive isotopes' which came with the MSV. Dinky's metallic red Spectrum Patrol Car (Spectrum Saloon in the series) offered only an 'engine-noise mechanism' as a special feature. Nevertheless, both the SPC and

the MSV are today almost as collectable as the SPV. In pristine condition, with the original boxes, the set would cost nearly three hundred pounds.

Pedigree Dolls was another Lines Brothers subsidiary which produced three figures based on the series. The 12-inch Captain Scarlet doll was made in the style of Pedigree's 'Tommy Gunn'

Just some of the many and varied items of merchandise.

soldier doll with a fabric costume and articulated limbs. The concept of the doll for boys was still very fresh in 1967, but the Captain Scarlet doll was doomed from the start. Unlike the original GI Joe and Action Man, the doll had no additional costumes or equipment; not even a jet pack to fly around with. The only enemy he could fight would be a Mysteronised Tommy Gunn.

Pedigree also issued two smaller dolls, roughly the same size as today's GI Joe toys. Captain Scarlet and Destiny Angel were moulded from soft rubber with a wire skeleton. Their costumes

were very detailed; Scarlet's cap included a perspex visor and pull-down microphone, and at his waist was a gunbelt and tiny pistol. Destiny Angel had a removable plastic helmet and removable artificial hair. Sadly, these very details meant that the dolls were quite fragile. Their arms and legs had a spindly appearance and were correspondingly delicate.

The third 'big-name' from Lines Brothers was Tri-Ang which issued a 'Captain Scarlet' set to add to its 'Minic' electric car-racing game (very similar to Scalextric). The rival firm of Rovex

Large plastic replicas from Century 21.

Industries also produced a similar 'Captain Scarlet Escape and Capture' set, which came with four pieces of track, an electric SPC and a Mysteronised sports car. Unlike the dolls, these car games were deliberately intended to be added on to an existing game.

In much the same spirit, Timpo Toys, who sold a fantastic range of plastic cowboys and soldiers at pocket-money prices, produced three Spectrum figures. Basically, the same detailed, 2-inch body with uniforms moulded in scarlet, white and green, the toys lent themselves to any number of battles with Mysteronised cowboys. Their other selling point was that they were almost in scale with the plastic Spectrum vehicles made by Century 21 Toys. At almost a foot in length, the Century 21 vehicles were much more delicate than their Dinky counterparts but featured additional gimmicks. The SPV incorporated roof-hatch ejector seats for Captain Scarlet and Captain Blue, while the wing mirrors of the SPC triggered missile launchers in the headlights of the car. Dwarfing both these toys was the Angel interceptor, which came with its own 'slot-in' friction motor. Definitely in the 'broken by Boxing Day' category, they were made from a much more fragile polystyrene than that used for present-day toy production. As a collector's item an Angel Interceptor in warehouse condition can sell for as much as two hundred pounds.

For those fans who actually wanted to 'be' Captain Scarlet, Century 21 Toys produced a polythene playsuit and a range of futuristic water pistols. For the girls, they commissioned Angels' Beauty and Jewellery sets as well as a transparent pendant which carried photos of the Spectrum Captains. Airfix also licensed a plastic construction kit of the Angel interceptor, made with the attention to detail for which Airfix was renowned. In fact, the Angel interceptor was probably the most enduring piece of Captain Scarlet merchandising, still on sale in chain stores until the early 1980s.

Quite apart from toys, Washington Potteries issued attractive cups decorated with transfers of Spectrum agents and vehicles, while Lone Star turned out a line of gaudy metal badges. Wonderama concocted a 6-foot wall frieze illustrated with scenes from such episodes as 'Spectrum Strikes Back', and Crown produced full-scale Captain Scarlet wallpaper.

John Waddingtons got in on the act with four 250-piece jigsaws based on colour stills from the series, but ironically, Captain Scarlet only appears on one of the jigsaws. Waddingtons also invented an elaborate Captain Scarlet board game. Played against the map of Europe, it involved four plastic SPCs transporting VIPs to the Spectrum Conference Centre in Yugoslavia. Moves were determined by a roll of the dice and

'Mysteron Cards' which required agents to miss a turn or return to base. The box artwork carries pictures of both Captain Scarlet and Destiny Angel. In fact, Destiny Angel, who was based on actress Ursula Andress, features in much of the merchandising, even though she did not have a particularly prominent role in the TV show.

Fans with a sweet tooth could buy Captain Scarlet biscuits with photographs of the Spectrum agents printed on the foil wrappers. Anglo bubble-gum also issued a set of sixty-six collector's cards – the front of each card showed either a photograph or drawing based on the series while the reverse made up a giant jigsaw painting by Ron Embleton, who had also painted the end-title sequence for the TV show. Barratt's Sweet Cigarettes (known to today's more healthy generation as Candy Sticks) issued a set of fifty smaller cards and also sponsored a special 24-page Spectrum Handbook, produced by Century 21 Publications and only available by mail order.

With his ice-cool nerve, it was inevitable that Captain Scarlet would promote Lyons-Maid's new Orbit ice lolly. J. Walter Thompson commissioned Century 21 to make a special TV advert for Orbit in which Captain Scarlet defended the newly completed Post Office Tower from Mysterons by turning the ice-lolly into a Mysteron-seeking missile.

Captain Scarlet was a natural successor to Virgil Tracy on the Kellogg's Sugar Smacks packet, and the loyalty of young consumers was assured by the free gifts. In-pack premiums included a set of small metal badges illustrated with the faces of Spectrum agents and snap-together plastic models (about an inch long) of the ever-popular Spectrum vehicles.

When it came to kits, nobody did it more comprehensively than the Japanese. Imai of Japan initiated a massive range of kits which were later repackaged in Canada and the United States. The Spectrum helicopter, Cloudbase and the Swift Removals SPV Transporter were just three of the items which Imai added to the usual range of character and vehicle merchandising.

Back in Britain, pyjamas, slacks, balloons, kites, slippers and a sketch pad were added to the merchandising list. The House of Romney's

A selection of the many books which were produced to tie in with the series.

'Captain Scarlet Asteroid Talc' is probably the most obscure item of merchandising while the award for the most ephemeral goes to the water transfers produced by Tower Press of London. Water transfers were generally sold in sweet shops during school lunch hours and as with stamps were torn off a larger folio. The individual pictures were based on paintings by Jim Watson and Malcolm Stokes and could be applied to the skin by wetting the back of the transfer under a tap. The transfers were produced in such large quantities that it is still relatively easy to buy a sheet from dealers today.

Slightly less common is the original *Captain Scarlet* annual, published in 1967 to coincide with the TV premiere. For many years, this annual was the *Scarlet* fan's bible, containing articles on Spectrum, its personnel, vehicles and enemies. Devised by Todd Sullivan and Angus Allan of Century 21 Publications the book is very much a snapshot of the original Captain Scarlet concept. In every comic strip, for instance, Captain Scarlet's 'sixth sense' causes him to 'sweat and sway whenever he comes near a Mysteron'. The TV shows quickly abandoned the 'sixth sense' concept because it gave the scriptwriters too many problems and yet the comic strips, with colour artwork by Jim Watson, Keith Watson (of *Dan Dare* fame) and Ron Turner (of *The Daleks*) demonstrate just how imaginatively the gimmick can be used. The strips also show the SPV power pack being adapted for use as a high-powered drill and one-man helicopter; ideas which are discussed in the pilot script but never actually used in the TV show. For these reasons, and Roger Perry's excellent design work, the annual is well worth hunting down.

Century 21 Publications also released 20 large-format booklets which included painting, sticker-fun, dot-to-dot and puzzle books for both *Scarlet* and *The Angels*. Two other books in the *Scarlet* range gave buyers a chance to build cardboard cut-out models of Cloudbase and the Spectrum vehicles, while *The Angels* range featured cut-out clothes dolls based on Destiny, Harmony, and Rhapsody. Last but not least, both *Scarlet* and *The Angels* had their own hardback storybooks illustrated in colour by Jim Watson.

In addition to their own-label books, Century 21 also packaged three novels for Armada books.

with CAPTAIN SCARLET

TV CENTURY 21

ADVENTURE IN the 21st. CENTURY

7ᵈ

UNIVERSE EDITION 152   DATELINE: DECEMBER 16, 2067   EVERY WEDNESDAY

WHERE IS SCARLET?

SPECTRUM MOUNT MAN-HUNT Mombasa, Monday.

Spectrum helijets and helicopters are whirling overhead, heading for the big game reserves of East Africa in a desperate search for Captain Scarlet.

The Alarm was raised this afternoon when Mombasa police discovered the body of Chief Pantula, who was the local Spectrum agent.

Colonel White of Cloudbase immediately tried to contact Scarlet and warn him of possible Mysteron agents in the area, but the Spectrum Captain failed to reply.

Continued on page twenty-four

Pacific Mystery

A SCHOOL teacher and his class of boys had to give up a deep-sea swimming lesson yesterday afternoon—because they were being chased by a strange 'sea-monster'!

Mr Edward Castle, physical education tutor at California High School, "saw something coming towards us. It was about ten feet long, not very wide, and fairly translucent. I couldn't make out any special features, but its mouth opened as it drifted slowly towards us."

Continued on page twenty-four

Photograph taken of Captain Scarlet as he sits in the Spectrum Helicopter shortly before its take off and disappearance

CORGI MODEL CLUB NEWS — Page 21

Written under Century 21's house pseudonym of John Theydon, the first book, 'Captain Scarlet and the Mysterons', is a fast-moving epic in which the Mysterons use a weather control machine to hammer the World Government into submission. This allows the author to tackle scenes which are beyond the budget of the TV show, such as a tropical rainstorm engulfing the crowds in a futuristic Trafalgar Square. As in the annual, the problem of Captain Scarlet's 'sixth sense' is tackled head on. Captain Black warns a Mysteronised World Space Patrol engineer that Scarlet can

Captain Scarlet was regularly featured on the cover of TV 21.

detect their unique radiation so the engineer fools Scarlet by donning his radiation-proof spacesuit.

Less satisfying is Spectrum File No.2, 'Captain Scarlet and the Silent Saboteur', a fairly uneventful tale concerning the disappearance of the highly advanced *Oceanus X* submarine and a plot by the Mysterons to destroy the world's circle of energy-producing Thermic Power Stations.

Apart from issuing *Captain Scarlet* material, Century 21 Publications had the weekly comics to create. Ron Embleton's *Captain Scarlet* comic strip continued in the centrespread of *TV21* with Spectrum battling Mysteronised WASP (from *Stingray*) and WSP (from *Fireball XL5*) agents. The Spectrum symbol was incorporated into the *TV21* masthead, and in the letters page readers were encouraged to mail in reports of local Mysteron activity. *TV21* even offered readers the chance to join Spectrum's junior division – the Shades. This ambitious operation began by dividing the map of Britain into 12 colour-coded areas. Each area was commanded by a Spectrum Captain to whom readers could report (additional characters such as Captain Cream and Lt Sepia being created for both the Shades and the comic). Readers could get their first Shade membership card, free of charge, just by writing to *TV21*. Shades then had the chance to trade in that card for one of a higher rank (a different colour naturally) if they passed an examination printed in the comic. It was a great idea; they had the cards printed up in all the colours of the rainbow, and the exam entries began flooding in. Only then did the *TV21* staff realise that they didn't have time to check the exam forms. In previous years, competition entries had been processed by a separate department and even that had been a much simpler task then checking 20 questions on each form.

Although they made sure that every correct entrant eventually received his or her new card, the *TV21* staff decided to drastically revise the promotion structure of the Shades organisation. Readers were distracted by a devastating storyline in the *Captain Scarlet* strip. Chris Spencer, who was editing *TV21* at the time, had noticed that most of the readers' letters seemed to come from 'Area Purple'; what is now the Yorkshire Television region. Since toy manufacturers also reported high sales in this area the explanation

seems to have been that there were more children in Area Purple than in any of the other regions. Whatever the cause, *TV21* swung into action with a story in which Captain Purple was promoted from answering Shades letters just long enough to die saving an underwater city.

Meanwhile, *Captain Scarlet* had changed the face of *TV 21* forever. The newspaper front page, which had made the comic so unique, was replaced by the opening panels of the *Captain Scarlet* comic strip. Boosted to four pages a week (two of them in black and white) the feature was now too much work for one artist alone. Ron Embleton was joined on the strip by several artists, each one tackling a different three-part story. Mike Noble, from the *Zero X* strip, contributed several 'Bond-style' adventures, featuring massive gun-battles and cross-continuity with the other *TV21*

'Hold it right there!' Stuart Evans' beautifully detailed Captain Scarlet sets his sights on Captain Black.

strips. Former *Dan Dare* artist Keith Watson contributed elegant views of 21st century London in a nightmare storyline about one of Scarlet's closest relatives being Mysteronised. Another *Dan Dare* graduate, Don Harley, drew the Captain Purple storyline. Even Frank Bellamy found a big enough hole in his *Thunderbirds* schedule to draw a *Captain Scarlet* cover (leaving Jim Watson to draw the interior pages). Working from scripts by Angus Allan and Scott Goodall, the artists produced an athletic version of Captain Scarlet that is today as fondly remembered as the series itself.

Now that they were TV stars in their own right, the Angels were used to promote the *Lady Penelope* comic in the TV adverts, and editor Gillian Allan boosted their comic strip to a two page length with guest appearances by Captain Blue and Captain Black. The comic also featured *The Spectrum*, a one-page strip by Tom Kerr, about the 'real-life' adventures of the group who sang the *Captain Scarlet* theme song. City Magazines, which distributed and co-published *TV21*, also published a comic called *TV Tornado*, which featured reprints of American comic strips and text features by *Marvelman* creator Mick Anglo. When *Solo* was cancelled, it was 'absorbed' by *TV Tornado* and Century 21 supplied the merged comic with a strip based on 'The Mysterons'. In fact, it was virtually a retread of *The Daleks* strip which had appeared on the back of *TV21* for its first two years. Each week, the 'giant computer' which ruled the Mysteron complex would blow up one of the Martian buildings and recreate it as a flying saucer. The Mysteron craft would then fly to another planet, where the atmosphere would cause the formless beings to 'take on their ancient Mysteron shape'. In the form of giant crystals, with a 'death ray' eye slit, the Mysterons would commence exterminating the alien races. Apart from the use of the Zero-X craft and the Martian City of Kahra, the strip had very little to do with either the Anderson universe or the TV series.

In the days before home video, the final piece of merchandising was perhaps the most satisfying. Century 21 released several 7-inch Extended Play records through ATV's Pye Records. Recorded at the same time as the actual film soundtracks, the first two 'mini-albums' were simply re-edited versions of TV episodes. The next four records

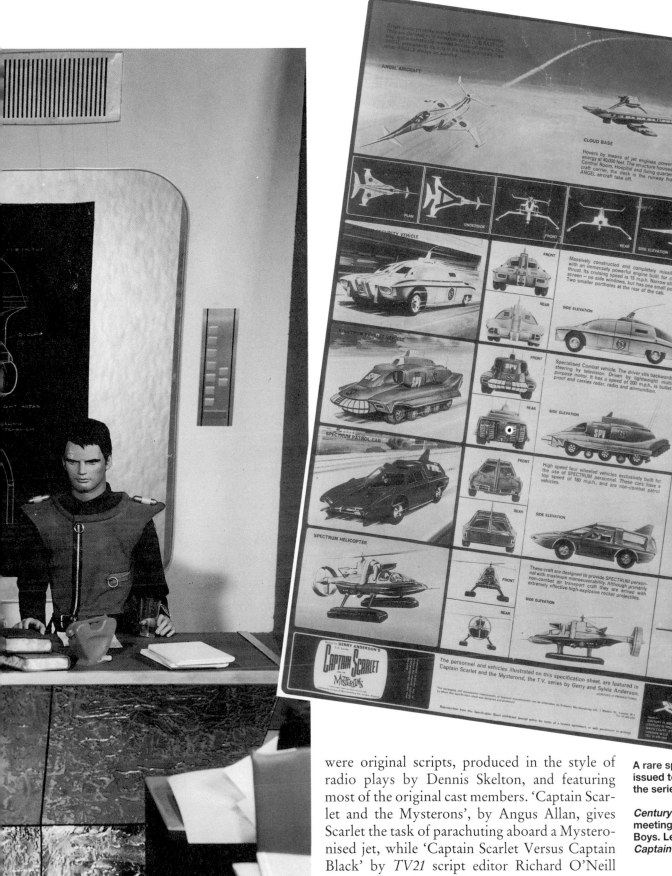

were original scripts, produced in the style of radio plays by Dennis Skelton, and featuring most of the original cast members. 'Captain Scarlet and the Mysterons', by Angus Allan, gives Scarlet the task of parachuting aboard a Mysteronised jet, while 'Captain Scarlet Versus Captain Black' by *TV21* script editor Richard O'Neill features Captain Black's attempt to lure Scarlet into a duel with electrode guns.

A rare specifications sheet issued to toymakers before the series was broadcast.

Century 21 sales reps meeting, August 1967: 'Okay Boys. Let's make this a *Captain Scarlet* Christmas!'

THE FINAL BATTLE
AND BEYOND . . .

As if to underline the merchandising slogan about making it a 'Captain Scarlet Christmas', the Christmas Day 1967 edition of ATV's game show *The Golden Shot* had a Captain Scarlet theme. A forerunner of Central TV's *Bullseye*, using crossbows instead of darts, the show was hosted by Bob Monkhouse, who had played the voice of Zero X navigator Brad Newman in the film *Thunderbirds Are Go!* The two hostesses, Carol Dilworth and Anne Aston, were outfitted in Angel uniforms, and the Spectrum pop group made one of their few live appearances in the musical break. The celebrity contestant, firing a crossbow on behalf of a disabled viewer, was none other than Captain Scarlet, relaying instructions by satellite from Cloudbase. To ensure that Captain Scarlet could exchange seasonal banter with Bob Monkhouse, the dialogue for the puppet was spoken 'live'. Francis Matthews recalls that 'I supplied my voice, as the show was being done, from the safe confines of a recording booth, well away from Bob!'

ATV Midlands broadcast the last episode of *Captain Scarlet and the Mysterons* on Tuesday May 14th, 1968, and by now, Century 21 Publications were already concentrating on their next production, *Joe 90*. As Gerry himself says, 'After the shock with *Thunderbirds* being cancelled, I'd just assumed that Scarlet would be cancelled after one series.'

TV21 continued to run the Captain Scarlet strips on the cover and inside pages, and in the October 19th edition it appeared that the Mysterons had actually conceded defeat. As the Mysterons complex shut down, Captain Black regained his old personality and President Younger disbanded Spectrum. The Angels and SPVs were turned over to the WAAF, Captains Blue and Scarlet transferred to the WSP as pilots of XL19, and Captain Black retired to a country cottage. Of course, there was only one way (apart from a dream) that the story could be concluded. It was all a cunning ruse! The Mysterons returned and Spectrum was hastily reconvened, with the help of Steve Zodiac, flying a new space-time machine.

In Autumn 1968, Captain Scarlet starred in the *TV21* annual and his second and last ninety-six-page annual. *TV2000*, a Dutch comic which reprinted the Century 21 strips had faithfully reproduced the Five Julias (Angels) and Voorpagina (front page) strips that introduced Spectrum.

Cloudbase goes down. Is this the end of Spectrum's floating HQ?

'Have I ever told you about the time I saved Colonel White's life?' Symphony and Melody exchange a knowing glance – they've heard it all before!

Unfortunately, the Dutch TV service only screened six episodes of Captain Scarlet, so the translated version of the comic strip was the greatest exposure most Netherlanders got to Captain Scarlet.

Meanwhile, in Britain the expense of equipping new colour studios was compounded by a Government tax on advertising revenue, and forced ATV to cut costs. Century 21 merchandising was streamlined; the toy company was closed down, and the publishing company was sold. Since City Magazines was still in operation at that time, *TV21* continued to appear, although the Century 21 content was gradually phased out. On July 12th the Mysterons were driven away after a scientist discovered a method of beaming cosmic rays down at their Martian settlement. Although they vowed revenge, they left Captain Black behind – a lifeless corpse. For the last few weeks Captain Scarlet continued as a kind of indestruc-

Destiny and Symphony prepare to leave Cloudbase in their rather attractive demob suits.

ible cop fighting Arcturan criminals. On September 6th 1969 *TV21* was closed down. Ironically, *Captain Scarlet* was already being repeated by some ITV companies, and his fight with the Mysterons would continue to be broadcast throughout 1970.

Although *TV21* had been cancelled, the liquidation of Century 21 publications had come too late to prevent the preparation of a combined *Thunderbirds* and *Captain Scarlet* annual. In the same format as previous annuals, it featured comic strips, cutaways of the Cloudbase computer and sick bay, plus a map of Mars which attempted to tie together continuity of *Thunderbirds are Go!* and *Captain Scarlet*. Century 21 had also packaged a 21st Century diary for Letts, which revealed that Captain Black and the Mysterons negotiated a peace treaty with the World President some years after the series ended.

In late 1970, Arthur Thorne, the head of Polystyle Publications, decided that the Anderson characters were too good to waste and he asked Dennis Hooper, the former art director of *TV21* to edit a new comic called *Countdown*. The first issue of *Countdown* came out in February 1971. Although Gerry Anderson's *UFO* and *Doctor Who* (with Jon Pertwee) were the main features, Captain Scarlet starred in a one-page strip drawn by John Cooper, the artist who had illustrated the final *TV21* episodes. The strip was very faithful to the TV concept with the Mysterons and Captain Black at full strength. After the first serial ended, Captain Scarlet became an irregular feature, illustrated by Malcolm Stokes and Brian Lewis.

Captain Scarlet also featured in the 1971 *Thunderbirds* annual (actually made up from the unpublished pages of the last *TV21* annual). In April 1972, *Countdown* became *TV Action*, with much of the science-fiction content being replaced by the likes of *Hawaii Five-O* and *The Protectors*. *Captain Scarlet* continued to appear, however, by way of reprints from *TV21*.

Although Granada, HTV and Tyne Tees continued to broadcast *Scarlet* well into 1972, this would be the last time that the show would be repeated for many years. The fact that *Thunderbirds* was re-screened as early as 1976 led to a rumour that Captain Scarlet had been banned by the ITV companies for its violence. This rumour was lent credence when special interest groups in

Spectrum's gang of four in civvy gear prepare to address the crowd at an early Fanderson convention.

America forced local TV stations to ban such 'violent' cartoons as *Batman* and *Superman*. Yet although British pressure groups have criticised everything from *Grange Hill* to *Doctor Who*, a lengthy search has uncovered no recorded criticism of *Captain Scarlet*.

This does not surprise psychologist Dr George Sik who says, 'kids are actually very sophisticated viewers, far more mature than adults tend to think. The idea of an indestructible hero will be interpreted in the context of the kind of programme *Captain Scarlet* is. Myths abound of children jumping out of windows and locking themselves in fridges, imitating the adventures of indestructible heroes but such instances are extremely rare.'

Stingray comic artist Lynn Simpson recalls, 'It never really occurred to me to ask how the Mysterons' powers worked or why Captain Scarlet was indestructible. All I wanted to know was if Captain Scarlet would get killed and if he'd come back to life at the end of the episode.'

In the early 1980s, the new market of local cable stations in America inspired Robert Mandell of ITC's New York office to repackage several Anderson productions as TV movies under the general title of Super Space Theater. *Captain Scarlet vs The Mysterons* (somewhat perplexingly issued as the second commercial video in Britain) cuts together 'The Mysterons', 'Winged Assassin', 'Seek and Destroy' and 'Attack on Cloudbase'. Britain's 'volume one' was *Revenge of the Mysterons From Mars*, which combines 'Shadow of Fear' with the Lunarville trilogy. A new prologue is delivered by an American Mysteron voice, reporting to the Mysteron High Council in deep space. Apart from that, the story is largely unaltered with the exception of some video laser effects superimposed over the original rocket battles. In Britain, the Super Space Theater productions were never aired on TV, instead being released direct to the fledgling video hire shops (at the time, commercial videotapes were still far too expensive to sell over the counter).

As interest in Gerry's series increased, a group of dedicated fans, led by Pamela Barnes, organised the first UK Gerry Anderson convention.

Held at the Dragonara Hotel in Leeds, 'Fanderson '81' was a three-day event, comprising screenings of selected episodes, a display of original models and personal appearances by Gerry Anderson and the voice of Captain Blue, Ed Bishop. Such was the popularity of the event that the organising committee approached ITC with a view to setting up an authorised fan-club and, a year after the first groundbreaking event, Fanderson – the Official Gerry Anderson Appreciation Society – was born. Eleven years later, under Chris Bentley's leadership, Fanderson has 1,600 members from as far afield as Iceland and Japan.

In 1988, the club issued an Extended Play 7-inch record as part of their yearly membership package. Designed to look like a Century 21 mini-album, the record featured original compositions by Barry Gray, many of which had not been available on record before. Alongside such favourites as the themes from *UFO* and *Thunderbirds*, compilers Ralph Titterton and Steve Kyte had included the Spectrum's 'Captain Scarlet' and 'White as Snow', a light, catchy jazz tune which turned up in the episode of the same name. More recently the second issue of Fanderson's *21st*

David Nightingale's *Century 21* – the indispensible magazine for Gerry Anderson fans of all ages.

It's all over: Captains Scarlet and Blue put their feet up and plan their holiday.

Century Fiction magazine celebrated the 25th anniversary of *Captain Scarlet* with a full-length novella 'Crisis' by Colleen Taylor.

Prior to the formation of Fanderson, Blackpool-based David Nightingale was authorised by ITC to create the first magazine devoted entirely to the world of Century 21. Dave's connection with Gerry Anderson goes back to 1979 when his exhibition in Blackpool needed relocating from the Golden Mile to the Pleasure Beach. 'The only economic way of doing it was to enlist the help of locally based enthusiasts. I was responsible for coordinating the move of the exhibition displays and the construction of the new venue. Philip Rae was responsible for renovating the models and designing the exhibition itself.' Through this Dave became firm friends with Gerry and, in April 1981, the first issue of *SIG* became available. That Spectrum's call-sign should be chosen as the magazine's title is indicative of just how familiar it had become; although as far as Dave's publication was concerned, it stood for 'Supermarionation is Go!'

Out of work and out of luck, Paul Metcalfe drowns his sorrows and hopes for a phone call from Gerry Anderson.

As the publishing concern grew, evolving, ultimately, into today's 'Engale Marketing', so the range of merchandise produced was increased. Calendars and postcards, all featuring Captain Scarlet, have proved to be extremely popular and, between 1988 and 1989, many of the original *TV21* Scarlet strips were re-printed in the glossy *Action 21*. Today, Dave's company publishes *Century 21*, a quarterly successor to *SIG*, edited by Mike Reccia and produced to an impressive professional standard. Dave ensures that regular coverage is given to Captain Scarlet and the Mysterions, which he describes as 'visually stunning and technically practically flawless.'

In 1985, the ITV companies began screening Captain Scarlet on Saturday mornings, and if nothing else, illustrated ITV's contempt for their audience, with episodes being screened out of sequence or slipped, without notice, into schedules when rain interrupted cricket matches. By now, however, Gerry Anderson had begun to receive the recognition denied him in the 1970s. Such varied venues as the Battersea Puppet Centre and the University of Belfast began screening selected episodes of the puppet shows, while the Institute of Contemporary Arts in London mounted a retrospective of Anderson's career including 'The Mysterons'.

By 1987, some of the original viewers of *Captain Scarlet* were old enough to be working in television on Granada's late lamented 'Night Network'. Scheduled for a late-night viewing audience, the series sandwiched five-minute segments of shows like *Batman*, *The Monkees* and *Captain Scarlet* between pop videos and celebrity interviews, while Polygram were now marketing the complete series of *Captain Scarlet* on commercial videotapes. Of course, all episodes of *Captain Scarlet* are going to be reshown on BBC2 during 1993. Following the successes of *Thunderbirds* and *Stingray*, *Captain Scarlet* is bound to be a hit with a whole new generation.

In the quarter of a century since his first appearance, Captain Scarlet has experienced the changing fortunes of all celebrities. A veteran of many battles, this remarkable character has beaten the odds time and time again; has triumphed over an apparently invincible enemy and risen phoenix-like from a graveyard full of forgotten heroes. As the 21st century draws near, Captain Scarlet seems certain to survive. Neither time nor the Mysterons have succeeded in defeating him and it is safe to assume that he will be fighting them both long after his mortal rivals have been laid to rest. Captain Scarlet is, after all, indestructible.

When will I see you again?
The cast enjoy an end-of-shoot party, oblivious to Harmony Angel's hovering helmet!

SEQUELANDERSON:

THE LEGEND

CONTINUES . . . .

"Look, Mum. No Strings."

While it would become a huge success *Captain Scarlet* received a less than enthusiastic reception from the critics. It caused a stir among parents, who condemned the show for its realistic carnage, and (some) children who were bemused by its gritty realism. Shrugging off the criticism, Gerry Anderson ploughed his resources into his sixth Supermarionation series, *Joe 90*, unveiled one year later.

Much like any other boy of his age, Joe has an ever-increasing sense of adventure – except for an ingenious invention which enables him to become the world's most audacious secret agent. With his special powers, Joe can become what every schoolboy dreams about – the world's greatest astronaut, a skilled pilot, or even a mathematical genius. Yet Joe is only 9 years old!

The adopted son of ace electronics engineer Professor Ian McClaine, Joe can achieve the impossible. He can do everything – brilliantly – thanks to BIG RAT (Brain Impulse Galvanscope Record and Transfer), an amazing electronic device invented by his father which records the knowledge of experts in various fields and transfers them into Joe's brain, giving him the specialist attributes of the highly skilled and experienced adult donor. This allows him to act as the agent for the World Intelligence Network, an organisation dedicated to maintaining the balance of power throughout the world.

When demonstrated to Shane Weston, Deputy Head of WIN, the intelligence man sees the device as a way of using the boy as a special undercover agent, one who can boldly go where no man could venture – and get away with it. Initially alarmed by the idea of sending his son on hazardous undercover missions, Professor McClaine is forced to concede that Joe is a formidable weapon for world stability and peace. Joe is enrolled as an agent for WIN.

Access to BIG RAT is achieved when Joe sits in a special chair, elevated into position inside a circular cage enclosure by means of a hydraulic device. Fixed in position, this revolves as BIG RAT is fed the donor's brain patterns, Joe dons his 'electrode glasses' and acquires everything he needs to become WIN's Most Special Agent.

On missions, he carries with him an ordinary-looking schoolboy's case which, with pressure on two small studs, reveals compartments containing his special BIG RAT glasses, pocket transceiver, WIN pistol and ammo, and identification badge.

Despite the beautifully detailed model work and exciting storylines, the series failed to pack the punch and vitality of Anderson's previous work and failed to arouse more than a passing interest with some Anderson fans. The show premiered in the Midlands (ATV) on 29 September 1968, and continued to a total of 30 episodes. Re-run several times in the mid-Seventies, the series turned up again in 1981.

Next in production was *The Secret Service,* a format Gerry Anderson saw as being the logical progression in making puppet films – a combination of live action and puppetry. Perhaps so, but he was out on his own in his thinking. The uneasy mix of live actors and puppets, combined with

Joe 90: (right) Professor Ian McClaine prepares his 9-year-old son, Joe 90 – the world's most brilliant secret agent – for another dangerous, undercover operation.

The Secret Service: Mrs Appleby is blissfully unaware of the secret shrinking habits of Father Unwin and Matthew, his seemingly backward gardener.

actor Stanley Unwin's gobbledygook 'Unwinese', failed to find acceptance with both Lew Grade and, later, the ITV network. Grade is understood to have cancelled the show after viewing the pilot (the first and only time that backer and producer failed to reach accord) and set a limit of 13 episodes. The programme was rejected by all but three of the ITV regions.

On paper at least the premise seemed irresistible. Father Unwin, an amiable parish priest, finds himself working for the British Intelligence Service when Professor Humbolt, a member of his parish, leaves an amazing device in his keeping, and requests that it be used for the good of mankind. Concealed in what seems to be an ordinary book which the priest keeps in his study, the minimiser (as the device is known) has the re-

markable power of being able to shrink a person or object to one-third normal size. Selected as recipient of the minimiser's miniaturisation ray is Matthew, Father Unwin's gardener.

Outwardly a slow-thinking, country yokel, Matthew is in fact a fully trained counter-espionage agent. An expert shot, he holds black belt in judo and is highly proficient with explosives and radio communications. When duty calls, Matthew drops his dim-witted persona and becomes the alert, athletic, intelligent counter-agent and embarks with Father Unwin on the next mission, more often than not in Gabriel, Father Unwin's vintage 1917 Model T Ford (both full size and a remote-controlled, puppet-size replica were used). Aided by their unique miniaturisation device, which enables Matthew to shrink to two feet

UFO: (top right) An Unidentified Flying Object poses a horrific threat to the inhabitants of planet Earth.

UFO: (bottom right) Commander Ed Straker (Ed Bishop) and Colonel Paul Foster (Michael Billington) of SHADO, a secret organization waging war against an alien terror.

The Secret Service: (below) Father Unwin – a priest with a mission – in Gabriel, his vintage Model T Ford.

high, Father Unwin transports his small-scale aide around in a specially converted briefcase, equipped with a chair and a periscope so that its hidden passenger can travel in comfort and see what is happening outside. The case also contains the miniature tools and instruments of Matthew's trade. Working independently of each other, but towards the same goal, the two keep in close contact via a communications device installed in Father Unwin's hearing aid.

Like other priests, Father Unwin is directly responsible to his bishop, in this case the Bishop being an acronym for British Intelligence Service Headquarters – Operation Priest, with the Bishop working not from his diocese, but from offices in Whitehall. Kept in the dark about her employer's extra-curricular activities, is Mrs Appleby, Father Unwin's loyal housekeeper. Only the Bishop knows of the set-up and directs his orders to Father Unwin via a cleverly camouflaged inter-communications system also incorporated into the priest's hearing aid.

One of Gerry Anderson's personal favourites, the 13-episode series premiered in the UK on 21 September 1969 to shallow acclaim. Tired of pulling the strings, but undaunted, Anderson took the decision to branch out into live action. The turning point was *Doppelganger* (USA: *Journey to the Far Side of the Sun*) a full-blown feature film that combined live actors with the model expertise attained with his Supermarionation puppet series – a production that would lead directly to his first live-action TV series, the highly inventive (and occasionally terrifying) *UFO*.

With a format that isn't too far removed from *Captain Scarlet and the Mysterons,* many Anderson fans see *UFO* as the classiest science-fiction TV series ever made. And why not? It certainly had everything going for it.

Transporting the viewer into 'the world of the future', the 1980s, when danger threatens from outer space, the series described how SHADO – Supreme Headquarters Alien Defence Organisation – was formed to combat the menace of a race of beings who had been raiding Earth in search of human organs. Sterile, the aliens cannot reproduce and require human body parts to keep their race alive. They visit the planet in UFOs – the Un-

identified Flying Objects of the title – kidnap humans and perform their spare-part surgery in brutalistic fashion before blasting off back to their homeland.

Waging war on the aliens from its headquarters beneath the bogus Harlington-Straker film studio, Moonbase – SHADO's moon defence arm from which Interceptor jets could be launched – is ex-USAF colonel, Commander Ed Straker. Alerted by the Space Intruder Detector (SID), a state of the art, computerised satellite which pinpoints the invaders within microseconds of the alien spaceships entering the Earth's atmosphere, his team of SHADO operatives puts its highly sophisticated resources into action as the first line of defence against the aliens. Besides the moon-based Skydiver interceptor – an atomic supersub/aircraft from which Sky One, a jet-fighter, could be launched into the stratosphere to seek and repel the UFOs in flight (or engage with the invaders in an undersea environment) – the team can call on a range of SHADOmobiles which, when air-dropped into action, pursue any alien craft that reach Earth. Little is known about the aliens themselves beyond the fact that they are humanoid and breathe a thick, viscous liquid during space travel. Without it, they die.

Heading up Straker's Earth-based unit are Colonels Alec Freeman and Paul Foster. Ex-RAF, Freeman is Straker's amiable and efficient right-hand man. He occasionally flies the Seagull X-Ray jet-plane. Civilian test pilot, Foster joined the team when he witnessed a battle between Sky One and a UFO. The sex symbol of the team, Foster is a man who will do anything to rid the Earth of the unwanted intruders – including mowing them down with bullets. Lieutenant Gay Ellis commands the Moonbase team. Proficient and pretty, like most female SHADO operatives on the moon, she sports purple hair!

With thought-provoking, adult and (sometimes) bizarre storylines, impressive hardware, virile actors and beautiful sexy actresses, *UFO* seemed ready-made to blast the Anderson team back to the top of the popularity charts. Such was not the case. Once again, the series is thought to have fallen foul of the ITV network gremlins. It failed to get a network launch and many regional ITV companies, unsure what to do with the programme's provocative subject matter (fare that

was far removed from what they had grown to expect from the 'Anderson/Century 21' banner), buried the series in their late-night TV slots.

Plans to do a second series were put on hold. Out, for the moment, went science fiction. In came detectives.

Lew Grade apparently called Gerry Anderson into his office, handed him a sheet of paper with four or five paragraphs written on it and gave Anderson twenty-four hours to decide if he wanted to produce the show outlined on the paper. Concerned that Grade might take offence if he turned the offer down, Anderson read the outline and agreed to make *The Protectors*, a series that Grade had conjured up with an eye on the international market, with big bucks from America foremost in his thoughts. Detective series were earning high ratings in the US at the time and Grade wanted a slice of the action.

Funded by Fabergé, Gerry formed a new company, Group Three, and shooting got under way in Europe on the first of 26 episodes, using the

The Protectors: Nyree Dawn Porter as the Contessa di Contini and Robert Vaughn in a part written specially for him – the 'danger-defying man of steel', Harry Rule.

talents of many of the Century 21 production staff. But not before Lew Grade had cramped Gerry's style by signing Nyree Dawn Porter for the second lead as the Contessa di Contini – instigating a hasty rewrite of the first 8 or 9 scripts, in which the second lead had been designated as a man!

The role of Harry Rule, the 'danger-defying man of steel', was written specifically for actor Robert Vaughn, who had made his name as Napoleon Solo in *The Man From UNCLE*, and was still bankable on US television. An ice-cold professional, and one of the world's top private detectives, Rule is the home-based member of the team, operating from a detective agency in the heart of London, sometimes working from his home in the country, which he shares with Suki, his au-pair, who helps the detective with his judo classes. Also on hand is Gus, Harry's pet Irish wolfhound.

The Contessa di Contini (formerly Lady Caroline Fitztempest Ogilvie) operates from her villa in Rome. Specialising in the theft of arts and antiques, she is equally at home in Europe's most glittering capitals or the criminal-infested backstreets of London. She, too, practises the art of self-defence, her choice being karate. The Contessa is schooled in the martial art by Dino, her oriental driver, who packs a mean punch himself when the occasion arises.

The youngest member of the team, Paul Buchet, operates from Paris. With dashing good looks, Buchet is the undisputed sex symbol of the trio. Women adore him. Crooks give him a wide berth.

Together they are The Protectors, three experts in their field, brought together under the banner of the 'Protector' organisation, to protect those in peril. 'No risk too great . . . No assignment too challenging', they hire out their skills to governments, businesses, and anyone else who is able to afford their fees.

Another break with the Anderson tradition was the absence of a musical score by Barry Gray.

The Protectors: **The Contessa and dashing Paul Buchet, the third member of the Protectors, played by Tony Anholt.**

Space 1999: Commander John Koenig (Martin Landau) leads his team of Alphans, Doctor Helena Russell (Barbara Bain), Tony Verdeschi (Tony Anholt), Alan Carter (Nick Tate) and beautiful metamorph Maya (Catherine Schell), in their search for a new world.

Space 1999: (opposite) Moon Base Alpha and its colony of earth scientists and researchers are set adrift through space, but time is running out . . .

This time around the music was provided by John Cameron, with the title theme 'Avenues and Alleyways' penned by songsmiths Mitch Murray and Peter Callender.

The series proved very popular with viewers and a second series went into production almost immediately. Indeed, it was so popular that a third series was planned. Apparently, this was never made due to a disagreement between Lew Grade and Fabergé – the company who were on line to finance a second series of *UFO!*

Disappointed to learn that Fabergé had withdrawn their funding and the proposed second series of *UFO* had gone down the chute, Anderson went to Lew Grade and explained the ideas that he had mapped out for the show. Indeed, he had gone so far down the road as to draw up sketches for the SHADO organisation uniforms. He had updated the Moonbase operation and had diagrams of the new vehicles he envisaged for the new series. The opportunity to use these for a new series was too good to miss. Convinced that the TV audience wished to see more aliens and space-orientated adventures, Grade agreed to contact Abe Mandell, ITC's head man in New York. Mandell contacted Anderson a few days later and agreed to finance the series providing that Anderson agreed to adopt a format for a series that made it impossible to do an earthbound story. Dreaming up the idea of a freak accident in the moon's nuclear waste dumps blasting the moon out of its orbit around Earth, Anderson telexed the idea to Mandell in New York. A reply was received a short time later. ITC would finance the show, known now as *Space 1999*.

The background to *Space 1999* is extravagant to say the least.

In the late twentieth century, man has established a colony on the moon. On 9 September, 1999, a freak accident in the moon's nuclear waste dumps creates a field of radiation that blasts Moon Base Alpha and its colony of 311 scientists and researchers out of its orbit around the Earth. Propelled across the solar system, the moon passes through a black hole and the Alphans find themselves drifting on an endless journey

through space. Lost in the blackness of space, their journey takes them through the galaxy and they encouter all manner of hostile aliens, bizarre scientific phenomena and strange new worlds. With their resources near to depletion, the travellers must search for a habitable planet that they can colonise . . .

The motivating force behind Alpha is Commander John Koenig, a tough, grim, no-nonsense task master. Competent but emotionless, he leads the Alphans through the reality of their spine-chilling situation in the company of Doctor Helena Russell, the colony's Chief Medical Officer, in charge of the physical well-being of the colony, and Professor Victor Bergman, Moon Base Alpha's scientific genius, whose sole handicap is his artificial heart.

Year Two (as the second season is known) saw changes in both format and cast. This time around the Alphans live in a gigantic underground complex beneath the moon's crust. Commander Koenig and Doctor Russell still head up the team, this time supported by Tony Verdeschi, Koenig's security chief and second in command, and Alan Carter, chief pilot of the colony's Eagle utility spacecraft. There is also the science officer, Maya. A sexy, alien metamorph from the planet Psychon, Maya has the power of transforming herself into any living form.

Despite being a visual treat – the programme's model work and special effects are among the most breathtaking ever seen on television – the series fared badly in the UK. Drawing consistently high ratings in the US syndicated market, the show was denied a network run in England and the ITV regions virtually ignored it altogether. The Anderson 'curse' had struck again. What had he to do to please his public?

Although eager to get back into production, it was almost a decade before the master puppeteer returned in a full-blown puppet series. For most of the Seventies his energy was directed to getting new projects into production. Though several formats were offered to the industry, none found a backer. Anderson's only venture into science fiction during this time was *Alien Attack*, a 30-second television commercial made for Jif, a food company, which used his Supermarionation technique to good effect and came complete with the

Space 1999: The spectacular sets and special effects helped create a stylish adult space odyssey.

theme tune to *Thunderbirds*.

But you can't keep a good man down. While none of Anderson's creations since *Space 1999* have been funded by ITC, presenters of the 'Supermarionation Classics', in January 1983 production began on *Terrahawks*, a format created and developed by Gerry and his new partner and co-producer, Christopher Burr.

After *Terrahawks* came *Dick Spanner,* the hilarious casebook of a private investigator in the classic tradition of Philip Marlowe. Also made by the Anderson/Burr Partnership, in association with Channel Four Television, filming of the

pilot took place in 1985, but Anderson had to wait until February 1987 for the green light to go ahead with production of the series.

In the intervening period between *Terrahawks* and *Dick Spanner*, Gerry Anderson has devoted his expertise to the production of two other pilots.

Little is known about *Inter-Galactic Rescue; Rescue 4*, Gerry's idea for a live-action series built around a multi-purpose, vertical take-off and landing craft, crewed by a four-man team. *Star Laws*, a 52-minute pilot film for *Space Police* was completed in 1987. Its characters are as weird as any created by Anderson: Bats is a cat-like female police officer with inborn sensory powers; Slomo is a quirky police computer; V. Lann is kingpin of organised crime in Precinct 44 with E. Vile and E. Vile's metallic guard dog Megabite as sidekicks. Star of the show is Lieutenant Brogan, commanding officer of the precinct and an old-fashioned, streetwise cop fighting to rid the neighbourhood of V. Lann and his gang.

At the time of printing, the future of either of these potential series remains unknown . . .

THE TELEVISION FILMS OF GERRY ANDERSON

Dates refer to year of production.

THE ADVENTURES OF TWIZZLE (1956)
52 Episodes. First puppet series
An AP Films Prod. for Associated Rediffusion TV.
Created and written by Roberta Leigh.
Directed by Gerry Anderson.

TORCHY THE BATTERY BOY (1957)
52 Episodes. First appearance of moveable eyes and mouth.
An AP Films Prod. for Associated Rediffusion TV.
Created and written by Roberta Leigh.
Directed by Gerry Anderson (26 episodes)

FOUR FEATHER FALLS (1958)
39 episodes. First Supermarionation series. Introduction of electronic lip-sync.
An AP Films Prod. for Granada TV.
Created by Gerry Anderson and Barry Gray.
Directed by Gerry Anderson (some episodes)

SUPERCAR (1959)
39 episodes. First Anderson production to be syndicated in America.
An AP Films Prod. in association with ATV for ITC Worldwide Distribution.
Created by Gerry Anderson and Reg Hill.
Produced by Gerry Anderson.

FIREBALL XL5 (1961)
39 episodes. Only Supermarionation series to be picked up by a major American network (NBC-TV).
An AP Films Prod. in association with ATV for ITC Worldwide Distribution.
Producer/Script supervisor with Sylvia Anderson.

STINGRAY (1962-63)
39 episodes. First UK television series to be filmed in colour.
An AP Films Prod. in association with ATV for ITC Worldwide Distribution.
Producer/Script supervisor with Sylvia Anderson.

THUNDERBIRDS (1964-66)
2 seasons.
32 episodes. First (and only) one-hour puppet series made for TV. Two films followed: *Thunderbirds Are Go* and *Thunderbird 6*.
An AP Films Prod. in association with ATV for ITC Worldwide Distribution.
Season One: Producer/Script supervisor with Sylvia Anderson.
Co-writer with Sylvia Anderson.
Season Two: Executive Producer/Script supervisor with Sylvia Anderson.

CAPTAIN SCARLET AND THE MYSTERONS (1967)
32 episodes. Introduction of highly advanced, 'stringless', perfectly proportioned puppets.
A Century-21 Prod. for ITC Worldwide Distribution.
Executive Producer and Co-creator with Sylvia Anderson.

JOE 90 (1968)
30 episodes. Action and machines (model effects) become secondary to the characters.
A Century-21 Prod. for ITC Worldwide Distribution.
Co-creator with Sylvia Anderson.
Co-writer with Sylvia Anderson.

THE SECRET SERVICE (1969)

13 episodes. First series to combine live action and puppets.
A Century-21 Prod. for ITC Worldwide Distribution.
Co-creator with Sylvia Anderson.
Co-writer with Sylvia Anderson.

UFO (1969)

26 episodes. First step into the world of live action.
A Century-21 Prod. for ITC Worldwide Distribution.
Executive Producer (Episodes 1 to 17). Co-producer with Reg Hill
(Episodes 18 to 26). Co-creator with Sylvia Anderson and Reg Hill.

THE PROTECTORS (1971)

Two seasons.
52 episodes. First non-fantasy, science-fiction TV series.
A Group Three Prod. for ITC Worldwide Distribution.
Co-producer with Reg Hill.

SPACE 1999 (1973-76)

Two seasons
48 episodes. Second live-action science-fiction series.
Season One: *A Group Three/RAI TV Prod. for ITC Worldwide Distribution.*
Season Two: *A Gerry Anderson Prod. for ITC Worldwide Distribution.*
Executive Producer, Co-creator with Sylvia Anderson.

ALIEN ATTACK (1977)

Thirty-second TV commercial using Supermarionation technique.
Produced for JIF.

TERRAHAWKS (1983-85)

Three seasons.
39 episodes. Introduction of Supermacromation technique.
An Anderson/Burr Prod. for LWT.
Creator and Co-producer with Christopher Burr.
Incidental music with Christopher Burr.
Writer "Expect the Unexpected" Parts 1 & 2.

DICK SPANNER (1987)

22 episodes. First stop-motion production.
An Anderson Burr/Channel 4/Virgin Prod.
Co-producer with Christopher Burr.
Creative Supervisor.

SPACE POLICE (1987)

One-hour pilot. Live action combined with animatronics and special effects.
An Anderson/Burr Pictures Prod.
Co-creator/Co-producer with Christopher Burr.
Music with Christopher Burr.
Co-writer with Tony Barwick.

ACKNOWLEDGEMENTS

The authors and publisher would like to thank the following:
Stingray
Steve Kyte, Ralph Titterton, Colin Bayley, Neil Alsop, Jim Millett, Dave Tremont, Christine Glanville and Bob Bell and Penelope Cream.
Thunderbirds Are Go!
Ralph Titterton, Cathy Ford, Dan French, Melvin Thomas, Frank Ratcliffe, Jon Keeble, Philip Rae (for pictures appearing on pages 146, 149, 156, 157, 158-9, 162, 164, 166, 172 and 173), Dee Conway/Taylors (for pictures appearing on pages 180, 181 and 183) and Gerry Heath (for the picture appearing on page 189).
Captain Scarlet And The Mysterons
Alan Howard, Pete Walker, Graham Bleathman, Katie Runciman, Lynn Simpson, Christine Glanville, Bob Bell, Alan Pattillo, Alan Perry, Francis Matthews, Elizabeth Morgan, Gary Files, Ed Bishop, Alan Fennell, Angus Allen, Milton Finesilver, David Nightingale, Ken Cameron, Ken Scrivener, Douglas Hurring, Anvil Films Ltd, Dr George Sik, Douglas Luke, Andrew Pixley, Sam Mitchell, Andy Allard, Roy A Wright, Mitch Ross, Stephen Brown, Chris Bentley, Ian Boyce, Frank Ratcliffe, Jon Keeble, Anthony McKay, Mike Richardson, Annette Buckley, Alan Gregory, Phil Willis, Joe Dunn, Krystyna Zukowska, Mr P Bassett, Mr W Reid, Mr and Mrs IK Drake, PA Davy and Lynn West.
Sequelanderson: The Legend Continues . . .
Dave Rogers for additional text.
And finally, Gerry Anderson himself.

Anyone wishing to learn more about the Anderson series is advised to send a stamped addressed envelope to:

Fanderson
PO Box 93,
Wakefield,
West Yorkshire
WF1 1XJ

As the official Gerry Anderson appreciation society, the club publishes a first-class, information-packed magazine, and offers its subscription members the opportunity to purchase merchandise exclusive to the club. Conventions are held which are attended by the people who created and produced the series. Non-profit-making, Fanderson supports several different charities, including International Rescue Corps.

Index